Praise for /

'An often chilling seri[...]
colleagues in Special Branch and CID, many of whom have never
spoken before about the Troubles.'

Belfast Telegraph

'Now that the history of the Northern Ireland Troubles is being
written, and sometimes rewritten for political purposes, it is
important that the voices of police officers are heard. This series
of books is a very human document of the tragedies of those
years and of some of the lighter moments too.'

Denis Murray, BBC Ireland correspondent

'A remarkable book. The story of the RUC is one that should be
told and it's told brilliantly.'

Mike Graham, talkRadio, London

'Fascinating and intriguing stories from inside a police force
on the front line of inter-communal conflict and violence, and a
reminder of the high price paid by its officers.'

Peter McDermott, *Irish Echo*, New York

'Fascinating story of cops trying their best to clear crimes and get
home alive to do another day.'

Washington Examiner

'Murders, robberies, terrorism, information gathering ...
paramilitaries and the black, defensive humour that kept
people sane are all here in abundance ... Compelling, frank
and often disturbing.'

*Policebeat: Magazine of the Police Federation for
Northern Ireland*

'If you like dark and inappropriate humour – pick up this book.
Great read, very moving and funny.'

David Feherty, columnist and broadcaster

'veritable page turners, by turns shocking and moving'

Joanne Savage, *News Letter*

'The RUC was a hero organisation to some and a villainous one to others ... a book like this helps to separate fact from fiction and reinforces that at the heart of our history, human beings make the war and make the peace.'

Joe Cushnan, *Belfast Telegraph*

'Absorbing stories from the real peacemakers of the Troubles. Humorous, sad, irreverent but always candid.'

Dr William Matchett, author of *Secret Victory: The Intelligence War that Beat the IRA*

'A series of frank accounts by men and women who served in a force that at times was stretched to breaking point, *A Force Like No Other* recalls the horrors of the Troubles but also some of the funnier stories of everyday life as a cop.'

Stephen Gordon, *Sunday Life*

'This should be compulsory reading.'

Former Special Forces Officer attached to the RUC

'A remarkable and valuable collection of personal reminiscences which capture for history what the brave men and women of the RUC went through to maintain law and order.'

Rt Hon Owen Paterson MP, former Secretary of State for Northern Ireland

'Without the contribution of those in this book there would have been no peace process. They can be proud of what they did to defend democracy and the rule of law.'

Lord Caine, Special Adviser to four Secretaries of State for Northern Ireland

'For some, the black humour which bound them together and kept them sane was not enough; flashbacks and nightmares of incidents are commonplace, illustrating the harrowing nature of the job and the terrible long-term toll it had on those who served the two communities.

County Down Spectator

A FORCE LIKE NO OTHER

THE LAST SHIFT

Colin Breen

·THE·
BLACK
·STAFF·
PRESS

If you are a former member of the RUC and have a story
to tell, please do not hesitate to contact me at
aforcelikenoother@gmail.com

First published in 2021 by Blackstaff Press
an imprint of Colourpoint Creative Ltd
Colourpoint House
Jubilee Business Park
21 Jubilee Road
Newtownards BT23 4YH

Cover photographs: 'An RUC officer on patrol in the nationalist Markets area
of Belfast' © PA Images/Alamy; 'Police come under attack during rioting in
the Sandy Row area of Belfast'.

Printed and bound in Great Britain by Clays Ltd, Elcograf S.p.A.

A CIP catalogue for this book is available from the British Library

ISBN 978 1 78073 331 9

www.blackstaffpress.com

Some names and identifying details have been changed
to protect the privacy of individuals.

I dedicate this book to the memory of police officers everywhere who have made the ultimate sacrifice, and particularly to the 302 members of the Royal Ulster Constabulary who died during the Troubles.

'For peace we served.'

In memory also of my brother Robin Breen, late of the Toronto Police Service.

Introduction

When I came up with the idea for *A Force Like No Other* in 2015, I thought it was going to be a book full of funny stories and anecdotes illustrating the black humour that kept us sane during the violence that plagued Northern Ireland. As I spoke to friends and colleagues, however, the book evolved into a more layered and broad-ranging history of what it was like to police a divided community on a day-to-day basis, and the danger that this work entailed.

Former officers and friends began to talk to me about experiences that had been locked in their heads for years, things they had never even told their families about. Some found it very difficult – emotions ran high and many were upset and tearful. But they were determined to speak, realising that it was important for us – and for the historical record – to tell our story in our own words. I like to think that that first book played a part in breaking the logjam, allowing officers to talk about their lived experience in a way that hadn't seemed possible before.

After *A Force Like No Other* was published, I immediately began work on the follow-up, *A Force Like No Other: The Next Shift*, largely in response to the demand from officers themselves. Many sent me stories or got in touch to ask me to contact them if I was considering a second book. As I gathered the material, I met a significant number of former officers who were suffering from PTSD and who very courageously and with searing honesty spoke about how it had impacted upon their lives and that of their families. Too often officers suffer in silence as it's not in our nature to seek help. I have no doubt there are many more out there who perhaps have not yet sought the help that is now available. I would strongly encourage anyone in that situation to go and speak to someone – there is information about the support that's available at the back of this book.

The Next Shift is a much darker book than its predecessor, and that darkness is very much part of the story of policing in Northern Ireland. In *The Last Shift*, however, which completes the *A Force Like No Other* trilogy, I was keen to bring back some of the humour, though not surprisingly the book still contains many heart-breaking accounts of events. In particular, I am pleased that for the first time the families of officers are given a voice here and describe what it was like for them – sitting at home listening to the clock tick, dreading a knock on the door, having to keep their own feelings bottled up and say nothing. One woman speaks about how her family's life was turned upside down when her father was badly injured and his colleague murdered while attending a burglary.

Next year, 2022, is the centenary of policing in Northern Ireland. In 2001, the Royal Ulster Constabulary was officially renamed, becoming the Police Service of Northern Ireland. I was all too aware that it marked the end of a remarkable era in policing. After all, over the course of many years, the RUC had evolved from a small rural-type service to the most internationally respected anti-terrorist police force in the world, and one whose former members still train other forces across the globe. It must never be forgotten that from the outbreak of the Troubles in 1969 until 2001, 302 police officers were killed; over 10,000 were injured; and hundreds were left disabled or seriously injured. Despite the dangers they faced, many of the officers I spoke to felt their years in the RUC were the best of their lives.

If anything, the sense of camaraderie that existed in the RUC is even more apparent now and is as strong among its former members today as it ever was. Trusting someone with your life as you ran towards danger, knowing that you all had each other's backs, creates an unbreakable life-long bond.

Like the previous books, *The Last Shift* shows the human face behind the uniform and how ordinary people coped in extraordinary times. Throughout the Troubles and all the years of violence directed towards the police, officers did their best with the cards they were dealt. These stories show how their career choice shaped, changed and sometimes ruined their lives – but they also show how the human spirit can triumph in the darkest of moments, against all the odds.

Earlies
07:00—15:00 hours

07:00 – DMSU, Drumcree

I was in the ebonies DMSU [divisional mobile support unit] which was based in Belfast. Among our duties, we were a very highly-trained public order unit and like other DMSUs were always being deployed all around the province to different trouble spots as needed. One year we were sent to the Portadown area during the Drumcree demonstrations and were tasked with securing the main field and the bridge in front of Drumcree Church overnight.

Conditions at the field were like something out of the Second World War; not what we were used to around the streets of Northern Ireland. There were reams of barbed wire that had been put in place by the military and the bridge had been blocked with containers, but there were no facilities of any sort for the vast numbers of troops and police present for the duration of the protest every year. The only thing missing was the trenches. Over time, pack lunches got better and Portaloos were introduced for the personnel at the heart of the demonstration, although there were never enough for the numbers involved.

One year we were sent down to secure the field. Nature took its course and in the dead of night, I had to go for a pee. This gave me the unfortunate chance to experience first-hand the state of the Portaloos! They were unisex and my male colleagues and the squaddies alike seemed to have aimed everywhere *around* the bowl area you could think of … everywhere except in it. On inspection, I thought my chances would be better in the hedges.

A quick look round the area, not much stirring, so off I set to position myself in the cover of the deep bushes. I was still dressed for a riot in all the kit that entails, so once in the bushes there was still work to be done. First to go was my flak jacket, followed by my gun belt. Next, we ladies had to unzip our flameproof boiler suits and undress to be able to go. Having performed the necessary ritual I hunkered for what by now was very welcome relief! Task completed I stood up to get dressed and went through the whole process again in reverse.

Then the bush I had been hiding behind got up and walked away.

07:06 – CID Office, Springfield Road Police Station, West Belfast

It was around 1969 that I was very happily covering Willowfield RUC station as a young detective sergeant when I was sent to the CID office [Criminal Investigation Department] in Springfield Road to help with an enquiry. It was supposed to be for only three weeks but after I arrived, there was never any sign of me being sent back. I found myself being increasingly integrated into the office and in the end, I didn't leave there until 1974.

The CID were living literally on top of each other. The army had commandeered all the original CID offices leaving us to operate out of bedrooms on the top floor – there were just no facilities whatsoever.

I worked very closely with a chap called Stanley Corry, a detective constable. He and I became very friendly as we ran our station football team together. We had organised a match for a particular day, but there were no facilities at Newforge, the force sportsground. It had a sports field but no facilities in the clubhouse, just changing rooms and showers. Food was not really available, so Stanley and I thought we could get a keg of beer organised for after the match. We went to a local business on the Grosvenor Road, ordered a barrel of Guinness and arranged to collect it on the morning of the match.

The morning of the match I arrived earlier than my usual time, about 7.00 a.m., to find there had been a report of a burglary in the Busy Bee, a shop in Andersonstown. Stanley was ordered by the inspector to attend and to take someone with him to investigate the burglary. I thought, what a golden opportunity that would be: we could attend the scene of the burglary then collect the keg of beer and keep it at the station until the afternoon.

We were both about to head off to the burglary when our inspector came in and told me that Rita O'Hare, the wife of the leader of the INLA [Irish National Liberation army] at the time, had been involved in a shooting on the Andersonstown Road the evening before. She had shot at a military patrol and wounded a sergeant major, but the army had returned fire. She too was wounded and taken to the Royal Victoria Hospital. My inspector said, 'I want you to go down to the hospital and interview this O'Hare woman.' I suggested that I go to the burglary with Stanley and then make my way to the hospital afterwards. He said, 'No, both calls are urgent. Stanley, you get someone else to go with you. George, I want you to go to the Royal immediately and there can be no change to those orders.'

A big chap called Bertie Russell had been transferred into Springfield Road that morning, coincidentally also for three weeks, to help with some inquiries. Bertie said to Stanley, 'I'll go with you. I haven't got started at anything else yet.' So, the two of them went to the Andersonstown Road to attend the burglary at the Busy Bee and I went to the hospital.

I spent an hour or more with Rita O'Hare and when I was coming out of the hospital, one of the staff – she knew me from being in and out of the place on different inquiries – told me, 'That ambulance that has just arrived has two of your colleagues in the back of it. They are both dead.' She told me that they'd both been killed near the Busy Bee. The call to the burglary had been a come on: gunmen

5

were lying in wait and had opened fire on both officers as they got out of their car – they died instantly. Twenty-one spent cases were recovered from the scene. A couple of weeks later a local sergeant stopped a car and found a Sten gun with two magazines and a Webley revolver. The Sten gun had been used in the murders.

You can imagine how I felt. One, I had escaped this terrible tragedy. Two, I had lost my very good friend Stanley and another colleague, Bertie. It was difficult to even take it in; it was a very sad three or four days in the build up to the funerals. Even after all this time I still think about that day.

07:30 – RUC Training Centre, Enniskillen

The Training Centre in Enniskillen (or the 'Depot' as it was more commonly known) was where new RUC recruits received their initial training.

In 1950, I travelled by train to Enniskillen to join my class of seventeen who were assembled before a justice of the peace. We were all given a last chance to back out and go home. None did. We took the oath of allegiance and were sworn in by the JP, taking on the powers of a constable.

Kitted out the next day, we were allocated a numbered rifle and I was surprised to be issued with a bayonet and sheath. I asked if I would ever have to insert the sharp end into someone's body and was told that it was only for drill and to give us something extra to clean. Drill was tough until we got used to it. The drill sergeants were strict and all had wartime service. They had served in the Irish Guards and Coldstream Guards, and had promised us they were not going to drop their standards ... and they didn't.

Food rationing still existed at the time, and we were allocated a ration of butter and margarine each week, but there were no fridges. They had to be kept in our bedside lockers alongside all our clothes and other possessions, but we were training in the summer and the butter and marg was often rancid before the next issue in seven days' time.

On Sunday mornings there was a compulsory church parade for all those not engaged in security duty, off sick or on weekend leave. On the parade ground you did not 'fall in' by having the tallest to the right, but by your religion and the location of your church. Presbyterians and Methodists fell in to the right, then the Church of Ireland and lastly Roman Catholics. The parade marched off through the town until we reached the chapel where we halted. The RCs dropped off of the end and we continued through the town, down the middle of the Main Street to the C of I cathedral, then carried on in a similar way to each church in town. When going through the town in uniform we were required to carry a swagger stick: a little black stick with a silver-coloured RUC-embossed knob. This was to let the Enniskillen residents know we were not full-blown police and did not carry a warrant card.

Towards the end of our six months training, our syllabus included the police driving course. Driving instructors and their cars stayed at the training centre for the length of the course. County Fermanagh roads were notoriously bad then and no one had to pass a driving test to drive a vehicle. There were many fairs held in the surrounding villages, and the instructors deliberately targeted these to give us experience of driving through crowds of animals and people.

At the end of the course that November, headquarters allocated me to County Antrim, and the Antrim county inspector allocated me to Toomebridge. I had never heard of the place and couldn't find it on most maps. I left Enniskillen by train and went to Great Victoria Street, Belfast. I left York Street by rail, went to Antrim Town station, and finally arrived at Toomebridge at about 20:30 hours.

The Toomebridge police station was primitive. The only heating in the whole building was a coal fire in the enquiry office: no such thing as power sockets for electric fires; no drinking water; no piped water other than a pipe that sucked water from the River Bann about twenty metres away. There were no mechanical pumps, just an exposed 'cow tail handle' pump behind the building. It was the duty of the station orderly to replenish the station water tank at 10:00 hours after he had completed his twenty-four-hour continuous stint ending at 09:00 hours. The water was not filtered or sterilised in any way and could not be used for anything other than washing the floor. I had seen dead cattle and dogs partially submerged leaving nearby Lough Neagh and passing by our inlet pipe.

There were just two members living in the station, the others were married and lived at home. I had to take meals at the nearby O'Neill Hotel and then return to the station. My bedroom was very cold. I had to bring my rubber hot water bottle to the hotel at supper time, fill it with warm water when leaving and return to the station with it under my arm. I put it into my bed and kept it there until morning. By that time the water was tepid and used for wet shaving.

Country duties generally consisted of cycle patrols, which were of about three and a half hours duration. There were two of these each day and were varied over the twenty-four hours. We were located on the County Antrim side of Lough Neagh and the River Bann. Water patrols were done in a boat with an outboard engine, and we had to recover bodies occasionally.

Communication was via one telephone; there was no radio. An informal method for contacting any passing police traffic cars was to place a large book on the crossbar of one of the enquiry office windows that faced the main road. This would alert the patrol to stop and call.

One day a colleague and I were about to leave the cafe where we took lunch. One of us challenged the other to race back to the police station. We were wearing sports jackets but police trousers – high collared tunics were part of the uniform then. We mounted the bicycles and raced along the road and started to turn round the traffic island at The Diamond. My bicycle lost grip and I fell in a heap along with the bike at the feet of some pensioners seated on the windowsills of the hotel. As I picked myself up, I found there was a hole in the knee of my police trousers. One of the pensioners pulled his pipe out of his mouth and said, 'Son, you'll have to get yourself a slower bicycle, that one's too fast for you.'

07:40 – CID Office, Lisburn Police Station, County Antrim

About three years after I first joined, I moved into CID. The first couple of days in the department I was finding my way, then came my first 'big case': the theft of a pair of jeans from a clothesline. A witness had even made a statement identifying a local youth who they said they saw taking the jeans.

Just what I wanted! A nice straightforward case to help me settle in. I arrested the suspect, brought him in for interview, but there was no confession. We spent the entire time talking up and down and round the houses, but still nothing. Almost in exasperation I said, 'I suppose you'll be telling me next you have a twin?'

Straight-faced as you like, he said, 'I do.'

I put him back in the cells and went out to his house and sure enough there was a twin. He was his double. I arrested the twin, recovered the jeans and headed back to the station. The twin admitted the offence, explaining this had been a one-off. He said, 'I was walking home at night, saw the jeans there on the line and thought, I'll have those.'

It wasn't the biggest crime in the world, but it got me started and taught me that sometimes things aren't what they seem.

07:55 – Border, County Fermanagh

Something that I found strange when I went to Fermanagh was the way they did their route clearances, in which we checked that remote roads in the area were safe for foot or vehicle patrols to use, that they had not been booby trapped with culvert bombs or landmines.

When we were doing route clearances in west Belfast, we had every culvert photographed and numbered. So, the first time I was doing a clearance at the border – it was from Lisnaskea to Newtownbutler, which took days to complete – I asked, 'Where is the culvert book?' That was answered with, 'What's a culvert book?', which I took as an indication that they did not have one. 'How do you know where all the culverts are then?' 'You just go down on your knee and have a wee look' came the reply.

I said, 'I want the entrance and exit to every one of the culverts in the area photographed and numbered so that when a new man comes along you can say, "There's the culvert book," and that way, none will be missed.' Whenever these route clearances are happening they should all be well documented with a photograph. You can also look at the photograph and tell immediately if a culvert has been altered in any way or if someone has been working at it. Those were the sort of things that city cops were able to transfer into practice in the country. They were all great lads, but just had a different, more easy-going approach than you'd find in the city. More a case of 'sure it will do'.

That said, at Newtownbutler, in an old part of the station, they had a detailed map of the area that showed every single house along the roads. These houses all had an orange or green flag sticking up from them, which contained all the information you could need: who lived there; number of children; make, colour of car and registration number. This meant if you were going anywhere in the Newtownbutler area you knew everyone who belonged there, and who didn't, including any vehicles that might be out of place. When I first saw that I thought, brilliant – this is the sort of thing we could do with all over the border area.

08:10 – Regional Crime Squad, Bessbrook, County Armagh

The Kingsmills massacre was a mass shooting that happened on 5 January 1976, near Whitecross, County Armagh. PIRA gunmen stopped a minibus driving along the road to Bessbrook and shot twelve Protestant textile workers. Only one victim survived.

I was an inspector in headquarters' crime squad under Bill Mooney when reports came in of a mass shooting just outside Bessbrook. I received a phone call from Mr Mooney to say, 'Get hold of someone and go down to Bessbrook to set up the investigation room,' and the next morning, I went to the scene of the shooting with a detective sergeant.

It was a very tragic-looking sight; a very deliberate slaughter. The road was thick with blood. The van containing the workmen had been stopped by a man wearing combat gear and carrying a red torch, giving the occupants the impression they were being pulled in at a normal military checkpoint. Once the van had stopped, around a dozen other men appeared out of the hedgerow and began to ask them their religion. There was one Catholic man there and his colleagues tried to defend him, thinking he was going to be shot. He was 'sent down the road' while his colleagues were ordered to line up outside the van and then were repeatedly shot. All died at the scene, except one victim who miraculously survived despite being shot eighteen times.

The attack was carried out by the IRA and was one of the worst killings of the Troubles. This IRA gang was operating from just south of the border and were involved in many attacks: maniacs who just wanted to do nothing else but murder. The weapons used were linked to 110 other attacks in the area. Names started coming through via Special Branch as to who this team of killers were, and I know the Garda did their best, as did we, in identifying the killers.

My sergeant and I decided to go to the scene again on Sunday morning and, while we were there, thought we would randomly call at a few houses nearby. We were very well received by the people, and I remember one man who wouldn't open the door to us but spoke to us through the window because he wanted to make sure we were who we said we were. I showed him my warrant card, as did my colleague. He took the sergeant's card, looked at it, and then was happy to speak to us – though, unfortunately, he couldn't tell us much. We went to the next house, where we were again asked for warrant cards. I produced mine, but the sergeant exclaimed, 'Oh my God, I left mine behind at the last house.' We drove back, but this time the little man was waiting for us and said, 'Is this what you're after?' holding up the warrant card.

The people we spoke to had heard the shooting but couldn't tell us anything else. I only mention this because people think that no one wanted to help us, but actually they were very friendly and I have no doubt that, had they known anything, they would have told us. But of course they had a problem in that they could not be seen to help or speak to us, for fear of the inevitable reprisal from the IRA.

08:20 – CID Office, Grosvenor Road Police Station, West Belfast

I was in CID in west Belfast for many years. It was one of the rougher divisions: very busy and with a constantly high threat level from the IRA. One day I was called out to yet another murder in the area. We always attended in quite large numbers when beginning our inquiries as it was much too dangerous, with the threat of snipers and bomb attacks, to even think of attending on your own. There was even a threat from local youths who would have stoned and petrol bombed you. Consequently, we were always escorted by uniform police and army personnel in bulletproof vehicles and as we arrived in these areas, with Land Rovers and personnel all over the place, people would inevitably come out to their doors to see what was going on.

I remember going to this particular murder scene to carry out house-to-house enquiries. People up there were too scared to talk to you face to face, generally, but they may have told you something discreetly if they felt neighbours couldn't hear. In some places, it was just hostile.

It was a typical winter's day: dull, very cold and, of course, wet. I had a long black Dexter-style coat on – some people would have described it as a 'detective's coat' – and I had it buttoned right up to the neck. I approached this house where a little old lady was standing at the gate. I said hello to her and before I could say another thing she said, 'Ah, come in, Father, come in.' She just turned and walked up to her door and I followed her with the intention of telling her, 'I'm from the police.' We ended up in her living room and she still had her back to me when she said, 'Tea Father, tea?' I replied slightly louder, 'No, not "priest" – I'm from the police!' She just said, 'I don't know anything,' and walked off. That was that.

During the same house-to-house enquiries, two of my

colleagues went to a house, their clipboards at the ready, and the lady invited them in. She started showing them the water running down her walls, the mould out in the hall and a damaged door. They said, 'No, missus, we're the police!' She replied, 'What? Get out to fuck!'

08:30 – Sion Mills Police Station, County Tyrone

One of the first murders I attended was that of a man called Ronnie Finlay, a former UDR soldier. He was shot dead by the IRA in the yard of a farm just outside Sion Mills in front of his wife and children as they dropped him off to work. It turned out that a six-man IRA team had taken over the farmhouse during the night, holding the family at gunpoint while they waited for Ronnie to arrive for work at around 8.30 a.m.

The terrorists stepped out of the house and opened fire just as Ronnie got out of his car. His wife [Kathleen Finlay] reported hearing a noise just as he had closed the car door but said that she didn't think it was a gunshot as she couldn't see anything untoward when she looked round. She could see that he was trying to keep himself upright on his feet, and she got out of the car to make her way to him, by which time he had fallen, causing her to fear he had taken ill. Just as she was about to go to him there was this burst of automatic fire and she knew immediately that they were under attack.

She told me at the time: 'All I can remember then is being back in the car and trying to force my children down onto the floor to protect them. Andrew, my youngest, clung to me and in that moment I thought, I've got to get them to the farmhouse for protection. As I ran to the house with Andrew in my arms, this gunman confronted me and told me to get back. I don't remember coming back to the car but remember standing beside it and shielding Andrew between the car and myself. The gunman stood at my right-hand side with his gun trained on me and then they just pumped Ronnie with automatic fire with the children there. I walked about three quarters of a mile for help. My legs were all punctured with shrapnel, streaming with blood.'

The gunmen escaped over the border, which was literally a field away, and went safely into Donegal. That whole Provisional IRA unit was known to us; they were mostly from one family. One of them, nicknamed Snake, was the main protagonist in the area. He was shot in Newtownstewart, when he went to try and kill a UDR man called Davey, but Davey saw him coming. Snake was on a pushbike, masked and fully armed, as he approached the builders' yard where Davey worked. Davey had his personal protection weapon with him, which he drew, then he turned round and engaged Snake, shooting him in the neck. Snake was convicted of attempted murder and was later released under the Good Friday Agreement.

Ronnie Finlay's brother Winston (43) had been murdered a few years earlier [in 1987]. He'd just returned home after visiting relatives with his wife. He got out of his car to open the garage door and he was shot. He was a former UDR soldier who had joined the RUC Reserve.

08:37 – Lisburn Road Police Station, South Belfast

In 1978, I joined the police and went off to the training centre at Enniskillen. I had joined straight from school and the first station I was assigned to was Lisburn Road RUC in Belfast. The only problem was that I lived in Dundonald at the time and didn't drive. I decided to ride my bike. I did all I was supposed to do from a security point of view – varied my route as much as I could, used a different bridge across the River Lagan every day – but, as it transpired, that was not enough.

One day when I was in the station, I received a telephone call instructing me to ring a certain office in Castlereagh RUC station, a Special Branch office. It turned out Special Branch knew I was riding a bicycle to work. They also knew it was a blue Peugeot cycle and the colours of the three tracksuits I wore. They also knew about my tactic of using different bridges over the Lagan to vary my route to the station.

Flabbergasted, I asked, 'How do you know all this and why?'

They explained to me in no uncertain terms that the Provisional IRA were watching and targeting me as I made my way to work and that I was in severe danger. They were planning to murder me on one of my commutes. Being new and only in the job a short time, this was very chilling news and I asked them, 'What should I do?'

The advice was simple: ditch the bike, learn to drive, buy a car.

08:55 – CID Office, Strand Road Police Station, Londonderry

I was stationed in Londonderry in the 1980s, including during the hunger strikes. I was in CID at the time in a city that was just a horrendous war zone. There was just no normality at that time because there were so many incidents. Many of them have stayed very strongly in my mind, including that of Reggie Reeves.

Reggie was a colleague of mine, we served together in the same station. Reggie, myself and another guy, Jeff, were the single men in the department, and we always thought we got called out to incidents more often than the married men. I don't think, now, that this was the case, but it certainly felt like it at the time, and of course 'living in' didn't help.

One morning I was asked to attend in the Shantallow area of the city, where what was thought to be a consignment of stolen televisions, radios and other electrical goods had been found by the military during a search of a shed. I unfortunately had to go to a Crown court trial in Belfast with another colleague, Jeff, and so someone phoned Reggie and he went out to it. An army dog handler had sent a dog in to search for traces of explosives and when the dog failed to find anything, control was handed to the RUC to carry out an investigation.

Reggie walked into the shed and lifted a TV; two uniformed lads were walking in behind him as he did so. The television was booby trapped and Reggie was blown to smithereens. He was a young man, just twenty-four – a really decent guy with his whole life ahead of him. Fortunately, the two lads with him, though badly injured, survived the blast. That could have been me, or Jeff, but fate had intervened. We didn't hear the news of what had happened until we arrived at the courts in Belfast, and we had to immediately turn back to the station to begin investigating Reggie's murder.

I will never forget attending his funeral in Portstewart. The pure emotion running among his police colleagues was incredible. Carrying his coffin, and the police band playing, had a big impact on us all. Sadly, reality stepped in and, when we came back to the office after the funeral, his files were shared out around the rest of us and everyone had to get on with life.

09:08 – Woodbourne Police Station, West Belfast

Stevie Magill was a really good guy. He was an even-tempered, mild-mannered young man with a warm smile and a dry sense of humour; an avid and practising Christian who let his character and his lifestyle be his witness. He had arrived on transfer to Woodbourne in west Belfast from Lurgan at around the same time I'd transferred from Dungannon: two young men wishing to be nearer to home in Belfast and both prepared to serve in 'B' division, west Belfast, to achieve it.

We were both assigned to C section in Woodbourne RUC station where we, at nineteen and twenty-three years of age, were both younger than most in the section. I remember Stevie to have been 'a good peeler', as we used to say; knowledgeable and naturally empathetic. A few months later, I was transferred to A section and my association with Stevie largely waned.

This transfer proved to be fortuitous for me in two respects: firstly, A section was full of younger guys with whom I identified more closely, and secondly, it meant that at just after 9 a.m. on 9 April 1980, I wasn't part of the crew that attended the bogus burglary at Suffolk Library. It was there that Paul 'Dingus' Magee, Joe 'Doc' Docherty and Angelo Fusco fired a hundred 7.62mm rounds on full automatic from an M60 machine gun directly at Stevie and three other officers: Davy, Barry and a policewoman named Alison, who I never met. She doubtless carries the mental scars to this day. Davy lost a chunk of his leg, Barry had his arm badly shot up and Stevie was killed. Forty years have passed since that awful day. I visited the library on 9 April, as I do most years, and the bullet marks are still on the wall of the library building.

A year and a half after that attack, two more colleagues from Woodbourne station made the ultimate sacrifice and twice as many were seriously injured. An RPG [rocket-propelled grenade] attack killed Alec Beck and severely injured Michael, and a booby-trap bomb claimed the life of Gary Martin and injured Cecil. Many others involved in these attacks have suffered years of PTSD as a result, scars that can't be seen, but that run deep nonetheless.

Belfast in the early eighties was a place of danger: a place run by terrorists, where law and order were difficult and dangerous to enforce. It has undergone an incredible transformation since the ceasefires – a transformation that Stevie, Alec and Gary gave their lives to achieve. I have often wondered what those lads would think if they could see the Woodbourne 'sub-division' now, largely normal and mostly peaceful. Would they see their deaths as being worthwhile, given fresh meaning and significance in terms of the eventual victory over the men of violence?

09:14 – Crime Squad Office, Castlereagh Station, east Belfast

There were six of us 'lady' detectives attached to the crime squad in Castlereagh during the early to mid-eighties. There was a tight bond between us and an unspoken sense of camaraderie, even though we rarely got to work directly with each other. But when we did, I must say it was great.

There was a fairly large travellers' camp in west Belfast, which was a great source of criminal activity, mostly involving the handling of stolen goods, and it caused big problems for the local police.

One week, in an attempt to curb the criminal activity that was rife there, our bosses decided that the camp should be raided, and anyone found in possession of stolen property of any sort should be brought in for interview. The local uniform branch raided the camp in the early hours and brought in a number of people for interview. One of these prisoners was thought to be a clairvoyant, which intrigued me and another colleague, so we volunteered to interview her.

She was fine to talk to, certainly a lot easier than what we had become accustomed to in the squad. We had quite a bit of craic with her and when we'd finished speaking to her about the crimes she had been arrested for, my colleague said to her, 'Tell us about your clairvoyancy; we believe you have the gift.' (Secretly we'd both been hoping for a wee session!)

She looked at us both very serenely then leaned over the table and said, 'D'ye not think if I was really clairvoyant, I would have seen you fuckers coming to lift us this morning?'

09:35 – Ballycastle Police Station, North Antrim

I was the head of CID for the North region, headquartered in Ballymena police station. I arrived there one April morning and almost immediately received a phone call to tell me a body had been found at a forest outside Ballycastle. I set out to the scene with a colleague and we arrived a very short time later, at around 9.30 or so.

The body had been found by a forest workman on a one-lane track. It was that of a young girl who had been pulled into a lay-by but left with her feet sticking out on to the road. There appeared to have been no attempt to conceal the body and her bag was very close to her. I guessed she was around eighteen. Her name was Ingar Maria Hauser, and she was from West Germany.

I put together an investigation team with a detective superintendent in charge who was very experienced and highly respected. It was decided that we would conduct the enquiry from Ballycastle RUC station. The superintendent went to Munich, where the girl's family lived, to see the police there and find out what they knew about the young lady – whether she had a boyfriend who might have followed her, for example, or anything else that might be of interest or help to us.

She had come over on an interrail trip, planning to visit

a friend at Cardiff University who was just finishing up her exams. Her friend had suggested that she 'visit the top end of Scotland for a couple of days' while she finished her exams. But for some unknown reason Ingar appeared at Stranraer ferry port and got the boat to Belfast. There were quite a large number of passengers and lorry drivers on board the ferry she travelled on. That was the last time she was seen alive.

Her body was discovered ten days later in the forest, although it is possible she had been murdered elsewhere and her body brought there for disposal. She had been badly beaten about her shoulders, chest and back. Her neck was broken, and she had also been strangled.

Mr and Mrs Hauser asked if they could come over to Northern Ireland and see where their child's body had been discovered. I spoke to the superintendent and said, 'We must facilitate them as best we can, better that they are with us at this time than wandering around the province by themselves.' John Herman, the chief constable of the RUC at the time, then sent me a message to say that all reasonable charges incurred by Mr and Mrs Hauser during their visit would be attended to by his office. We'd already had them booked into a hotel in nearby Portballintrae and they were with us for two nights. One of my colleagues went to the hotel to speak to the owner and to see our visitors safely off. He spoke to the hotel owner and said, 'Can I have the bill please?' The owner replied, 'What bill? There is no bill.'

A post-mortem was carried out on Ingar's body to determine the cause of death and scenes of crime officers conducted a very thorough examination of the scene. Nothing was left to chance. We also had a scientist there from the forensic department who carried out a most meticulous examination, as you would expect them to do in these cases. Evidence of seminal material was found on her body, so we had something with which to identify the person if they were found or we had a suspect.

We did a reconstruction in and around the Ballymena area and anywhere connected to the port where we felt she may have travelled in or through but nothing concrete ever came out of it. We identified every conceivable person we could find from the boat. We covered every car and every lorry driver. We covered army camps and personnel who were travelling as well. We never saw her coming off the boat on CCTV or anything, nor could we get any evidence of her being in a car or a lorry. She had a Europass ticket with which she could go anywhere.

The investigation at the time was carried out very thoroughly by detectives with a vast array of experience in these matters. Police enquiries extended to Germany, England, Wales, Scotland, the Republic of Ireland and, of course, extensively in Northern Ireland. I was even sent to England to appear on *Crimewatch UK*. It was the first time anyone from the RUC had taken part. I went over with a team: one from the press office and four from the murder squad we had set up for this inquiry. Nick Ross was the presenter who interviewed me, and he has enquired about the case from time to time over the years.

There was a lot of feeling and speculation in the area at the time that the little girl had been held in one of the villages near Armoy on the way to Portrush in north Antrim. I find that hard to take in. If she'd been kept in a village, even going out to buy food would have sent a flag up: people would have known there were strangers, or that people were buying food they didn't normally buy, as if someone had been staying with them. Similarly local speculation that two men arrested over potential involvement in republican paramilitary organisations had kept her, abused and then killed her, but there's no evidence of that.

It's been forty years now since the incident. I kept up contact with the family, but sadly, both of Ingar's parents are now dead. They went to their graves not knowing what happened to their daughter.

There have, of course, been suspects but no evidence to convict someone. A couple of years ago police arrested a man and a woman who live locally and they were interviewed about the murder, but again, there was insufficient evidence to bring any charges. It has not been helpful in the years since to have had people speculate in the press, often without foundation, about what may or may not have happened – it serves only to build up unrealistic expectations.

However, the DNA is still there and it's valid – thanks to the excellent work carried out by the forensic scientist and scenes of crime officers at the time, police were confident they had secured sufficient evidence that would one day lead to the conviction of the killer.

10:20 – Uniform Patrol, Springfield Parade, West Belfast

I was in uniform up in west Belfast during the hunger strikes of 1981. At the start, a crowd would have just appeared after each death, but by the middle to tail end of them, local IRA and Sinn Féin representatives got people out into the street to make the protest look bigger.

When a hunger striker died, a man would appear out in the streets with a big bass drum. He would then walk round the area, giving it a slow beat like a death march. There was no time to go round the area, knocking doors would take too long. Off he would set down the road – boom, boom, boom – the locals would all come out and fall in behind him: a funeral procession while he beat the drum until they got a big enough crowd for a decent riot.

Young fellas would burn buses, cars, lorries and set up barricades to mark the hunger striker's passing.

One day we were standing at the top of the street when out came the man with the bass drum. He was the smallest bass drummer in the world, and it would have been a fairly close match as to which was bigger, him or the drum. An army patrol turned the corner and walked down the street towards the crowd. There was the normal shouting at the troops, though because of the hunger striker's death it looked like things were going to develop into a bit of trouble. The next thing, a soldier fired his rubber bullet gun, putting a round straight through the centre of the drum. I can see the drummer's face yet. I honestly thought he was going to cry. He just stood there with no skin on either side of his drum and his arms down his side – he just did not know what to do. He was like a child whose moment in the sun had just been taken away from him.

It probably ended up the quietest part of the day.

10:35 – Foot Patrol, Strand Road Police Station, Londonderry

I had gone into the Depot in February 1981. I passed out that May and was given a one-week woman police course. We never did a driving course because of the H-Block disorder and hunger strikes; we were all sent out to our stations as soon as possible as they were trying to maximise manpower available. I was fired out to Strand Road station in Londonderry. I had to phone my dad to find out where it was when I was told where I was going. I had no accommodation, nothing. I arrived at the station and that was it. They didn't let females live at the station in those days, so a girl put me up for a month until I could find somewhere of my own to live.

A year later, on 4 May 1982, three of us, Alan, Davey

and myself, were detailed beat patrol in the city centre. We were probably on quite a heightened alert because the following day was the anniversary of Bobby Sands' death and there was word that there was going to be an attack on the Londonderry courthouse, or something.

The three of us set off. We walked from the station towards the city centre and went up Shipquay Street. For security, we had to walk separately, we would never be allowed to walk together: one had to be on the footpath on one side of the street and the other two on the footpath on the opposite side. We got to the top of Shipquay Street and had just reached The Diamond area. At that stage Davey had to go into Austins department store on The Diamond to take a statement from someone in relation to a shoplifting case he was dealing with.

Alan and I remained outside covering him. We stood apart as we waited for him to come back out. A red van pulled up alongside us at the corner of The Diamond and I thought they were looking for directions to go somewhere, so I walked over to the passenger side of the van to see what the fella wanted.

As I was walking over, the side door opened up and there were gunmen in balaclavas poised to jump out. I think there were three of them. As soon as I saw them I shouted, 'Alan, run!' I turned away and ran as fast as I could. Obviously, I didn't get very far. I heard gunshots, and then I felt extreme pressure and a burning sensation in my back. I was knocked to the ground but there were gunshots still being fired. I froze and pretended to be dead because, subconsciously, I thought, well, I'm still alive and I want to remain alive. I was going in a completely different direction from Alan, so I didn't see him being hit or anything. Then they came over and must have seen that I was still alive as they put another bullet in me while I was lying on the ground. It went into my leg. Then the van drove off (I'm assuming it drove off because all the noise stopped).

Whatever way I had fallen I had put my radio on to a permanent transmit mode. I believe a few randomly selected swear words came out of me and were broadcast over the entire network, but I don't really know. I radioed for assistance and very soon afterwards there were cars coming up the street to help us. A fella who was in my section came in the ambulance with me to Altnagelvin Hospital. I told him, 'My mummy is away on a school trip you'll have to phone my daddy,' and I give him my dad's phone number at work. 'Let him know what has happened.'

I was still conscious when I got to Altnagelvin and I remember them cutting all my clothes off me. That was the last thing I remember. I woke up in intensive care to find my mum and dad were there. I said to my mum, 'What are you doing here?' She said, 'Do you think I'm going to look after somebody else's children and not be here to see my own?'

I was in intensive care for ten days. Then they moved me to a side room off a main ward somewhere. I found out that intelligence had been received through Special Branch that there was a severe threat against my life. I had to be transferred out of the hospital I was in, but it had been deemed too dangerous to go by road.

I think the reason the threat came in was because the terrorists thought I could identify them. The two in the front of the van hadn't been masked or anything, but I couldn't have told them from Adam. I mean, with shock and all the rest of it, I couldn't have told you one thing about them. But I was to be airlifted from Altnagelvin Hospital by military helicopter down to the military wing of Musgrave Park Hospital in Belfast.

I was out at the landing pad in an ambulance waiting for the helicopter to come. The first helicopter that arrived had to do an emergency landing – it had caught on fire – so I had to go back to my room on the ward again. Apparently, it was then, while I was waiting for the second helicopter to arrive, that gunmen came into the ward to finish me off. The two police guards who had been placed outside my door gave chase and they didn't get me, thank God. Then the second helicopter arrived and I was transferred to the military wing, which I was in for another week.

I had skin grafts for the flesh wound on my leg but when the doctors took the dressings off it appeared black. They weren't happy with it and were going to redo the entire skin graft. Fortunately, my dad played golf with a specialist in the Plastic Surgery Unit in Dundonald Hospital and phoned him so that we could get a second opinion. Consequently, I was discharged from Musgrave Park and taken to the Ulster Hospital in Dundonald. Mr Slater, I think it was, took all the black bits off and actually it had taken perfectly. It's not pretty, but it's entirely fine, and I was very grateful for that. I didn't need more surgery.

I was extremely lucky. Because the bullet was high velocity and went in through my back, and because of the flak jacket I was wearing, it deflected up through my lung. The entry wound is the size of my fingernail but the exit wound is a very large thing at the top of my shoulder.

Alan, who was only twenty-one, wasn't so lucky. He was shot several times at point-blank range – killed at the scene. He was only out of the Depot six months. Davey knew nothing about the incident as he was in Austins shop at the time – I don't know whether he came running out; I don't know what happened with him, but he was unscathed. The funny thing was the supervision car that was out that day was actually parked on the other side of The Diamond but they heard nothing. Maybe that's why they were so quickly on the scene. I think there was a nurse, maybe, who came over to give me first aid.

Jack Hermon, who was chief constable, had come into the hospital to see me and I thought he was stupid because he walked in wearing full uniform. I think I might even have said something to him along the lines of, 'Are you wise, sir?' Or something like that. I told him, 'I want to come back, I have to come back to Londonderry,' and he passed it off with, 'Oh, sure we'll see about that.' At nineteen years of age, you don't want your career to be over; you're stubborn and you're strong. I was off work for five months on the sick to recover and when I came back, I did a month stuck in the station, attached to CID. It was not for me. I had only been in there for two weeks when I knew I just had to get back to my section; I had to walk the beat again. It was a psychological thing with me, and I think that by facing it, I have managed to get on with things over the years. When I had to walk up Shipquay Street I was absolutely scared stiff, but I did it. If I hadn't done that I would never have known how I would have coped.

I was still in hospital for Alan's funeral, but his parents and family came to see me that day. I met them later when they presented a clock to the station in his memory. I think I felt guilty because I had survived and their son had died. The gunmen must have thought he was the greater threat to them because he was armed. I wasn't armed.

I don't think there is enough put out about women not being armed in the police back then. We weren't even issued with a baton. Probably because the men were armed, they thought we were armed. It was possibly thanks to me going on about this that the sergeant wouldn't put females in a vehicle when we were on night duty, because the man would have had to protect us and that wasn't right; we didn't want the fellas to have do that because they had to look out for themselves.

I was really pleased when we were armed, much as I hated the training.

10:47 – CID Office, Dungannon Police Station, County Tyrone

A fortnight after I had arrived at the CID office in Dungannon, a woman called Fiona Conlon reported she had been raped and abused by her husband, Anthony Conlon. She made a long and comprehensive statement detailing the abuse that she had suffered, which had been going on for an age. He was just a complete control freak and used to beat her with an electric cord he had taken from a Hoover.

The couple had two young children and he had put them into a bath of cold water for so long that they had to be taken to hospital suffering with hypothermia. When alarm bells went off in the hospital, he then forced his wife to confess and admit that she had done this to the children. She was actually convicted in court of cruelty.

Eventually she hit her breaking point and plucked up the courage to come to the police. He was charged with varying offences but got out on bail, a condition of which was that he was to move to and stay in Omagh.

I came into work one morning to be told by uniform officers that Fiona Conlon had been reported missing and they had been looking for her during the night but hadn't found her. I had two detective sergeants and I asked one of them, 'Can you liaise with the uniform section who were working during the night and find out what exactly has been done to find the husband?' I said to the other sergeant, 'You may set up the incident room, this isn't good.'

Sure enough, her body was found lying in a stream near her home and the husband was also found. Fiona Conlon had drowned in a stream 22 inches deep, but she also had a deep stab wound in the right side of her back. A bloodied, black-handled kitchen knife was found close to her body, as were traces of her blood. Her husband had taken us to the scene and told us he had been knocked out by a knife-wielding attacker, who had turned up while they were having sex in the field around midnight. Ms Conlon, he claimed, had gone by the time he came around.

However, after his sixth interview, Conlon changed his story and admitted stabbing her. He had returned to the town, met her, and stabbed her in the back, then brought her body over to a stream where they'd had sex – he said she had consented – then he left her lying in the stream. At some point, she had drowned. When her body was found it was frozen. Conlon was probably the most sinister, most evil non-terrorist I have ever spoken to. He was not remorseful in the slightest.

There was a long series of interviews conducted with him, all of which were recorded on tape in the presence of his solicitor. There was some forensic evidence, fibres that matched various things, all of which were put to him during the interviews. We told him where semen was found in order to prove the rape, but every single piece of evidence we put to him, he changed his story to account for it, hoping the explanations would acquit him.

This became the first time where a conviction for rape was given where the injured party was dead. At the court in Enniskillen, he was sentenced to life imprisonment with a recommendation that he serve at least sixteen years – he was released on licence in 2014 and works for a charity now in Portadown.

I remember going to a case conference with the prison staff – these are held when somebody is sentenced to life for murder. They have an officer as a point of contact who takes responsibility for them. Conlon had been in prison a few weeks by that stage and had been a model prisoner. He had told his welfare officer that it had been a crime of passion: he had found out that his wife was having an affair, they had an argument, she grabbed a knife, and he took it from her but unfortunately in the struggle she was accidentally stabbed. This, of course, was a load of nonsense and I had to sit there as the prison staff believed everything that came out of his mouth.

10:56 – Crumlin Road Courthouse, Belfast

A loyalist assassination team was intercepted in Armagh on their way to Kilkoo to murder a republican target who was supposed to be very active in the area at the time. At the trial in the Crumlin Road Courthouse, one of the accused said he had been offered a deal by a detective: 'You tell the truth but you'll be let out. There'll be nothing more about it'. While someone else was giving their evidence to the court, he attracted the attention of his barrister. There was a bit of frantic waving and the court paused while his QC came round to speak to him in the box. The barrister then got up and said to the judge, 'Do you see that gentleman standing just at the entrance to the court with the moustache and dark hair? That's the detective who offered him the deal.'

There was a bit of looking, straining all around to see who this detective was. The judge looked over the top of his glasses and asked, 'Is that the man in the blue suit and white shirt?' 'Yes, that's him,' came the reply. This person was known to the judge who said, 'That's a constable from the close protection unit who has been with Judge X for some years. I don't think he would have been in Gough barracks, offering deals!' There was a bit of slinking down in his seat from the QC and laughing from everyone else in the court, including the press.

Another one of the defendants in the same case was complaining rather loudly to his barrister, Desmond Boal, that he did not feel he was doing enough to fight his case and, really, he should and could be doing an awful lot more to prove his innocence. Boal looked at him and said, 'I'm not the one who made the statement of admission,' and walked off.

11:00 – Coffee-time Reflections

I was stationed in west Belfast twice, once as a sergeant and then a few years later, as an operational chief inspector. It was a very violent area when it came to terrorist activity and it got a bad press. I found that when I was there, there were a lot of ordinary decent people who just wanted to get on with their lives but weren't allowed to by paramilitaries.

When I was a sergeant, I remember going to the door of this house as the residents had phoned in wishing to report a crime. It transpired that their car had been stolen and the only reason they needed to report it to the police was they needed a crime number to tell their insurance company. The problem the locals had was the IRA had it ingrained in them that they were never to speak to the police or have anything to do with them. To be fair, a lot of them ignored this, but they couldn't be seen to speak to us. They were just frightened of what would happen to them or their families.

I went to the house and this woman opened the front door and she started on me: 'What the fuck do you want? There's nothing for you here!' Of course, all of this was screeched at the top of her voice; the neighbours couldn't have missed it. I walked on into the house as she was moving backwards, and explained to her that I was there about the car. She said, 'I know you are, love. Sorry about all that shouting, but we have to do that. You know what it's like.' She followed this up with, 'Will you take a wee cup of tea?'

So then, I had a cup of tea and took down all the details of the car and where it had been stolen – how much it was worth and all the rest of it. I got up as it was dangerous to hang around one place too long and as I stood, she said, 'Now I'm going to have to shout at you again.' True to her word, as I was going back out through the door, she screamed, 'Right, now, don't come fucking back here. If you don't get my car, you are fucking useless, the whole lot of you. A pack of bastards!'

The thing is, it was people like her who, even then, would have phoned me to try and help. There were people in west Belfast that saved so many lives and I know because I was getting phone calls from them constantly, especially when I came back as a chief because I was seen at more community gatherings and different things in the area. I had given my mobile number to quite a few people in the Andersonstown/Whitburn policing area, and at maybe two o'clock in the morning, my phone would ring with a message: 'Watch yourselves around the Mona Bypass, be very careful there's something there.' I would have phoned it through right away to put the area out of bounds. The next day we would have appeared to be casually in the area and discover a bomb planted at the side of the road, waiting for a passing police and military patrol to come along so they could detonate it.

The majority of people in those areas just didn't want it, they wanted to live normally. It was just a small group of Provos, the rest of the people were just frightened. If it hadn't been for those people phoning in and tipping you off, there would have been a lot more murders, and the Provos knew it was happening. They knew we didn't just stop patrolling the streets. They probably suspected that it came from leaks within their own organisation, rather than the public (of course, it came from both). It must have unsettled them to quite an extent.

My last duty before I left west Belfast on promotion to inspector was on a Sunday at a republican parade: Easter Sunday or whatever it was. Then the next day I was standing in Cookstown as an inspector at a parade. The contrast always sticks in my head as, when I was standing there, these guys are going past saying, 'Hello, how are you, inspector? You're a new face.' People were talking to me again.

11:15 – Donegall Pass Police Station, South Belfast

I joined the police in May 1969. I was part of the last squad to pass out from the RUC Depot in Enniskillen carrying a rifle with a fixed bayonet. Over the intervening years I served in many areas and in many different stations. What I am about to tell you happened in 1979 when I was a section sergeant attached to Donegall Pass RUC station in Belfast.

It was a Friday, and we were on the early shift. I was short on constables that morning, particularly ones who were authorised to drive police vehicles. My normal commitments left me with a female officer as driver of the station patrol vehicle, and a male constable as observer. It was a busy morning; the calls had started coming in thick and fast, so we were pretty stretched.

I was in the station about 10 a.m. when a constable from the neighbourhood patrol unit came in to catch up on some paperwork and I decided to commandeer him to assist with calls. We'd planned to use the supervision vehicle, but unfortunately it was required by the enquiry officers, so instead we decided to take the newly allocated armoured Hotspur Land Rover. In those days, armoured Hotspurs had just come out and were still a relatively rare sight on the roads of Belfast. We answered a couple of calls then were tasked to attend a reported burglary at 54 Benburb Street in the Village area of Belfast. It was a well-known loyalist stronghold. We got there about 11.10 a.m. and I completed my notebook entry recording our arrival. I looked around the place and all appeared normal but I knew there was something not right. I could just sense it, though at the time I could not figure out what it was. I got out of the vehicle, walked across the footpath, stepped inside the entrance gate, and knocked the front door. No answer. I knocked again, a bit louder. I heard the sound of gunfire as I did so, then I felt what seemed like a really heavy thump to the top of my head.

It felt as if my head had been hit from behind by an axe. I remember falling backwards and thinking that if I fell on to the gate, I would hurt myself. I collapsed backwards on to the footpath and fell against the back wheel of the Hotspur. As I lay on the ground, I probed around the wound on my head with my hand and realised that I had actually been shot. I immediately radioed for assistance but I could not hear any response. I radioed again.

I have no idea how long I lay there. I drifted in and out of consciousness. I was blind and I remember hearing two-tone horns [police sirens] in the distance. My sight slowly began to return and I saw the blurred green of one of my colleague's shirts and then gradually, as my vision improved, I recognised one of the constables from my section leaning over me. I asked about my driver and I was told he was all right. I have some recollection of him assisting me on the footpath just before an ambulance arrived and I was lifted on to a stretcher to be taken to hospital. I remember holding my left arm by the cuff of my shirt using my right hand. I had no control over my limbs apart from my right arm. I was paralysed apart from that arm. Other colleagues appeared at the scene and I was accompanied to the hospital.

I was taken into casualty – or A & E as it is now called – and I remember the surgeon telling me to move my limbs as he was examining me, but I was unable to do so. Eventually, after a lot of effort, I was able to move my left arm and my legs. I asked the surgeon if I would be able to play football when this was all over, and he confirmed that I would. I replied – I suppose trying to lessen the tension I was feeling – by saying, 'That's brilliant because I wasn't able to play before this happened.'

My family was summoned to the hospital. My son was away on holiday with my parents and they were due to return to Northern Ireland that day on the ferry. My father was paged by name and asked if he had any connection with the police. They arrived at the hospital some hours later by police transport. My mother was distraught. My eight-year-old son was in shock. I still remember the expression on his face as he walked into the hospital ward that day.

I had been shot twice in the head and recovery would be slow and difficult. I was discharged from hospital after a week because they could do nothing more for me, but I had to do a lot of rehabilitation. For a year I could neither talk nor walk. I was paralysed down the left side, my speech was slurred, and memories were very jumbled; they still are sometimes. I've been more emotional since the shooting.

I now know that the call to the burglary was a hoax to lure us into the area. The call had been made by a young girl pretending to be the householder's daughter. Gunmen had hijacked a Housing Executive van that morning in west Belfast and driven it to number 43 Benburb Street, opposite number 54. Someone in a suit, pretending to be from the Housing Executive, had called with the eighty-year-old owner of number 43 the day before and let him know to expect the workers.

The workmen arrived with various bags at number 43,

but immediately produced guns and told the occupier they were taking over the house. They also held his home help at gunpoint when she arrived. Two of the terrorists had gone upstairs to wait by the bedroom window, from which they would open fire on the police arriving at number 54. After they had shot me, they fired some shots from a handgun and drove off up Broadway to the Falls Road and made good their escape. An Armalite rifle and a Woodmaster sniper rifle had been used in the well-planned attack.

I was very lucky to have survived. The driver and I had both been saved because we'd taken the brand-new, bulletproof Hotspur Land Rover rather than a soft skin car. The Hotspur was struck several times, but it had protected the driver and it also offered me protection when I was lying on the footpath. One other thing that I think really saved me was that I had just returned from holiday and had let my hair grow a bit before I went so I would look less like a cop. Then when I had got back, I was straight on to twelve-hour shifts and hadn't had a chance to get a haircut. I had thick curly hair in those days and because it was longer than usual, my RUC cap was not on right: it was sitting too high on my head. Snipers always aim for the band of the cap because that is usually the middle of the head and the terrorist was, ironically, a good shot. I still have the hat with the bullet holes.

I was able, later on, to work out what had been bothering me when we initially arrived at the call: there was no one about. In a small, close-knit community like that, if you'd had a burglary at your home people would know. Neighbours would be over offering support, and certainly watching what was going on as the police arrived and went about their business. The fact that there was no one about, no one out in the street, should have set off alarm bells.

It would be fifty-three weeks before I returned to work.

In my first week back I was asked to undertake uniform duty and walking out of the station in uniform for the first time since the shooting was a very big step for me. I later took up a position as an RUC transport manager until I was told I was no longer wanted.

Nobody has ever been made accountable for the shooting, but the rifle used was recovered a short time afterwards. A soldier had been shot with it and it was established that it had been used in several murders prior to the attack on me. I am just another statistic – some might not even describe me as a victim!

11:18 – Strand Road Police Station, Londonderry

One morning in the office, a colleague and I were briefed about some intelligence that had been received indicating that a part-time member of the UDR, Lieutenant Leslie Hamilton, was under serious threat. We went to see him, advised him about security and explained that he should make changes to his routine and be more careful about his habits. Unfortunately, he didn't believe anything would happen to him and carried on with his normal routine.

A couple of days after we had been to see him, I was on duty. I had started work at 8 o'clock in the morning. I heard the nearby gunfire but didn't know what it was. Reports of the incident came into the office and I was sent to the scene of the shooting. When I got there, I realised it was Hamilton. He was dead. He had been ambushed near the supermarket entrance in the Waterside area as he was unloading bread from his van. He had been shot at point-blank range. Witnesses said the gunmen, after shooting him in the head, chest and abdomen, stood over the dying man and fired at least eleven more bullets into him. Another witness told us they ran over to see if they could help, but he was lying in a pool of blood. The ambulance was there very quickly, but there was nothing anyone could do for him. Mr Hamilton had worked for a Coleraine bakery firm for thirteen years and called at the supermarket daily. A colleague who was with him managed to escape without injury.

The gunmen had driven into the supermarket car park at approximately 8.30 a.m. in a stolen car, which was later found abandoned at a nearby housing estate. The Provisional IRA telephoned a local newspaper claiming responsibility for the murder.

Leslie Hamilton had been a member of the UDR since its formation in 1970. He was accorded full military honours at his funeral service, which was held in the family church at Bready. He was thirty-six, and married with two sons, aged eight and thirteen.

11:30 – Newry Police Station, County Down

A number of years ago I was working in the unit that dealt with child abuse. We received a call about a cot death, which of course we have to investigate to rule out foul play. It turned out the call related to a three-month-old baby girl who had sadly passed away. When we received the call, the family were at Daisy Hill Hospital in Newry.

I made my way to the hospital as quickly as possible and when I got there, spoke to the duty sister who warned me that the family did not want the police anywhere near the place – she made me aware that they were a staunch republican family who had no love for the police. I was told they had said that if I went into the room there'd be trouble.

I rapped the door and went in and explained who I was and why I was there. The atmosphere in the room was really tense – you could almost feel the hatred directed towards me. Nobody was really speaking and I was told to get out of the room. The mother was sitting holding the wee baby, which she was nursing, and then she said to me, 'My baby is gorgeous. Isn't she lovely?' She was nursing her and gently rocking her. I stood beside her, looking at the child, then she handed me the wee baby.

That was nothing you could ever have been trained for; nothing you could have expected to occur in a situation like this. I said, 'Yes, she is gorgeous. She's beautiful.' I had a conversation with the mother, I then kissed the baby on the forehead and handed her back to her mum. It was just instinct and compassion for the mother's despair.

The instant I handed her back to her mum the whole atmosphere in the room changed. The father and grandfather came outside and spoke to me, thanked me and saw me to my car. They explained that their opinion had been that, if the police arrived, they would be gloating; delighted that they had lost the baby because of their background.

From that moment on they worked with me. I got all the details required for the pathologist and for the coroner, which is always a terrible job in such circumstances, but has to be done. There was just something in that simple act that made them realise that we are human, that we weren't the enemies the propaganda they read said we were. When I was handed that wee baby it could have been anybody's baby. I don't even remember kissing her on the forehead, it was just one of those instinctive things and obviously meant more than a thousand words.

The next day I had to call out to their house and when I arrived there was a group of youths on some high ground overlooking their home. Even though I was in plain clothes, they knew what had happened and guessed who I was. They immediately started to stone me and the vehicle, and I remember a paint bomb exploding just a couple of feet in front of me. Family members came out of the house and chased the young thugs away. One of my shoes was covered in paint, so I took it off before going into their home. The family were very apologetic about it and insisted on taking my shoes away and cleaning them while I gathered the information I needed. When I was leaving, they all thanked me profusely for my help and for the compassion I had shown in their time of grief. I told them not to hesitate to phone me if I could be of help to them at any time and we parted friends.

11:33 – CID Office, Strand Road Police Station, Londonderry

I was called to an incident in the late autumn [of 1981] – the murder of James McClintock, a fifty-seven-year-old married man with three children who worked as a driver for British Telecom. He was a country man who had spent quite some time in the UDR but had left it some fifteen years earlier. The IRA had been waiting for him in a blue Ford transit van that had been hijacked in the Shantallow area of the city. They had parked at a bad bend in the road where they knew their victim would have to slow down to get safely round it, and as he did so, they opened fire and completely riddled his car. They also opened fire on a farmer who happened to drive into the scene moments after the UDR man was murdered. The farmer was also shot but fortunately was only slightly injured.

I arrived at the scene and looked into the gentleman's car. I remember that he looked as if he was just sitting there, slumped forward, asleep. He had the most incredible expression of calm on his face, but from the eyebrows up half his skull was gone. What I saw that day has haunted me for many, many years. A dreadful scene that filled my dreams for a long time and still does to this day.

11:42 – MSU, Drumcree, Portadown

The protests at Drumcree Church developed after the Orange Order were prevented from returning along the Garvaghy Road to the Orange Hall in Portadown after attending a church service. The ensuing stand-off between the Orange Order, their supporters and the security services made international headlines the world over.

What became known simply as 'Drumcree' was without doubt one of the worst and most difficult periods in my police career. It was the knowledge that we were truly alone: that our communities, our friends and even relations had all turned against us. There was no longer a feeling of safety in our own homes. Colleagues were being attacked, their houses and vehicles damaged, and their families and children abused at work or school. In many cases, police officers were being put out of their homes and the towns they had lived in all their lives, never to return. It was a really nasty, hurtful period, but our determination to do our duty never wavered.

During the 1997 protest I was in one of the Fermanagh MSUs [mobile support units] and spent the days before the actual parade guarding the little bridge below the church, with the army engineers building the large CCO [crowd control obstacle] behind us. This was a huge construction of corrugated iron, steel girders and barbed wire, built as only the army can build, its purpose being to prevent anyone coming through, over the bridge or around it on to the banned route into Portadown.

While it was being constructed, we had to maintain a buffer zone in front of the bridge, as members of the public were coming down to watch, jeer and hurl abuse at us. When the working week drew to a close, the crowd would swell as protesters finished work on Friday and made their way to the area. As a result, Friday evening and all day

Saturday would see increased protests before the actual parade on the Sunday. At its worst, we were confronted with twenty thousand protesters; busloads even travelled over from Scotland and England to lend their support.

As dusk approached on Friday evening and the numbers grew, we prepared for the expected intensification and increased hostility from the protesters. By mid-evening we were in full riot gear – helmets, pads, shields and flame-retardant balaclavas and suits – standing in a line in front of the CCO while work to get it finished continued behind us. The protesters came down and stood right in front of our line. They were chatting and huddling in little groups, but as the numbers grew so did their courage until, eventually, we had quite a crowd standing in front of us, shouting insults, trying for weak spots in our ranks, pulling at shields, trying to kick our feet or stamp on our toes. We just stood there, in silence, resting our shields, waiting for the real rioting to start, as it inevitably would.

I had a male standing in front of me; at one point he was right up to my visor. He couldn't see my face due to the balaclava I was wearing and the reflections off the Perspex, but then he started playing to the crowd. Where was my wife? Who was with her while I was here? Who was she entertaining, and how many? He spent quite a while extolling her virtues, or lack of them, to the men around him, calling her the most offensive names he could think of, and accusing her of the vilest activities possible while I was standing there, miles from home, and blocking his path. The thoughts running through my mind during this extended tirade were mostly all the same: You should know, mate. She's your sister.

He was my brother-in-law.

The most hurtful thing about it all was that when I finally got home and told my wife, she sided with her brother. Only for the fact that she was pregnant with our first child, I'd have walked out there and then. I was so close to divorce, and I can understand why so many of my colleagues' relationships and marriages broke up in those years. It was all too close to home.

12:17 – MSU, Drumcree, Portadown

It was the very last Drumcree that G1 MSU were at, the now infamous Junior LOL [Loyal Orange Lodge] parade on 26 May 2000. I remember it was a really, really hot day, which was probably the straw that broke the camel's back for me. We knew we were going to be the front-line unit that day and we knew that the parade would go off fairly peaceably; it was only kids, the juniors, after all. They used to march off from what was the Prod end of the Garvaghy Road.

We sat there all day, toasted in our full public order flame-retardant gear, ready to go at a moment's notice. Then we ran out of water. It was extremely hot by late afternoon and I had a banging headache. As soon as the parade was over, the trouble started and we moved into position.

We had our five trucks and another unit, J1 or J2. A large crowd appeared very quickly after the parade dispersed, followed by salvos of petrol bombs and then acid bombs. I had to warn a couple of journalists about the acid as I could see they were getting little holes in their suits, which were smoking. I told them, 'That's acid,' but there was a female journalist there who didn't believe me and just laughed, saying; 'Acid, acid?' I said, 'Yes, you do you know where you are, don't you?'

We placed our riot shields up at the back of the Tango doors [a type of bulletproof Land Rover] to give us some sort of protection. I told the reporters, 'If you want to report from here, can you do it from somewhere reasonably safe?' It was very unusual that the reporters would actually be behind our lines, they normally chose to report things from the rioters side.

As the afternoon wore on the trouble really began to intensify. This was happening at the time when our authorities were insisting that we do public order duties without baton rounds being discharged. They would not give us permission to fire them to protect ourselves. Some bright spark in the command room, realising how bad the disorder was going to look on TV, decided we had to make some arrests. We all looked at each other and said, 'Make arrests with petrol bombs and acid bombs being thrown at us by the dozen?'

They sent the J1 unit out, but they only had twelve men fit to go on duty that day as they'd been hammered on their previous deployment. They were immediately surrounded by a crowd of four or five hundred people. Our inspector, who was probably the best inspector I ever worked with in the MSU, said, 'We are going to have to go and get these boys back. They're completely cut off and getting a hammering.'

We went out in open order [during a riot, police would move in close order, forming a tight, impenetrable unit, bound tightly together with shields connecting; for open order, there would be gaps in that formation] but it was too a big the space for us to cover it properly, so we were really restricted. We got the boys back but then we started getting hammered. In fact, they actually managed to grab one of my colleagues by the helmet and pull him over a hedge. He was quite badly beaten and they tried to take his gun from him as well, but he managed to hang on to it. He was probably the oldest member of our unit, but he never came back to the job after that.

We struggled to get behind the trucks that were very tightly packed together. There were five or six units behind us at this stage, but no help was forthcoming. I don't know why, but I assume the commanders did not give them permission to move forward. We got back in behind the trucks. We were the last crew back in and my skipper [sergeant] was just behind me. I noticed that a truck to my left was exposed on its own. The crowd had pulled the door of the Tango open and were throwing breeze blocks in on top of the driver. His own unit was out on the ground over on the other side, but they had driven their trucks so tightly together to prevent the crowd breaking through, they couldn't get past them to come to his assistance.

I said to my crew, 'Come on, we can't stand here, he's getting hammered there,' and we drew batons and moved forward. I just thought, they're going to kill this driver. We've got to save him. By the time we were able to get close to him, there were only three of my crew left behind me. I could see that the driver's arm was badly broken, and the blood was pouring out of him. We just leathered into them and got them far enough back to get his door closed. Don't ask me how we managed to get the truck back, because when I looked there were no drivers in the vehicles behind him, everyone was out on the ground. He was trapped. I shouted at him to stick the truck in reverse and plant it [drive with speed and force to get out of the danger zone, pushing other vehicles out of the way], that it was the only way he was going to get out of there. He managed to do that and pushed the truck behind him far enough back to get an opening and we were able to get him out of the vehicle and off to hospital. There was blood everywhere.

We were left then with the job of getting ourselves back. I was the last one to make it – they had managed to grab my shield and actually break it so that I had half a shield left. They started attacking my feet with breeze blocks. I remember getting hit repeatedly and the pain in the top of my feet was unbearable; I thought every toe I had must be smashed. I went down on my back with the remains of my shield pulled across the top half of me and that was the only thing that protected me, because I had no leg shields on. They were hammering and hammering at me. All I could hear was, 'Get the bastard. Get his legs, get his legs.'

One of the boys who was in operational training was a big, big giant of a man who came forward and got through to me. He pulled me back through the gap at the vehicle by my flak jacket. I couldn't stand, so they put me in an army Saracen, a medical one. The big man had effectively carried me back and set me in the rear of the Saracen. I had half a shield and half a baton, that's all that was left and an indication of how furious the hand-to-hand fighting was.

We had been tasked to come out and do our duty, and we were proud to do so, but we ended up having to attempt to rescue another unit because of the tactics used. The fighting lasted seven hours and we had no permission to fire baton rounds. One of our boys eventually got fed up with the mess and did open fire with the baton gun, discharging a round. That ended it. Seven hours of rioting spent asking for permission to defend ourselves was resolved by one baton round that someone decided to fire anyway.

I was brought to A & E at Craigavon Hospital by my colleague. Rioters began arriving in number and we ended up hiding behind the curtains. A row started in the hospital and we had to call for back up, and no fucking baton, nothing, just a gun. We were grossly outnumbered as the place became swamped with rioters.

I could barely stand properly, and I left the hospital that night on crutches, arriving home at about 5.30 in the morning. I was supposed to be going on a fishing trip over to England – a big lad from work had organised it – and I was so determined that these rioters would not stop me that I turned up on crutches, having had an hour's sleep.

That day destroyed our unit. There were boys who never came back and, of the twenty-six of us who went on duty that day, twenty-one were injured. It was embarrassing because of the reputation we'd had as a first-class unit – we just thought, that's us, we're finished here. It must have been around six weeks before most of the boys came back to work after their injuries.

We were sent straight into the Drumcree stand-off. We were parked up on standby in Lurgan police station when we heard on the radio that squaddies were being attacked down on the Lake Road in Lurgan and could we make our way there to assist ASAP. When we arrived, we were immediately attacked. A pipe bomb was thrown at us from the cul-de-sac at the railway – this backed on to a railway bridge where they could carry out their attacks and get away into the estate with relative safety. It was a well-thought-out location to attack us from.

Just as we got there, who arrives at the scene but John O'Dowd from Sinn Féin with four or five Provos in tow. He appeared beside a derelict building from where a pipe bomb had been thrown at the squaddies but hadn't detonated. He lifted the pipe bomb, or had it in his hand, as we came over to him. He was waving it at us shouting, 'I'll deal with it.'

Our inspector said, 'Fucking sure you won't. You put that down or I'll arrest you for possession of explosives.' We were concerned that any evidence that may have been on the device would have been destroyed by his handling of it. It turned into a bit of a stand-off and he actually had the balls to stand there with the fucking thing. He could have been shot.

I had to threaten him to make him put it down and eventually he did.

12:33 – Musgrave Street Police Station, Belfast City Centre

During the 1990s, and the planned campaign against Orange parades in interface or nationalist areas, Drumcree, Ardoyne, Dunloy and the Ormeau Road all became scenes of protest and confrontation. Undoubtedly there was a clear strategy behind these developments; the campaign also depended on local involvement to present a façade of deep injustice and hurt caused by these parades. Consequently, local people in each area were thrust into the media spotlight as the opponents of these parades. A suitable local resident, usually unemployed and/or a pensioner was selected to take a judicial review against any decision by the Parades Commission that did not go their way. Also, many of the local people who were against violence but did not want these parades in their area were at the fore in discussions with police and well-meaning negotiating groups such as the Quakers etc.

As a prelude to the season's parades, we discussed likely scenarios and what assistance we would need from the army. Some of this was in engineering and the creation of barriers that would minimise the exposure of police and army to large numbers of hostile elements from both sides.

The Parades Commission subsequently imposed conditions on the Twelfth of July parade on the Ormeau Road, Belfast – prohibiting it from using this main thoroughfare to travel to and from the city centre. The army immediately produced their blueprint of a barrier to close the Ormeau Road at the Ormeau Bridge. This looked very impressive, and we were assured it would withstand attacks by mechanical diggers etc. As the date of the parade approached, local police viewed this barrier within the confines of an army base. It certainly looked impressive, both in height and robustness.

Prior to the parade the army installed their barrier at

49

the Ormeau Bridge and it certainly was impressive. The road was completely blocked and, as the parade was about to start, we instructed the army to insert, we assumed, the two remaining blocks for the footpaths on either side of the roadway. The engineering officer looked aghast and immediately stated that he had only been asked to block the road – no one had mentioned footpaths! So here we had this massive obstruction but two large gaping holes either side of it. In fairness, the army quickly assembled a number of vehicles to plug these gaps.

As it turned out, the parade did not approach the Ormeau Bridge and the barrier was not needed, never mind tested, and the local community returned to normal everyday activity with the continued interaction between local police and residents.

In the aftermath of the parades I went into a travel agent in the city centre to enquire about a family holiday. Imagine my surprise when I bumped into one of the leading spokespersons for the resident's group. After a few minutes conversation I casually said to him that it would not do my reputation any good if I was seen chatting to him. He, much more seriously, said, 'You might be worried about your reputation, I would be more worried about my kneecaps.'

12:45 – CID Office, Armagh Police Station, County Armagh

I was in the office when I got called to Orangefield estate on the unionist side of the city. A lot of policemen and UDR men used to live there – members of the security forces felt it was safer than a lot of other places in the area. The call was to the apparent suicide of a part-time UDR soldier who lived in the house with his elderly mother.

I brought a uniform policewoman with me in the hope that she would be able to comfort the mother while I investigated the scene to try and work out what exactly had happened, and to rule out any foul play. We went into the house and, understandably, the man's mother was in quite a bit of a state. She informed me that her son was lying upstairs in bed. We got the lady calmed down a bit and I asked her to make a cup of tea. It was more to give her something to do really while I got on with what I had to. She was immediately much more settled. The policewoman and I went upstairs into the bedroom and there he was, lying in bed with his .22 pistol [a personal protection weapon] in his hand, lying back on the pillow with his eyes open. It wasn't gruesome or anything; he could well have been alive, so I leaned over and put my ear to his mouth to see if I could hear any breathing, in which case I would send for an ambulance straight away. I wasn't confident that his mother would have called an ambulance or checked his condition when she saw him at first. She must have been out of her mind not knowing what to do. But he was dead.

The next thing, he just suddenly sat bolt upright. The policewoman started screaming and ran out of the room down the stairs and into the street. While I didn't run away, I must admit I nearly shit myself. He lay down again and that was the end of it. You hear stories about headless chickens, but people with a gunshot wound to the head jumping about? The policewoman who'd been brought to console the mother ended up in a worse state than her, and this lovely old lady had to comfort her.

12:48 – Lurgan, County Armagh

It was the Twelfth of July and we were in full riot gear, trying to prevent potential disruptions to the main parade as it passed through Lurgan centre. It suited Sinn Féin if local youths caused trouble, as they could point to the statistics and claim that there was always violence associated with the annual parade, in the hope of yet more restrictions.

We had a crowd throwing stones at us from a distance, then the stones turned to petrol bombs and we took cover behind the vehicles. It was a lovely sunny day, and we were quite relaxed, standing in the sun eating our packed lunches, watching the rioters through the open rear doors, then the windscreens of the vehicles as they approached the police line to throw their missiles. There was the usual mixture of stones, bottles, bricks and petrol bombs, but the danger is always that there may be blast bomb among them.

One young lad was throwing repeatedly, though not particularly accurately, and as the day progressed, he came ever closer. We weren't too concerned, being safe behind the armoured vehicles, but eventually he began to become a nuisance. A mate and I stripped down to bare uniform – no flak jacket, pads or gun belt, no shield or helmet, just a three-foot baton. We watched as the young lad approached and then, as he drew back his arm to throw, we sprinted out between the Land Rovers.

He stood, transfixed – should he throw, or drop it and run? By the time he had decided which, we were on him. My colleague rugby tackled him to the ground then, as he tried to rise towards me, I hit him with the full weight of the baton. The rioter went down, was restrained, and we took him to the nearest available custody suite.

As soon as we got him to the station to be processed, he visibly deflated and started to cry. 'You've ruined my life,' he told me. 'I'll never get to America now.' He could see nothing wrong with his own actions but the police, by arresting him for what he did and subsequently securing him a conviction for riotous behaviour, had ruined his chance of an American visa. It was always our fault.

12:50 – Special Patrol Group, Belfast City Centre

It was 26 May 1972, and I was a sergeant in the Special Patrol Group [Riot Police]. Back then it was illegal to park and leave a car unattended in Belfast. Unattended cars would be opened by the army using a Carl-Gustaf rocket launcher with a non-explosive head.

That day, we were in an armoured Land Rover with seven occupants: five police and two soldiers. The soldiers were our heavily-armed protection. We turned left on to Oxford Street from Chichester Street – Oxford Street runs close and parallel to the river Lagan; Laganbank Road also runs parallel to the river and joins Oxford Street on its right – and saw two council workers painting white lines on Oxford Street to facilitate a new one-way system. There was a large grain truck entering the intersection on our right from the Lagan side. There was a woman, Margaret Young, walking on the pavement to our left. She was passing between a car showroom and a parked green Volkswagen Beetle. I saw the car was empty.

I said, 'We better check that car,' and, as we approached, I opened the door of the Land Rover. We were about four metres from the car when it exploded. We owe our lives to that armoured Land Rover.

I did not hear or feel anything. I was, however, totally aware of my surroundings. I saw the large grain lorry explode and I saw the driver fly out through the windscreen. Grain when exposed to massive heat will separate and each kernel burns instantly creating a low but powerful explosion. I immediately made a radio transmission to report the blast. Later, I spoke to the radio operator in Castlereagh, about five miles away. He told me he had left his position to stretch his legs and was looking out the windows over the city when he heard my transmission. He turned his head toward his radio and then the blast hit the windows. My transmission reached the radio room before the blast.

At the scene I grabbed a first-aid kit and went immediately to Margaret Young. She had lost her legs and waist just below her midriff. Her body ended and evolved into where the rubble began. She subsequently lived for six hours. I left one of the men with her and told him to hold her hand and to talk to her.

I ran over to the grain truck and found the driver sitting on the road, shaken, but otherwise okay. I went back to the area where the men had been marking the road. They had parts of the car sticking out of them. I tended to them to stop bleeding; their breathing, which is the first consideration, being nearly normal. The ambulance, fire department and other police arrived within minutes. It was thought the explosion was remotely detonated by the bomber who was observing from nearby. Another two seconds and I would have ended up like the unfortunate Margaret Young.

When we left the scene, we retired to the canteen at Donegall Pass station. There we had tea. We spoke about everything except that which we had jointly experienced. A common thing among trained people who have just gone through trauma. We carried on as if nothing had happened, just like every other RUC member did on a daily basis.

12:57 – Coalisland Police Station, County Tyrone

On 26 March 1997, two men threw an explosive device at Coalisland police station. Unfortunately for them the Det [Military Detachment – an army plain-clothes special reconnaissance unit] were carrying out an operation in the area in relation to something else. They saw these two guys with hoods over their heads throw something and then heard the bang from the explosion. They immediately challenged the men, were ignored, and so subsequently opened fire. One of the men, Gareth Doris, was wounded while the other, Paul Campbell, was grazed by a bullet.

Doris was arrested at the scene and later sentenced to ten years for possession of an explosive device – believed to be a home-made device containing about a pound of Semtex or similar – and causing an explosion. Campbell, however, made off by hijacking a vehicle being driven by the local parish priest who was unaware of the incident and just told to drive. That night Campbell was taken across the border, by others, and admitted to hospital in Dundalk under an assumed name.

The following day I was approached by Special Branch who told me that they had received intelligence to say that one of the perpetrators was in Dundalk Hospital. I rang a Garda that I knew, explained what had happened and he told me he would get back to me shortly. True to his word he rang me back and said, 'Yes, there's a fella in here with a gunshot wound who was brought in on the night in question. He threatened staff, demanding treatment.'

Blood had been recovered from the back seat of the priest's car, and we were very fortunate that it *had* been recovered because, believe it or not, the forensic scientist who initially looked at the car was colour blind. I thought that if we could just get the bandages used in the hospital, we would be able to match the blood with that found in the car and it would prove that this person was the one who carried out the attack. This would give us enough to begin extradition proceedings. There had been a long history of difficulties in obtaining extradition of terrorist suspects from the Republic of Ireland to the UK, but I was confident that this would give us a fairly good case. I made sure that every i was dotted and t crossed, knowing that with the courts everything had to be absolutely correct. I was determined to leave no loopholes. However, it transpired that before we could get the bandages, the authorities in the south had to ask the defendant to give his permission for them to be handed over. Unlikely, to say the least.

It was years later before Campbell was arrested in Northern Ireland. In 2015 he was arrested coming off a train in Portadown. [In February 2020, he was sentenced to seven and a half years in prison for his part in the attack.]

13:06 – CID Office, Strand Road Police Station, Londonderry

I got called out to an incident in which four IRA men had tried to kill an undercover soldier at the junction of Southway and Lone Moor Road in the Brandywell area of the city. Earlier that day, they had stopped a civilian, Daniel Moore, in the Creggan estate, taken his car and held him captive for an hour and a half.

The lone soldier was driving an Opel Ascona car and had been spotted in the area by the IRA active service unit. They pulled up in front of his car intending to challenge him but, as the terrorists got out of the car, he managed to fire at them first. Two of them were shot dead and the third gunman was seriously injured. The fourth member of the gang drove off, leaving his colleagues behind.

A colleague and I were the first detectives on the scene, and straight away we were given information telling us where the wounded IRA man had allegedly been taken. We went immediately to the house to see if we could catch him. All we found was a chair, the cushions of which had been saturated in blood from where he had sat, bleeding out. The whole area was soaked in his blood but he had clearly been moved. He was believed to have been taken away in a 'Provo ambulance', which was trying to get him across the border into Donegal, but he was so badly wounded they had to take him straight to Altnagelvin

Hospital in Londonderry. There, he was dealt with and arrested. He later pleaded guilty to having two Armalite rifles with intent and attempting to hijack the soldier's car. The court sentenced him to five years imprisonment.

Meanwhile I had gone back to the scene, which by now had a fair number of police present. I remember one of the uniform lads opened the driver's door of a Land Rover to call me. He said, 'You better watch out, they have a habit of opening fire on us when we are on the ground.' Just as he said it, the first high-velocity round hit the back of his Land Rover. I took cover, as the gunfire was quite intensive at that stage, but he drove off. It was funny looking back, him driving off, leaving me totally exposed at a time when I was seeing bullets hit the road, not even knowing where they were coming from. I ran for cover and got behind a small wall. Speaking now, the weird thing is how much we accepted these things as normal, yet I could have been killed.

13:25 – Crime Squad, Castlereagh Police Station, East Belfast

The regional head of CID was giving a briefing to the crime squad about a major investigation that was going on. There were quite a number of officers there of varying ranks and, of course, the squad themselves. The chief superintendent had a fairly ferocious reputation, which he played on to a certain extent, to try and get things done. As part of this inquiry he had sent a detective over to headquarters to get three albums of material printed immediately. The detective was to use his name if necessary, to ensure that it was done.

Of course, the relevant people in headquarters were busy, or may well have been making a point that they weren't going to jump to get things done ahead of other work just because this person had requested it. They said to the detective that they would get on the phone when the material was ready and that he would have to call back. He returned to the crime squad briefing empty-handed.

The boss turned round in front of the assembled crew and said, 'I don't know, sometimes I think those people up in headquarters think I'm nuts.' Then one of his detective inspectors responded by saying, 'You know what, sir, I wouldn't restrict that just to headquarters.'

13:30 – Coffee-time Reflections

I come from a Catholic background and I must say that, never once from the day I started did I feel any animosity from my colleagues. Over the years I have heard a lot of nonsense talked about this, and myths have sprung up, usually manufactured by the republican movement who tried to create their own narrative, which, as far as I experienced, was just lies. I never had one moment of anti-Catholic feeling – it just did not exist. In fact, I would say quite the opposite: I enjoyed great friendships; friendships that have lasted a lifetime. There was fantastic camaraderie and a bond that never leaves you.

Looking back, my time in the RUC was very enjoyable. All I wanted to do was catch the bad guys and be a policeman. It just so happened that I was going to be a policeman in Northern Ireland, which came with its baggage. There were times that it was tight, and it was certainly dangerous as we know all too well, but that was all I wanted to do and I like to think, I suppose, that I caught a few bad boys along the way.

13:48 – Lisburn Police Station, County Antrim

When I was stationed in Lisburn, a local man, Paul Gault, was murdered in his own home. The scene of the crime had been staged to look like a burglary gone wrong, but we quickly figured out that it was a domestic-related crime. It transpired that the man's wife, Lesley Gault, had been involved in an affair with Gordon Graham, an assistant chief fire officer in Fire Brigade HQ in Lisburn.

It was the talk of the place because Paul and Lesley had had triplets, and reporters from the *Lisburn Star* newspaper had made this into a big local story when they were born. The pictures were the story: beautiful newly-born triplets pictured with a very proud mum and dad at their happy family home.

Fast forward five years, the husband's dead and we have arrested Mrs Gault. Lisburn was just abuzz with this unbelievable twist in the tale. From a police point of view it was a really interesting investigation to be confronted with, largely because of the sequence of events that led to the murder.

It all began on 1 May 2000 when Paul found out about the affair – Lesley had purportedly confessed to him when he'd caught her on the phone with Gordon. According to Lesley, after a full-on argument, the pair had agreed to keep trying for the kids' sake and some days later had decided to go away for the weekend to the Killyhevlin Hotel in Fermanagh in an attempt to reconcile.

Some eighteen days after the affair was uncovered, on the morning they were due to leave, Paul and Lesley returned to their home having dropped the children – who were in P1 – off at school. Lesley then went to leave some of the children's things at her parents' house, as they were looking after the kids that weekend. Paul went into the house through the back door, went into their bedroom to pack some bags, whereupon he was beaten to death with a hockey stick. He was beaten to an absolute pulp – his head was completely crushed.

According to Lesley's version of events, she had then

returned from visiting her parents and gone to the back door – the Gaults very seldom used the front door – and noticed that the window in the door was broken. She said that she'd decided not to go into the house but instead ran round the front to go to the neighbour in the adjoining semi-detached house. She told the neighbour what she had found and the two of them came round to her back door. The neighbour went into the house, stepped over broken glass and called for Paul but got no answer. Strangely, Lesley stayed outside at all times. The two went back around to the front and the neighbour called the police to report a burglary. Then he returned to the rear of the house on his own.

He went through the house, including upstairs to the bedroom, and eventually found Paul. He made a second phone call to the police, this time telling them there was a dead body in the house. This triggered our standard procedure for such calls: uniform police arrived at the address first, confirmed that there was a body and set up a crime scene.

Meanwhile Paul's father, Paddy Gault, had arrived at the house and pushed past the uniform police at the door. He made his way up to the bedroom – and this is the bit that just gets you – he held his son's body. Then he ran downstairs, covered in blood and says to the police, 'That's not a burglary. My son has been murdered.'

I distinctly remember getting the phone call about the case. I was on the late shift and wasn't due in yet but when my boss filled me in on what was happening, I did a U-turn, dropped my wife and kids back home and said, 'Sorry, I'm going into work.'

We were doing house-to-house enquiries and usually on a case like this, the neighbours will all tell you how terrible what has just happened is; but all we kept getting was, 'Mr Gault? That's dreadful. Do you know about the fireman?' and 'Oh aye, the fireman.' They told us that this fireman drove a white Vauxhall Cavalier, and we even got his licence plate number. By coincidence my next-door neighbour was also in the fire department – he was also an assistant chief fire officer – so I phoned him up and said, 'Do me a favour, check this number for me. I think it's one of yours.' He says, 'Yes, it's owned by Gordon Graham.' I asked, 'What does he do?' He replied, 'He's in charge of health and safety.' Pretty ironic.

Thanks to my neighbour we knew that Gordon was at work and less than three hours after Paul Gault's death, we were knocking on Gordon Graham's door. We sent detectives round and they informed him they wanted to speak to him about Lesley Gault. He soon admitted their relationship. Then we said we wanted to talk to him about her husband, adding, 'Her husband's dead,' but he was calm as you like. The only thing he said was, 'What, and you suspect me?' He was cool as a cucumber the whole time.

Thankfully we had been able to get to Gordon quickly and seize all his clothes. However, not one spot of blood was found. We knew, given the blood distribution and the brutal way that Paul had been killed, that the murderer should have been covered in blood himself, but the assertion we later made (which was broadly accepted in court) was that, thanks to his role as lead health and safety officer, Gordon would have had access to forensic suits. We did find *some* forensic evidence – a piece of glass that was embedded in the sole of his shoe. It hadn't been worn down in any way, which meant it had been freshly acquired. If we had waited any longer, that evidence would have been lost. There were also tiny fragments of glass in his work shirt pocket.

In the same way, there wasn't one spot of blood outside the bedroom where Paul had been killed, yet we knew that if someone was to beat someone to death in their bedroom unexpectedly, they would be certain to leave a trail of forensic evidence out the door. The fact that there was no blood anywhere else in the house was inconceivable ... unless there had been prior planning. In addition, a bedroom is quite a confined area. You only have certain spaces in which you could do something like swing a hockey club – otherwise you'd be hitting wardrobes and all things – yet miraculously Paul had been killed in the spot where the best opportunity could present itself. It was a kill zone; it was an ambush, which again pointed to prior planning. And if there had been prior planning, then it couldn't have been a burglary that *had* gone wrong. Who had the motivation to kill Paul Gault? That brought us back to the affair.

As far as we were concerned – and this was our proposition to the DPP and Crown Court – three things had to happen for Paul Gault to be murdered. One, he had to be off work that day, a Friday, which had happened because Lesley had suggested they go to the Killyhevlin Hotel for the weekend, a holiday that she had booked. Two, he had to be out of the house to allow the attacker to get in. We had evidence from the school teachers that the triplets had been taken to school by their mum every single day apart from the day of the murder. They had never even met Paul Gault, except for the one occasion that got him out of the house. Three, he had to be home alone and walk into the kill zone, something that was achieved by having him go home and pack their bags. Lesley had dropped him off at the driveway, told him that she was going to her parents, then watched him walk to the back of the house.

We zeroed in on Gordon Graham. Before lunchtime on the day of the murder we'd got him locked in as best we could – the clothes had been taken off him, and we'd been given the first account of his movements, allowing us to have something we could then pick apart. He was so precise about all of his movements except for the period of time when the murder had actually occurred. We'd been able to pin that down thanks to the Gault's next-door neighbour who said he remembered hearing all this noise from next door. He'd looked at his digital clock and, though he couldn't remember the actual time, he told us that 'it was nine-zero-something.' We now had a nine-minute window in which the murder could have happened; between 9.01 and 9.09.

Gordon claimed that he'd been in work early that morning, then gone to Bow Street in Lisburn town centre to get a birthday present for his wife. But that was where his story became vague. All he could tell us about that time was 'I was up and down the shops in Bow Street trying to find a birthday gift,' but for other times he was much more precise, saying things like, 'Then I went to Marks & Spencer's at Sprucefield because I needed to buy something.' We did find CCTV footage of him walking in the front door of Marks & Spencer's: he looks straight ahead but just for a moment he looks up, not only checking that he can see the cameras but, more importantly, that they can see him. He walks through the shop and buys a little carton of blackcurrant juice, the receipt for which he readily produces. It is, of course, dated and timed. A very peculiar thing to keep a receipt for! He then, for some reason, chooses to drive home to Ballygowan, which is over fourteen miles away from Lisburn, to leave some wood off. He speaks to the babysitter and fiddles about in the house for a while. But while he could give us a very strong account for most parts of the day, he had nothing for the bit in the middle, the time of the murder.

We had to prove that he wasn't walking up and down Bow Street at the time of the murder or, if we did find him on the CCTV between 9.00 and 9.10, well then we'd know that it couldn't have been him and we'd be starting again from scratch. Thankfully, we caught a break.

We'd done a complete sweep of CCTV footage from all round Lisburn and were confident he was not there. The only potential issue came from the video from the Orange mobile phone shop. The shop had a camera over the front door that looked all the way across the full breadth of Bow Street, so if someone walked from left to right, or right to left, you would see them. The detective assigned to the CCTV trawl started the video at about the 8.45 a.m. mark or so and that's when disaster seemed to strike – the view of Bow Street had been completely obscured by a promotional poster for the latest mobile phone stuck to the front door. The detective says to himself, 'You are kidding me. This is the best video we have and it's been blocked by that stupid poster.' People talk about Maradona and the hand of God, but they have nothing on the Orange mobile shopkeeper who, just at the moment it turns 9.00 on the tape, opens the door, leaving it wide open and taking the poster out of sight. We now had a perfect view and were able to prove that Gordon wasn't anywhere near Bow Street when he said he was.

We think that Lesley Gault had also been banking on CCTV to give her an alibi. After she'd gone to her parents', she'd driven into Lisburn and walked around a pharmacy that happened to have CCTV. She is seen buying Calpol [children's paracetamol]. We immediately asked her, 'Why did you get Calpol? None of your kids were sick.' 'It was just as a precaution,' she said. We thought that it was nothing to do with precaution – we believed she wanted to be seen on CCTV.

We carried out a further examination at the rear of the Gault's home. The apparent point of entry was through the back door, which had a solid bottom half and a double-glazed glass top half. When police arrived, the glass in the door had been broken in a similar fashion to what a burglar would do, though we had concerns in this case as double glazing is very difficult to break. The glass was also marked like someone had cut at it and left scratches. No one had ever heard of a burglary being done that way, with scoring to the glass, apart from in the movies. We looked at all of the crime reports across the entirety of Northern Ireland and found no evidence of a burglary being done like that. It just didn't make any sense.

We had to work really hard to disprove the burglary gone wrong plan. Had this been a genuine burglary there were only two options: either the burglary happened before Paul came home or it happened after he arrived home from the school run. If it had happened before he came home, he would have seen that the glass was broken, which would have immediately put him on alert, but still decide to walk into his small three-bedroom semi-detached house. He would have had to walk in and, on not seeing any sign of the burglar, carry on into the bedroom and start packing a bag to go away for the weekend. He doesn't ring the police to report what has happened. In fact, he doesn't do anything. He is taken by surprise by the would-be burglar, who for some reason hadn't been disturbed by Paul returning home. Then the burglar decides in that instant that his best course of action would be to kill him. He happens to come across the deadliest weapon he could: a hockey stick that is just sitting outside the bedroom he is in (the stick was used to open the roof-space hatch). Now, that's a lot of things that have to come together by coincidence. But all of that aside, we could rule this out as an option because, when we checked Paul's shoes there was no glass on them. He hadn't walked through any broken glass on his way in.

That left us with the second option: Paul's already in the house, packing away, when suddenly, *smash*, the window is broken (unnecessarily as it happens, because Paul didn't lock the door behind him when he got home). Had there been a smash, he would have been immediately alerted, yet for some reason this man – who was on medication for anger management issues – on hearing this breaking glass, decides to ignore it and continue to pack the bag. The burglar, meanwhile, unaware that he may have alerted someone, carries on with the burglary and moves further into the house. He would have been surprised to find Paul, who is equally surprised, but the burglar still finds the hockey stick and, critically, decides to kill Paul. It was just nonsense.

We were certain the killer had broken the window after the murder and that he'd done it from the outside so that the glass fell inside the house. It had to have been the last thing he did otherwise he would have put Paul on alert as soon as he arrived.

For us, the burglary theory had been eliminated: we knew this had to have been a murder committed by someone with a motive. This led us back to the lover and the wife. But then, how did the murderer get into the house? Had a key been provided?

During the house-to-house enquiries we spoke to a mother and daughter who lived across the street from the Gaults. Their evidence was to prove vital. On the morning of the murder the mother had been outside, waiting to drive her daughter to the train station to catch the 8.15 train. The girl was running late. Lesley Gault drove past in her car and, as the woman told us, 'She didn't slow down or wave or anything … I had to sort of squeeze in to let her car get past me, while I'm shouting at the daughter to hurry up.'

The significance of this information came when we interviewed Lesley. When we asked if she'd gone anywhere the morning of the murder she said, 'Oh, I didn't go anywhere, I was at home.' We told her we'd two witnesses who said she'd gone out, but she kept denying it: 'No, I didn't go out.' This went back and forth and back and forth so, in a switch of questioning, we jumped to another detail: 'Well, what were you having for breakfast?' 'I don't know, I think Paul had cereal.' 'What did you have?' 'Special K.' She was then shown a photograph of a saucepan with scrambled egg in it. It can always come down to the detail really. Now you could say, how would anyone remember a detail like that about the day their husband was murdered? But equally, maybe she didn't remember because she wasn't there, she was out driving. Our theory was that she and Gordon came together somewhere during the time she was out so she could hand over a key to her house. Then whenever she and Paul went out to do the school run, Gordon was able to use the key to slip in, locking the door behind him. Then he waited; the trap was set.

We now had to prove that the whole thing was a staged crime scene – the first time we'd ever had a staged crime scene presented as evidence in Northern Ireland.

Paul's body was left with his back to a wall and his side against a chest of drawers, on top of which were Lesley's jewellery boxes. The police photographer had recorded the scene: the first picture was taken as found; the second picture had items lifted out of the way to prove or disprove there had been blood underneath them. Through this we were able to show the flow of blood at the time of the crime and whether it had been the case that the burglar had killed Paul, but not intended to do it; or having killed Paul was calm enough to lean over his dead body and select things out of the jewellery box. Then, having done all that, he doesn't actually take anything because, downstairs in the kitchen, he leaves his sports bag, full of the family's valuables: an Xbox, a PlayStation, a video recorder and two crystal glasses. Having gathered all that stuff in the bag, why would he leave it? Perhaps if you wanted a big sign that said to the peelers it had been a burglary gone wrong.

We did something that was a first, certainly for Northern Ireland. We'd already got evidence back from forensic science that showed that the glass found on the sole of Gordon's shoe, and glass found in his fire rescue suit, were a match for the outer window of the Gault's back door. But now we did a low copy DNA test, which is extremely sensitive. Blood, semen, hair and so on are the sort of thing you usually get DNA from, but low copy DNA is taken from trace evidence. We submitted the sports bag for examination, requesting that the handles and the lining of the bag be looked at in particular. Six months later I received a phone call informing me we'd got a double hit on the baseline test. The likelihood of the handles on the bag being handled by somebody other than Gordon Graham was one in a billion. Now we had strong forensic evidence.

The two suspects had also written love letters and had a high volume of calls and texts to each other, which showed the intensity of the relationship, and right up to the day before Paul Gault was killed, including when Gordon Graham had been at a training course with the fire service in Nottingham, there was a record of phone calls back and forth between them. Then, on 19 May, the day of the murder, radio silence, absolutely nothing. After the murder, we put the two of them under surveillance. We had watched Lesley running around Lisburn as we waited for the two of them to come together but the closest we got was Lesley going to a phone box and calling his number while holding her mobile phone in her hand.

Gordon Graham was charged with the murder of Paul Gault, but the DPP [director of public prosecutions] would not allow us to charge Lesley with murder and instructed that she would be reported to them for a later decision. I think they were afraid of charging her then maybe having to withdraw that charge. We told them about the call she had made from the phone box, but unfortunately the judge ruled against putting that into evidence.

This had all been at a time before family liaison was built into the procedure for a case like this, so throughout the investigation I had liaised with the Gault family; mainly Paul's father Paddy, a solid, decent man who had worked in the docks all his days. Paul's mother was such a gentle lady. Every time I arrived at the house, she would take herself off to the kitchen and make a cup of tea. She didn't want to talk; she couldn't bear to be involved in the conversations she knew I would have to have. One day Paddy said to me, 'You're not thinking that Lesley might be involved?' and I had to go silent because I was absolutely thinking Lesley could be involved.

On the day we had arrested the two of them, I went to Paddy's house and said, 'We've made two arrests this morning: we've arrested a man from the fire service ... and we've arrested your daughter-in-law.' There was a lot of emotion from him – relief, disappointment and anger all rolled into one. Apparently, he'd found out about another affair that Lesley had been having but hadn't told Paul. He'd felt guilty: 'If I had said to Paul then about her involvement with so-and-so, this might never have happened.' But only a day and a half later, I was back at the house to tell Paddy that we'd had to let Lesley go. I tried to reassure him that we were not finished, that we were reporting her to the

DPP, but I don't think he even heard the last bit.

She was released from the custody suite in Grosvenor Road RUC station, where she'd just been interviewed for a day and a half over the murder of her husband – and wouldn't you think she'd lie low for a while? Wrong. She comes straight up to the grandparents' house to get her kids back. Instead of waiting outside in the car and having her solicitor or someone else come to the door, she marches up to the front door as brazen as you like to demand the kids. Jim, Paul's older brother, opened the door to her, while I stood at the living room door with Paddy, Paul's two sisters and several other family members behind me, all of them wanting to kill her. They really wanted to lynch her, and I had to hold them all back, but she just marches in and happily goes on up the stairs. The triplets were in their pyjamas so, while they were getting ready, she came back down. Then, from nowhere, a big fist thumped her in the face and a whole fight broke out. There's hair being pulled; there's legs being kicked; she's squealing, hitting the sisters and they start squealing; and there I was, with my boss, right in the middle of it, trying to get them broken up, while the three kids sit at the top of the stairs watching. It was horrendous. She then marches off taking the kids with her, leaving me to sort out a shellshocked Paddy and family.

Twenty-four hours later, the DPP confirmed that they were content to proceed with the murder charge against Gordon Graham. It would have been my job to charge him, but I'd had to leave for a prearranged family holiday. As fate would have it, though, I had to write the report for the murder file when I returned, which resulted in another first for policing in Northern Ireland. Because we'd thought this case had been a staged crime scene, we needed to get independent expert analysis to prove it, and so we went to the FBI. My boss and I boxed up as much of the evidence as we could – crime scene photographs, post-mortem photographs, scenes of crime examination reports, intelligence that we had gathered related to the case – and sent it through the American embassy in London to Quantico, the FBI headquarters. We flew over to the United States for a case conference, the detail of which was incredible. We were to present our evidence to the behavioural analysis unit, the experts that deal with serial killers across the United States. Four senior supervising special agents came into the room and produced magnifying glasses. We thought, 'Come on, what is this Sherlock Holmes stuff? Magnifying glasses?', but they went through every photograph in granular detail. They were looking at one of the photos of the bedroom when one of the FBI agents asked, 'What's that length of wood sitting in the middle of the bedroom?' Well, Phil and I looked at each other – we couldn't remember any length of wood, and we were worried we had missed something. Turns out, an extendable ruler, which is used when a crime scene is mapped out, had been left in the shot. We had to explain what it was, but my heart had skipped a beat for a moment! They were really on the ball. They were also very complimentary about the examination and the report on the crime scene, and they provided expert analysis to confirm that this was a staged crime scene. That was the first time the FBI had been involved in that sort of behavioural analysis work for a Northern Irish case.

Eventually the big trial came along. One of the points that came up was the use of the hockey stick as a weapon. The defence counsel argued that a hockey stick wouldn't really do any harm, but the pathologist insisted that it was a formidable weapon. It was the language that he used in his evidence that was so compelling to the jury. We made the point that, of all weapons he could have used, why choose this hockey stick? It still had the dyno tape on it with Lesley's name written on it in her own hand. It was because it was like a final two-fingered salute to Paul Gault – this thing's going to kill you and it belongs to your wife!

I remember sitting in the Crown court in Belfast, thinking about something Paddy Gault had said to me. He'd told me that he came from a very republican family – old-school IRA in the 1950s/1960s; probably stickies [Official IRA] back in the 1970s – and, though he'd assured me that he'd never been involved in anything himself, some of his family members had. He was just letting me know that 'This guy, Gordon Graham, has to be convicted. This court has to do the right thing ...' and he let that linger, saying nothing but saying everything all at once. I was thinking, here's Paddy, his entire family are old-time IRA from the lower Falls, who no doubt know some new-time Provos ... if Gordon Graham walks out of court one day, he might not make it to his car.

Gordon Graham was convicted of murder and given a life sentence. For Lesley Gault, though, there was a hung jury, and a decision was made to have her re-tried alone. A second trial took place just for her and this time the jury convicted her of murder by a majority ruling. She was sentenced to life in prison. They both lodged appeals against conviction: his was held first and was dismissed. But at Lesley's appeal, her lawyers raised seventeen or eighteen disputed matters, one of which related to the summing up by the judge on her second trial.

That judge had told the jury that for Mrs Gault to be convicted of murder, a number of scenarios had to play out. If the jury believed that Mrs Gault dropped her husband off at the gate of their home knowing he was going to be murdered, they could convict of murder. If they believed

72

that she knew he was going to be the subject of a grievous bodily harm, they could also convict of murder. And finally, if they believed that Mrs Gault dropped her husband at the gate of their home believing or knowing that he was going to be subjected to an assault that *might* end up with him being killed, they could also convict of murder. The first two points he'd made were fine, absolutely solid. But he had gone about twenty words too far. [For her murder charge to stick, the murder or a GBH that might cause his death, and not merely assault for which death is not the intended outcome, needed to have been premeditated.] Defence counsel picked up on those last few words and, along with the other points, made it part of Lesley's appeal.

The appeal lasted for three days and was heard by three judges, including the Lord Chief Justice Brian Kerr, who was chair. The case was broken down line by line and, in his summation, Kerr worked through every point raised by the defence. He dismissed every one of them except the final appeal point which pivoted around the third point made by the original judge in his guidance to the jury. He ruled that on that one point alone the appeal must be allowed to stand, and overturned the conviction. He then added that it was a matter for the DPP whether they wished to consider a third trial. And then he did something unexpected – he remanded Lesley Gault back into custody until such time as the DPP had made that decision. By keeping her in custody, he forced the hand of the DPP who had to make a decision within days whether to go for a third trial, which they did.

The defence lawyer requested that the third trial be held outside Belfast because the jury panel there was tainted. Consequently, the trial was listed for Omagh courthouse and lasted for five weeks. For clarity, when deliberating, a jury must try to reach a unanimous verdict first, but if that cannot be reached, it may then consider a majority verdict. However that can only happen if the judge permits them to move to the majority verdict option. The accepted minimum time a jury must deliberate before a judge can grant this is two hours and ten minutes. In this case, the jury was given the majority option immediately after the two hours ten minutes minimum. Shortly after that, they returned with a majority verdict of not guilty. In my view that seemed to be a rush to judgement, barely outside the statutory minimum timeframe. How can you go from a hung jury in one trial to a majority guilty in another trial to a majority not guilty on the third trial – and all based on the same evidence? That's the vagary of the jury system.

The outcome of that trial marked the culmination of four years' work and now I had to handle passing the news to the Gault family, who had sat through each day of the three trials. 'That's it,' I said. 'Unless there is new and compelling evidence from somewhere, it's over.' They were just devastated from having to live with the incredibly heavy toll those dreadful events had taken on their lives.

I remember standing outside Omagh Courthouse and in front of me was a car containing Lesley Gault and her solicitor. As I turned away, the press doorstepped me, asking me what I thought. I told them, 'There were two people involved in this murder; one has been properly convicted. We are not looking for anyone else in connection with the crime.' That was the headline that ran, and to this day I have no doubt that she was involved.

Several years after the acquittal, we decided the best course we had open to us was to pursue a civil action against her as by then she had received her dead husband's life insurance. We referred her to the Assets Recovery Agency, or as it was then the Serious Organised Crime Agency, to stop her from being the beneficiary of a crime.

As a result, we seized and sold her house, the proceeds from which, along with any money we could find, were placed into a trust for the children. She is now married to an Elim Pentecostal pastor working down in the Shannon area in the Republic of Ireland, happily spreading the gospel as a pastor's wife.

I kept up the connection I had made with the Gault family, though, sadly, Paddy has since died. I went to his funeral service at the chapel in Lambeg. When my father died, the triplets came to his funeral; they're in their twenties now. And when my brother Alan, who was a sergeant in the RUC, died suddenly, Paddy turned up at the funeral in Roselawn completely out of the blue. His remaining son Jim and his two sons-in-law came too. But that's just the kind of connection I had made with this family; a connection that came from the direst of circumstances. The first Christmas after the murder, my wife and I returned home one night to find a Christmas hamper at the front door. I opened the card to discover it was from the Gault family. I cannot express how moved I was by the humanity of that kindness, thinking of us at such a terrible time for themselves.

There was a moment after the arrests, when we were waiting for the report to be approved by the DPP in order to charge Lesley. I had written the report, which was 230 pages on its own; the file itself was fourteen volumes. I had brought Paddy and Jim into my office as I wanted them to know how much effort had been put into the investigation. They sat to one side of my desk in a couple of soft chairs. Opposite them, all along the wall, were all these fair-sized black boxes. I said to them, 'By the way, that's the amount of evidence that we presented to the DPP and court to secure prosecutions in Paul's case. I know you don't, but please don't think we didn't put our heart and soul into this case.

This mattered, it mattered to you most of all, but it mattered to us as well because we were your advocates in this.'

13:56 – Mobile Patrol, West Belfast

We were out on patrol one day and came across a lovely looking S-Class Mercedes parked up in a wee laneway off the Lagmore Road near Twinbrook in west Belfast. We thought it must have been stolen because you wouldn't normally find an S-Class Mercedes up there. We got out to have a look around, watching out for any sign of bombs, disturbed ground, and so on, just in case it was booby trapped and was being used to bring us into the area. We checked the surrounding area and when we got to look in the car discovered a local boy giving another fella, who turned out to be a doctor, a blow job.

I took the young guy to one side to find out who he was. I did a check on him, and it came back that he was a heavily-traced terrorist [meaning that, if he was spotted, officers had to fill in a sighting report containing details of the encounter, including who he was with]. He was involved with the Provisional IRA. I asked him, 'How much do you get for doing this?' He said, 'Fifty quid,' then added, 'Times are tough.' I just said, 'Right, we'll leave you to it,' and we left.

When I got back to the station, I went to see a guy in Special Branch that I was friendly with and said, 'Here's a boy might be of interest – if he's going to suck a fella off for fifty quid, what will he do for five hundred?' The Branch man nodded, replying, 'Good man. Leave that with me.'

It turned out that the guy was quartermaster for the Provos. He went on to facilitate the Sneaky Beakies [Branch] by telling them the location of a hide, so that undercover officers could enter and remove the firing pins from weapons or file them down so they wouldn't fire. They also placed a device so that they knew when the hide had been opened to take weapons out, effectively informing them if there was going to be a job on in the area. Their response was to put the area out of bounds for a couple of days. That seemed to be happening weekly. Every time, the Branch man would wink at me and whisper, 'That's your guy.'

Years later I met the Branch man in court. We were having a bit of a chat and he asked me, 'Did you hear what happened to our friend from Twinbrook?' I told him no, as I had moved out of the area, and he said, 'They [the Provos] eventually worked out that there was something up. They brought the fella and his wife to a house where they were interrogated and, eventually, they took his wife out to the back entry and raped her while making her husband watch. They shot her in the head, then him, and left their bodies there.'

That was the way the IRA cleaned that up. It was a sad ending, but there is no doubt that that man saved a hell of a lot of lives.

13:58 – Lurgan Police Station, County Armagh

I was a uniform section sergeant attached to Lurgan RUC station. One of the other sergeants stationed there, Billy, was put into an operational support unit, which was like an anti-crime group that worked round Lurgan. Their sole mission was to identify and target members of terrorist groups and, when they were seen, stop and search them, find out who they were with, and so on. The unit worked very well, but the sergeant was a really highly strung character who didn't always take well to people winding him up, which given the unit he was in and the characters working there, was a really bad combination. He liked to keep himself fit, so quite often

77

at lunchtime he would go down and use the gym in the station. One day, before he went down, he made a point of telling everyone that this bottle of Coke was his and that no one should touch it. He would, of course, have been better off saying nothing.

He came back to the office to find a ransom note for his Coke, left by the boys in the unit. They also left a photograph of two of them in balaclavas holding a gun to the bottle of Coke, while another held up a copy of the *Lurgan Mail* to prove the day's date. Big Jim couldn't see the funny side of it and went immediately to the station tannoy [a public address system] to announce, 'Whoever's got my Coke better return it immediately,' making a complete tit of himself in the process. He may as well have left a big sign saying, 'Please take my Coke' in the first place!

I enjoyed my time there in the section, which had some really good, decent members in the team. They used to have permanent station duty officers back then and a great guy called Dennis was one of them. I think you would need to have carbon dated Dennis, he had that much service, but there wasn't anything he didn't know in terms of local knowledge about Lurgan and its people. He knew every nook and cranny, every townland, every street, and yet I don't think he'd left the station in years.

Of course, all things come to an end, and I found out I was moving to Belfast to take up a post as a detective sergeant. Dennis was the SDO [station duty officer] when I was leaving. Three years later, I was promoted to inspector and was sent back to Lurgan. Dennis was still the SDO when I came back. He was the first person I met as I walked through the door. It was like a time warp. I had walked out the door three years before and he'd said, 'Right, skipper, good luck. See you later.' Now, as I walked back in, he said, 'All right, inspector, good to see you.' It was like time hadn't moved, I had just nipped out, got changed and come back in.

14:00 – Grosvenor Road Police Station, Belfast City Centre

The Weapons Intelligence Section (WIS) would monitor, and attempt to trace the origins of, the types of weapons being used by terrorists, test firing any that were seized.

My section was on the late turn, but we were told to come in an hour early and assemble in the parade room at Grosvenor Road RUC station to receive a briefing from the army. Two members of WIS had come into the station to give us a talk and show us the various weapons and explosive devices that had been recovered in the division. The items concerned had been laid out over several desks that had been pushed together.

The army guys gave us a talk about the weapons and different explosive devices, including booby-traps, that we might encounter. It was fairly informative and much more real when you see how the actual devices the terrorists might use to kill you are made up. The talk lasted about half an hour and when they had finished, we were invited to examine all the items on display and ask questions.

As the group moved toward the tables on which the seized weapons and explosives had been displayed, I was aware of a colleague to my left. He had a pistol in his hands, which he was pointing in the direction of a locked glass cabinet. In it was displayed a vast array of information on terrorist suspects: photographs, addresses, dates of birth, types of vehicle they drove and registration numbers.

Seconds later, I felt the breeze of a bullet flying past the back of my head. There was a massive bang, after which the room went completely silent. What seemed like a long time later, the large pane of thick glass from the cabinet crashed to the floor.

It transpired that the two army experts had failed to clear their weapons when they came into the police station and before giving their talk had left their pistols on the display tables among the array of weapons. Their magazines were attached and there was a round in the chamber – commonly referred to a round 'up the spout' – meaning the guns were ready to be fired. You simply had to pull the trigger, you didn't need to 'cock' the weapons.

Fortunately, only one of those pistols had been lifted from the table, because the other weapon was in exactly the same condition. A crime scene was declared, and I heard subsequently that the two army personnel were demoted in rank and given a massive fine for negligence.

Ironically, that afternoon in a west Belfast police station was the closest I ever came to being killed in my twenty-six years in the job, and it was very nearly done by a fellow officer and friend. Thankfully, I heard that round being fired. Apparently, it's the one you don't hear that removes you from this world, although I've never understood how we know that!

14:06 – Oldpark Police Station, North Belfast

One time, up in Oldpark, we made a dreadful mistake. It was the summer; it was very, very hot and the vehicle we had at the time was the single long-wheelbase prototype Hotspur. It was an absolutely terrible vehicle – although a lot of improvements would be made to it with the passage of time – but at least it was bulletproof.

The heat inside, particularly in the back, was outrageous and even though there was a kind of air conditioning, which was a new thing, no one knew what it was or even how to work it, which seems ridiculous now. The vehicle essentially turned into an oven on wheels – it was just stifling. To try and resolve this problem we drifted slightly out of our sub-division and went to the grounds of Belfast Castle, where we stopped literally for five or ten minutes just to get out of the vehicle and get some air.

A couple of days later we had another really hot day, so of course we did the same thing and went to our new spot to cool off. Another couple of days passed and when we were being paraded for duty, Special Branch appeared to warn us not to do it again. Disturbingly, the Branch guy was able to tell us details of everything that had occurred when we had stopped, including how we had taken off our flak jackets.

Turns out, the IRA had spotted us the first time and then, because we went back so quickly to do it again, they intended to place a device beside where we had parked and have a gunman open fire on us as we stood around in the air without our flak jackets. Fortunately, intelligence from sources in the IRA meant Branch were able to wire us off, which saved us from getting bushwhacked. It was a stupid mistake for us to have gone back there the second time, but a lesson well learned never to do anything like that again.

14:09 – Tennent Street Police Station, North Belfast

On 17 November 1971, while I was in the White Section SPG [special patrol group] based in Tennent Street RUC station, nine republican prisoners escaped from Crumlin Road Gaol. The next day, two of them were recaptured at a VCP [vehicle checkpoint] outside Omagh. The two escapees were dressed in the garb of Cistercian monks. The two other males in the car were actual Cistercian monks and were also arrested. As a result, we were told that we would be taking part in a search of the monastery in Portglenone, County Antrim, where the Cistercian monks were based.

On arrival at the monastery we were met at the entrance to the main building by the abbot who was friendly toward us. He was a very imposing individual, well over six foot, with a deep commanding voice. Apparently, he had been a professor of theology in his former life. His name was Aengus Dunphy and he had been abbot from 1958. The rest of the monks also seemed friendly enough, but they had taken a vow of silence so would only nod or smile at us. The abbot was the only monk who could speak to us.

The plan was that White Section would search the main building, other police the outbuildings, and the army would search the 150 acres of land. The communal phone near the entrance was taken over by one of our boys and, interestingly, while we were there, he received quite a few anonymous calls warning that the police and army had practically taken over the town.

It wasn't very long before word got round to our position that a hide had been found in the chicken shed. It wasn't a normal shed – it was big, had heating and lighting and housed a few thousand hens. A stud wall had been built at one end of the interior, which left a space big enough to hide two men. Sleeping bags and other items indicating the hidden room's purpose were found. It was pretty obvious that this was where the two escapees had spent the night. It was later learned that the two monks who had been arrested had looked after the chickens.

The abbot invited us to lunch, and we accepted. We ate separately in a room just off the dining hall. We hadn't realised that the monks did not eat meat, although they raised cattle, sheep and chickens, and so on. for sale to the public. They ate in complete silence and we, as a sign of respect, ate our potatoes and cabbage without speaking (very much).

In the afternoon, I was one of a party detailed to search the monks' quarters; I think they were called cells. Naturally, each monk accompanied us to their own cell.

These were very sparsely furnished: no mattress, just a thin palliasse over wood; a wooden 'pillow'; a bedside locker; and a simple wardrobe. Once the monks were in their cell, the vow of silence went out the window. They chattered away and some were visibly nervous. Didn't take long to figure out why. In one we found a small radio hidden behind a false back in a drawer. An aerial had been cunningly threaded round the framework of the wardrobe and he got great reception. He begged us not to tell the abbot as only certain senior monks were allowed contact with the outside world. In another we found a store of porno mags, and in another a large collection of empty wine and spirit bottles. We did not tell the abbot. It was none of our business.

I searched the sickbay in which there was one monk that I was told was on his deathbed. He was an older gentleman who seemed glad to see someone different. I chatted away to him for about half an hour and found out that he was English. He had been an officer in the British army during the First World War, and the sights he had seen during the conflict had sickened him so much that he had joined the Cistercian monks when the war ended and never gone back to his original life as a banker.

In the end, the search went on for three days. We found nothing apart from the hiding place for the 'on the runs' and items of clothing. The vast majority of the monks were decent men and were not involved in anything other than working their land and being self-sufficient. 'Politics' did not interest them.

14:10 – CID Office, East Belfast

I arrested a postman in Belfast one day because somebody had reported to us that he was throwing letters into the River Lagan instead of delivering them. It's actually a very serious offence to interfere with the Royal Mail and will nearly always attract a custodial sentence.

Back at the station, he was taken out of the cell to an interview room and I went down to see him. He told me his name was Rocky. He was about four foot nothing and very cocky on it. I asked him the obvious question: 'Why did you throw the letters into the Lagan?'

He explained to me that in his delivery area there were several blocks of very tall flats and he'd had to go up and down the stairs because the lift was out of order. I persisted and said, 'But why did you throw the letters away?' He said, 'Up the fucking stairs, down the fucking stairs, up the fucking stairs … fuck the letters!'

14:15 – Mountfield Police Station, County Tyrone

I was just nineteen when I was stationed in Mountfield RUC station and, like a lot of young fellows, I bought any new gadget that came on the market. On one of my trips into Omagh I bought a portable cassette tape recorder. It was state of the art back in the sixties and cost me £19-19-6d. I fiddled about with it for ages and wasted a lot of batteries hiding it and taping the boys in the station. I taped Sergeant Walker taking the weekly school and he thought it was great when he found out, as he overheard me replaying it to a couple of the lads in the guardroom.

Anyway, courtesy of an impressed Sergeant Lipsett, I got a phone call from Crime Special [forerunner of Special Branch] in Omagh station one day to ask if I could tape an Easter Rising commemoration speech due to be given in Carrickmore, which was about six miles from Mountfield. Tomás Mac Giolla, president of Sinn Féin, was coming up from the Republic of Ireland on Easter Saturday, to celebrate the fiftieth anniversary of the Easter uprising. Without thinking much about what they were getting at I said, 'Aye, no problem.' In 1966, the IRA didn't really raise any alarm bells with the young, inexperienced me. Their last campaign had fizzled out around 1962 and had been a six-year failure, so I reckoned a trip to Carrickmore would be a bit of a day out for me.

On the Saturday in question, I was picked up in front of the station gates (very aware of personal security in those days!). I was in civvies, naturally, with an old topcoat on. The recorder was slung across my shoulder, hanging by my hip, and concealed under the coat. The microphone was threaded down my left sleeve with the head lying in the palm of my hand. My disguise was completed by the addition of an old duncher [flat cap] that had been lying around the station.

I was dropped off on a narrow lane and told to walk the rest of the way. Apparently, I couldn't miss the field, which was off the main road out of Carrickmore. They were right: there were hundreds of people all gathered around an old flat-backed lorry with a few loudspeakers randomly dotted about the place. I joined in and nobody gave me a second glance. My duncher obviously completed my 'Volunteer' look. I moved near one of the speakers to help with the recording getting picked up and when Mac Giolla took to the platform to speak, it was easy to click down the two toggle switches that started the contraption recording.

Mac Goilla made his speech for the faithful – his blustering blarney lasted about thirty minutes – and when all the rebel yells and flag waving had died down, I made my way back to where I had been dropped off. My first secret mission complete, I gave my recorder to Crime Special but had to write the instructions out so that they could work the machine and not erase any of the content. They sent it back in a few days, minus the tape. I suppose funds must have been tight in those days!

An official report followed in due course and was put on my personal record. Might have helped when I joined Special Branch a few years later. Might not.

14:18 – MSU, Enniskillen Police Station

On 16 November 1990, Prime Minister Margaret Thatcher came to Fermanagh to visit a military base, after which she was due to visit the town of Enniskillen. As is always the case with any prime ministerial visit, security in the town was very tight. Thatcher was a hate figure for republicans and would have been a very prestigious target for the IRA. Even managing to cause some disruption to her visit would have made world headlines.

I was in L5 mobile support unit at the time and our task was to saturate the town with a very visible presence to deter any terrorist attacks. Thatcher visited the town hall, which was right in in the town centre, and we patrolled the streets and roads around the area. I was walking along the front of a church hall, almost opposite the courthouse, when there was the unmistakable crash of breaking glass, followed immediately by pieces rattling off my legs and boots. My immediate thought was that someone had thrown a bottle or something at the sergeant and myself as we walked along. This would have been a regular enough occurrence. I was looking around for anything or anyone out of the ordinary but, of course, there was no trace of anyone, bar the usual crowds of shoppers in the street.

As we stood there scanning the area, a little old woman approached. 'Excuse me, is this anything important?' she asked as she handed something to the sergeant. It was a shiny metal cylinder, maybe six inches long. We looked at it, but to be honest, we had no idea what it was. It looked like someone's lunch wrapped in tin foil, so the sergeant set it on top of one of those green telephone junction boxes on the footpath and we left it there.

We walked on for a few hundred yards and then, without saying anything, the sergeant decided to go back to the green box for another look. Suddenly, the penny dropped and we had a full-scale security alert: the glass breaking had been a coffee jar bomb that had been thrown at us from the cover of the side of the church building. Fortunately, we had been lucky that it had failed to explode on impact as was intended and equally lucky that it had failed to explode when handled by both the little old lady and the sergeant.

Thatcher's visit continued as planned and she was completely unaware of the incident or how close we and the old lady had come to being a world headline. It was to be her last visit to Northern Ireland as prime minister as just days later she was forced to resign after eleven years in office.

14:29 – Cookstown Police Station, County Tyrone

Albert Cooper was a part-time UDR sergeant major who lived in Cookstown. Our paths had crossed on numerous occasions during the course of our work, and I'd always found him extremely helpful and pleasant to work with. He owned a car repair garage in the town and was well known.

One day he was in his garage working when a young woman drove her Vauxhall Astra car into the premises and parked it facing a wall. It had a defective exhaust. She apparently told Mr Cooper that she needed the car and asked, 'Could you do anything for me?' He replied, 'Leave it with me, I'll have it done this afternoon for you.' She handed him the keys and away she went. That afternoon he began work on the exhaust. He started the car, put it in reverse gear then *bang*, up it went. An under-car booby-trap bomb had been connected and primed to explode when the car was put into reverse, which was why she had parked the vehicle facing the wall.

I was first on the scene and we literally had to peel bits of his body off the wall. I had been speaking with him the night before, and as I was working, I felt as though I could hear his voice from our conversation, yet I can't remember his name now. I still have to go to *Lost Lives* [a 1999 publication that tells the stories of the men, women and children who died during the Northern Ireland Troubles] every now and then to look it up, but within an hour it's gone. It's almost like a mechanism to survive that I can't control.

The girl who left the car into the garage was a nineteen-year-old student nurse who was a very active member of the IRA. She was subsequently charged in connection with the murder and convicted along with her co-accused. Commenting at her trial, the judge said, 'You have displayed a youthful and somewhat demure appearance in court but you are a person of steely resolution who could hand Mr Cooper the keys of the car knowing they were, in fact, the keys to oblivion.'

14:35 – CID, Garnerville Police Training Centre, Belfast

When I was in the CID – I'd only been there for a few years – I was asked to give training a go. I agreed and was taught the ins and outs of the lecture circuit. I enjoyed it and felt reasonably confident at it.

One particular class came in for training and I happened to know many of them, having worked with them before. I ended up being talked off the subject and we got on to what was happening in their respective areas. A girl who was on the course, whose name I won't mention, asked me about her upcoming CID course in Wakefield, England. Coincidentally, this had been where I had done my own

CID course and with great enthusiasm I declared, 'You'll love it – you will be lifted and laid the whole time you're there.' Well, of course the whole class just burst out laughing and, thirty seconds behind them, I finally realised what I just said, and could feel my face getting increasingly redder the longer I stood there. The more my embarrassment became apparent, the harder my colleagues laughed. It was a great way to lose the attention of the class.

14:37 – CID, South Armagh

When I was working in CID in County Armagh, we got a call to a burglary in a primary school way out in the countryside, a really rural area. We realised that, in all likelihood, it had probably been the army who had broken into the school. Usually when they were sent out on patrol, it was on a five-day alert mission to see what was going on in the area. Their rations were pretty crap back then and this unfortunately meant that they would break into any place they thought they could get some proper food.

When we turned up at the school, we spoke with the caretaker to find out what was missing. He said, 'Well, it's not just food that has been stolen this time; the fridge is gone.' We searched around the area and nearby fields, and it wasn't long before we found the fridge. It was lying on its side in such a way that the door, once opened, would have fallen on to the ground. Then someone suggested that this might be a set up; that the IRA might have booby trapped the fridge guessing that, when it was recovered, the instinct would be to open the door, whereupon it would blow up.

The scenes of crime officer [SOCO] with me had a bit of a discussion about our best options. We hoked about trying to find a rope, and in the end we got a load of skipping ropes and tied them together. I tied one end of a skipping rope to the handle of the fridge and we moved about 50 yards away from it. The SOCO man chose to hide behind a large tree, leaving me to pull the rope while standing out in the open.

The door fell open and we saw all this gelignite packed up the side of the fridge door. As soon as I saw it, I just thought, 'Oh my God, it's a booby trap!' But nothing happened – no loud bang, no smoke, no nothing! We eventually crept over and looked inside. It was 4lb of pork sausages!

The following week we were searching a hay shed in the same area, not far from the school. We were just finishing up and coming down the ladder having found nothing. Then the SOCO man who was with me said; 'Can you hear something ticking?' I thought he was just messing about but I listened. Sure enough I could hear a ticking noise quite plainly. We got offside fairly sharpish and were standing around outside, wondering what to do, when the entire hay shed blew to smithereens, knocking us off our feet.

That was life working in the Armagh area: you just never knew the minute.

14:48 – Sion Mills Police Station, County Tyrone

The lady who cleaned the station in Sion Mills was an absolute gem. We were only in our twenties at the time and she was like a second mother to us all. Nothing was too much trouble for her. She made buns, and she would have made breakfast for the section on the early shift.

Big Marty had been out on patrol and managed to rip the backside out of his trousers one day. She came immediately to the rescue when she saw him: 'Look, you big lump, throw those trousers off you and I'll stitch them for you. You can't run about like that.' He was told to stay at the enquiry desk as station duty officer that day, but of course the rest of the section knew he was running around the station with no trousers on.

We were in the sanger [reinforced security post] at the front gate doing station security while this was going on and, as luck would have it, there was a buzz at the front gate: somebody wanting to come in to report something. It turned out that it was a woman who wanted to report a missing dog. So, we buzzed her on in and directed her to the enquiry desk. She seemed to take an age to tell Marty about the dog, giving him half her life story. He had to stand at the counter, right up to it, unable to move in his police shirt tails and boxer shorts, growing redder by the moment. He was like a traffic light by the time she'd finished!

14:50 – Border, County Fermanagh

Whenever we were out operating around the border in County Fermanagh, we always tried to know the Garda's location in the south. If we were cratering roads, we would leave one open and while we had a team on our side covering us, we would ask the Garda to give us cover as well. However, they never knew in advance where exactly we would be.

I can say, hand on heart, that relations between us and the Garda were excellent. The Garda saved my life on a number of occasions with information they passed through to us. Though, when we'd meet them for a chat, there would be no risks and no nonsense with them. They would bring some of their detectives with them armed with machine pistols. That would have been enough to cause a major incident in itself, never mind if they actually fired a shot. I can remember thinking to myself, 'The border's only just up the road, should we all not just move?'

I met up with an ops planning sergeant from Monaghan –

he came to us on the northern side of the border – to discuss 'Operation Blue Eyes' (a name taken from an Elton John hit at the time). It was a joint operation that had already been operating for a few months, and the relevant order, signed by me and by the Garda sergeant, had an RUC crest on one side and the Garda crest on the other. It was part of a coordinated approach to try and follow terrorists who were operating here in Northern Ireland, but based and hiding in the south, the so-called 'on the runs'.

Shortly after this meeting, the chief constable, Hugh Annesley, was at some inter-governmental function down in Dublin. There were allegations made at this meeting by some politician – I'm not sure if they were English or Irish – that referred to a lack of cooperation between the RUC and the Garda. Hugh Annesley triumphantly waved the joint operation document at them and replied, 'Well, look at that. If that's not cooperation, what is?' That went down very badly because the superintendent in Monaghan had not told Dublin Castle that they were carrying out joint operations. This had been a purely local arrangement between those from Monaghan and Lisnaskea, and was being kept quiet. The senior Garda in Dublin were very annoyed that they had known nothing about this, and the politicians were equally annoyed for the same reason – basically there was egg on the face of the entire southern contingent. Hugh Annesley, on the other hand, thought it was brilliant and a complete coup for him because they had been pointing the finger at him, but he was able to show that there was good cooperation between the forces, causing everyone to look bad except him. As a result of this, the superintendent was sent somewhere in Connemara and the ops planning sergeant was moved to Donegal. They effectively cleared the whole station out. Meanwhile, the success of Operation Blue Eyes would have confirmed me as a target for the IRA.

14:57 – Springfield Road Police Station, West Belfast

It was 19 December 1978 and I was a sergeant stationed at Springfield Road. I was on early shift as a standby crew. It was really supposed to be a rest day [due to manpower shortages rest days were regularly worked as overtime], so we were an extra vehicle on the road, which was a bit of a novelty for Springfield Road station – we were always shorthanded as it was so busy. There were four crew members in the wagon: myself and three constables in an armoured Hotspur Land Rover. We got a call to pick up another crew member who had been at the Crown court on the Crumlin Road for a case he was involved in. The case had been abandoned or cancelled for the day and he needed transport back to the station. We went to Crumlin Road and picked him up, so now five of us were in the vehicle. This was the typical sort of job an extra vehicle would get.

Coming back from the courthouse a call came over the radio reporting a suspicious car in Forfar Street, just off the main Springfield Road, behind the main admin building at Mackie's foundry – a massive employer in the city. The district mobile patrol vehicle said they couldn't take the call as they were about to go into Musgrave Street station to get refuelled. I said, 'We are en route back from the Crumlin Road. We're in Tennent Street at the moment; we'll have a look on our way back.'

We arrived into Forfar Street. There was only one car there, which was strange as normally there would have been a solid line of workers' vehicles parked on the street. They were always parked half on, half off the footpath because it's a very narrow street and you're only allowed to park on one side of it. We found out the workers in Mackie's had decided to call a wildcat strike that morning – they had all downed tools and left, which meant all the workers' cars were gone. But there was this one vehicle was sitting there on its own: a green Vauxhall Viva, Mark 2 (the Coke bottle-shaped one).

We stopped short of the vehicle, a good bit back from it because we were worried about remote-controlled detonation of a bomb either in the car or in the immediate area. There had been an incident with a bomb several months before when the remote-controlled detonation hadn't worked properly and the bomb had exploded prematurely. Before I got out of the Hotspur I flicked about on the radio channels, pressing the transmit button to send a signal on each of them because if one of those remote-control bastards had been waiting on us, we could set it off with our own radio transmission if it was on the same waveband.

I sent a couple of crew members with rifles to various points around us because the other difficulty we faced in a place like that was the possibility of sniper attack. With two men in place to cover me from snipers, I approached the car. I had checked that the vehicle was not on the stolen list, but information about the registered owner wasn't available at the time ... or wasn't known because the car had not been taxed for a while. I approached the car, then went round it without touching it and looked inside as best I could. No wires were hanging from it and it had not been hotwired. There was no obvious sign of any damage to the car. It didn't look like it had been stolen as nothing actually appeared wrong with it apart from the fact it hadn't been taxed. I couldn't tell if there was anything in the boot because the car was sitting at an angle, half on the footpath and half off it. It was impossible to tell if there was any weight – in other words, explosives – in the boot.

On my second time around the car one of the crew members said, 'Wait a second. It's parked on a storm grating.' At the time the IRA were putting bombs in the storm gratings and attaching a detonator to the axle of the car, or to the bottom of the car, with fishing line. When you moved off, you pulled a piece of wood or something from the end of a clothes peg, causing the ends of it to spring shut, completing the circuit and detonating the bomb that was underneath you in the drain, or attached to your car. I stopped moving, he came forward and got down on his hands and knees, which allowed him to look down into the storm drain. He declared, 'There's nothing there.' I told him to move back, which he did, and I went around the car again.

Third time around, I looked at the downspout on the nearby wall. The previous bomb I mentioned had been behind or inside a cast iron downspout and I knew that if cast iron has been broken recently, the edges are shiny. The downspout beside this car had a hole in it, which was indeed shiny so had therefore been made recently. I thought, 'There's a bomb in this pipe,' and I started to walk backwards from the wall. As I passed the rear of the car, I half-turned to shout to the crew to move back.

Whoever was watching me knew that my next move would be to call the army to get the ATO [army technical officer] down to check out the area for explosives so they detonated the bomb. It turned out there was a 50lb bomb packed into a beer keg in the boot of the car.

I went flying through the air. I thought to myself, 'This must be what it's like when you're dying,' then I hit the ground and thought, 'I'm not dead yet.' I didn't know that I was on fire. The crew member who had been looking down the drain came forward and started hitting me with his big rubber overcoat. I was lying there on the street thinking, 'What the fuck are you hitting me for? I'm bad enough, leave me alone.' But I didn't realise I was on fire: my hair was on fire, face, uniform, the whole thing.

My right arm was very, very sore. I was in extreme pain. I knew a bomb had gone off because we'd had the orange flash. You get the flash first, a big orange light, then you get the wave from the blast that goes up the street. The last thing you get is the sound of it. The sound just went rumbling on and on; it kept repeating like it was going off into the distance somewhere, but it kept going *bang, bang, bang* until eventually it got less and less.

I knew my arm was in trouble – it was really sore. I was really sore all over. I didn't know at that stage that my arm had been blown off. I just couldn't move at all, couldn't even move my eyeballs for a good while. I eventually managed to move my head very, very slightly and looked down to see if my feet were still there. I could see the toecap of my left boot and I thought, 'Oh, at least my feet are still there, my legs are still there,' but in actual fact, my right leg was gone and my left leg was hanging on by bits.

A military patrol had been dispatched to the scene and arrived very quickly after the explosion. They were fit and well trained, so better able to deal with battleground injuries. They started working on me immediately. The factory also had medical staff and two nurses came out; they were also working on me. An ambulance arrived – as it happened, it had been driving down the nearby Springfield Road, returning to the Royal Victoria Hospital [RVH], and when the paramedics heard the explosion they diverted themselves to the scene. I remember thinking, Christ, the ambulance was quick. Then they opened the back doors of the ambulance and took out a couple of blankets. Normally if you weren't too bad, they would use red woollen cellular blankets, but I knew from experience that if you were a bit of a mess, they would use grey army-type blankets. So when I saw them coming towards me with army blankets I knew, 'I'm in trouble here.' Luckily enough I wasn't too far from the RVH and was in the hospital in a matter of minutes. They slid me into the back of the ambulance and just as the ambulance driver was closing the back doors I thought to myself, 'I'll just go for a wee sleep until we get to the hospital,' and that's the last thing I remember for some considerable time.

The explosion had happened on a Tuesday. By Thursday, they had to amputate the bottom half of my left leg because it was in such a state – the blood they were pouring in at the top of me was pouring out the bottom of my leg. My injuries were a combination of blast damage and shrapnel, even though they hadn't packed the bomb with shrapnel, nuts and bolts, which they often did. The boot lid had blown off, hitting me and causing soft tissue injuries on my right-hand side. I was wearing a Rolls-Royce set of body armour which I'd only got the week before. I had been very reluctant to give up the old army flak jacket I already had because it had pockets and I was a heavy smoker at the time and needed somewhere to keep my fags. They eventually prised it off me the week before the blast and gave me this Rolls-Royce thing: two slabs of Kevlar with Velcro straps round the waist of it. There were two sides that came together under your armpit and the boys nicknamed it 'tortoise shell'. The slice of the car boot lid that hit me had carried the armour shell inside me. I heard the surgeon telling one of the junior doctors that the intrusion had stopped three eighths of an inch from the lining of my stomach, so another three eighths of an inch and my guts would have been out on the road. I didn't see the boot coming towards me, I was out of it. Just the orange flash. It was one of the crew who told me there was a big piece of the Kevlar plate stuck in my chest, pushed into me by the car boot.

I was in the RVH for a very long time. When I'd come

out of the operating theatre, the nursing staff really hadn't liked my chances of getting out of the recovery room, then when I got out of the recovery room into intensive care, the sister there – I always listened to the sisters rather than the doctors – said that I wouldn't make it through the night. Though not to me obviously, I was out of it.

I'm not sure how many weeks later I woke up. I do remember a stage when I started waking up a bit, just little interludes of being awake when they started taking me off the medication. I had a huge haemorrhage on my right side – I remember my blood hitting the ceiling then dripping down off it. There was a whole panic with people flying about everywhere, some with crash carts, then I went to sleep again.

I had an out-of-body experience. I didn't get any bright light drawing me away from my body at the moment it happened, but I remember, in intensive care, being pulled towards this tunnel on the ceiling – I was just floating along on the ceiling. I didn't want to go down the tunnel, I was very aware of that. Nobody seems to know whether this was some spiritual thing, or to do with the drugs or what it was. Some people say it's your spirit trying to leave you, I just don't know, but I remember fighting to get back to my body. I had been very badly burned in the explosion and they used 'wet bandages' to treat the burns. These had to be changed every three hours and it took an hour to change them. I remember being on the ceiling, watching the nurses as they changed these bandages. They were telling me to turn over, reach round – giving me instructions that would allow them access to do their job. In the end I had to have a skin graft on my back – they took skin from my chest and used it as a patch on the back end of me, but for that to heal I had to lie on my face and stomach for two weeks, which I can tell you was no easy task. I got addicted to morphine; you can get addicted to morphine very quickly and you imagine all sorts of shite going on which is as real as it could possibly be.

I think it must have been about three months before I made it out of intensive care into a room in a side ward, Ward 37. The first time I sucked in fresh air again was Easter, when somebody wheeled me out to the door. I remember it was Easter time because I got more Easter eggs than would have been needed to fill a shop. I sent most of them over to the children's ward in the hospital. The following September, the end of September 1979, they moved me to Musgrave Park Hospital and started to fit me up for artificial limbs. I was there until sometime in the next year, 1980, then it was a case of just getting used to the artificial limbs.

While I'd been in intensive care, I had two people, two peelers, guarding me twenty-four hours a day. When you go into intensive care in the Royal, immediately to the left there is an alcove for relatives to sit, but obviously being intensive care, very few relatives would have been there at any given time, so that's where my two police guards normally sat. I'd had to go for another operation and so was taken from the intensive care unit through the back doors and upstairs to the operating theatre. I was accompanied by one of my police minders; the other one had been left sitting in the ward in the alcove. He'd decided to stretch his legs and had gone for a wee dander around the ward. As he did so, two IRA men came into the ward and swung to the left, expecting the two policemen to be there in the alcove. Instead there were no policemen and my bed was empty. As the policeman came back round the corner, there were these two IRA men – they all just stared at each other. He realised what they were at as he saw their guns and he turned slightly sideways to draw his own gun. One of the IRA men shot at him, striking him in the chest, but because he was standing sideways the bullet went underneath the skin of his chest across the front and out the far side. He pursued them through the doors, running up towards the Falls Road. He got about halfway up the road when he realised he'd been shot. I have no doubt that, had the three of us been where we were normally, we would all be dead.

After I'd finally been released from hospital the continuing threat on my life from the IRA was so severe that police with sub-machine guns spent every night waiting for them in my house, protecting me, my wife and children, in case they came for me. I subsequently had to move house because I was under threat, even though I had already been blown up. Special Branch had very detailed information about the threat, down to which junction on the road in east Belfast they would kill me at – they'd planned to get me when my car stopped in traffic. They were going to say that, because I had driven out of a police station in plain clothes (I'd been working there as a telephonist), they'd thought I was a detective. That was going to be the excuse they would use in the press – they'd say that they hadn't realised I'd been injured before, which of course was a lie. They knew perfectly well all about my injuries. One of the guys who was with me when I got blown up got a job working with the army as a liaison officer in west Belfast. He actually got stopped in the street one day by a terrorist who said, 'I thought you had been blown up.'

And the other people who were in the patrol that day? One of them had his ears badly damaged in the blast and another suffered severely from shock because my arm had gone flying up the street past him and he hadn't been sure whether it was his own arm, or my arm, or whose arm it was! The woman who had initially reported the car as being suspicious – she'd told the security man at Mackie's – had been walking back towards her own house and been hit in the leg by a piece of flying metal when the car exploded. She suffered a broken ankle as a result of the incident.

The police paid me off in due course and gave me a civilian job. I became a telephonist, which I wasn't terribly impressed with. I used to do the boys' files for them to give me something to do. I was at Buckingham Palace with a group of disabled police officers, and we met the Queen. There was a guy from the Police Federation there with us, I suppose to keep an eye on us. He was introducing people to the Queen and when he got to me he said to her that the police had been good enough to give me a new job. He was very lucky he didn't get a dig in the jaw.

Lates
15:00–23:00 hours

15:00 – Warrenpoint Police Station, County Down

I was still in my first year of service when we were notified that John Hermon, who had just been made chief constable, was coming to carry out an official inspection of the station. He was due to inspect Kilkeel station before he got to us at Warrenpoint. His intention at that time was to upgrade the accommodation in all the stations throughout the country and I think he visited everyone in the course of this exercise.

I was on a late shift and Mike Maguire, the station sergeant, instructed me to get into my uniform, wear a civilian coat over the top of it, and drive my own car to the edge of our sub-division, as near to Kilkeel as I could. He wanted me to bring a radio and transmit back to them as soon as the chief constable's car had entered the area. This I did, but the trick was then to get back to my station before the chief constable's party arrived – I needed to be there, and in uniform, when they entered the station. This wasn't as easy as you may think because there is only one road between Kilkeel and Rostrevor, but it splits into two at one point and I just had to hope that they wouldn't have the local knowledge to use the upper road, the one I'd planned to take, which would allow me to pass them before they reached the junction at the far end. Thankfully, I managed to get to the station before they did and was in with the rest of the station party in time to parade and go through everything that was normal for an inspection of that nature.

As Mr Hermon was leaving the station he spotted above the houses on the far side of the street, the top of a crane in the docks area. He turned to Sergeant Maguire and said, 'That man has a bird's-eye view into the station, I would like to think that you know who he is.' Whereupon the sergeant, who had over thirty years in Warrenpoint by that stage, said, 'Ah now, sir, that fella's called–' and he mentions a name. 'He is a son of so-and-so and he is married to a local girl. She is the daughter of so-and-so.' He gave Mr Hermon a full family tree for the crane driver. Hermon was really, seriously impressed with this, and duly went on his way. I turned round to the sergeant and said, 'Skipper, thank heavens he asked you that question. I wouldn't have had a clue who the person was.' The sergeant replied, 'Cub, I don't know who that person is either, but I will by tomorrow!'

Sergeant Maguire remained in Warrenpoint until somebody put a bomb under his car. He was picking his wife up from work and she spotted it as she was getting into the car. They moved house as a result. He was originally from Fermanagh but could never go home again after he joined the police. At one stage, some terrorists had arrived to take him out as he was walking down from his house to the station. He always did this in full uniform throughout his service, every day that he was on duty. This particular morning, a group of approximately nine local women circled him and marched him down to the police station, preventing the terrorists from getting near him. That was the esteem he was held in locally. He was a Catholic, and these women went to Mass with him. He didn't tell me who any of the woman were, he just told me that they appeared out of nowhere and said, 'Sergeant, you have to get to the station right away.' It was only when he arrived there that he knew something was seriously wrong. They told him, 'Those fellas over there were waiting to shoot you.'

He gave me one particular lesson that I have never forgotten: 'When you give your word, young fella, never break it, because you only have it the once.'

15:03 – CID Office, Springfield Road Police Station, West Belfast

I was attached to the CID office in Springfield Road in the early seventies. In those days there were so many murders taking place on both sides it was almost impossible to keep track of them. We didn't have the manpower we have now, and if you were the only CID officer available you attended the scene of the murder, even if it was not your area. You would deal initially with all the various aspects of the crime, handing over to a detective from the area when they became available.

I was just coming from the station when a report came in. The army were billeted in Springfield Road police station at the time and had bedrooms and an ops room in the station, so when their patrol radioed into the ops room informing them of the incident, they were able to get hold of me quite quickly. They took me up to some waste ground opposite the West Circular Road at the Springfield Road end. The army had been patrolling the area and had heard shots in the vicinity of Corry's timber yard, just up from where the fire station is now. There was quite a lot of waste ground near the yard, and they'd found this young fella lying on his back with his rosary beads in his hand. He had been shot but was still alive.

It was terrible and had a huge impact on us. The equally young soldier who had been told to guard the young lad was standing there crying. I went over and lifted the injured lad into my arms to try and comfort him. I said a prayer with him, not the Last Rites or anything because I didn't know how but I tried to say an Act of Contrition with him and told him not to worry as God would look after him. He died in my arms.

It was a Saturday afternoon. The UVF or UDA had randomly picked him up, walked him round the back of the shops to the waste ground and shot him. He must have had his rosary beads in his pocket. It was an ideal place to take someone because the grass and weeds had grown up to pretty much head height. To this day, I still see that young lad's face as he died.

15:07 – Castlereagh Holding Centre

By the time we got called in and made our way to Castlereagh holding centre in Belfast, which was used for the interrogation of terrorist suspects, all the people that could have been arrested in this particular case had been. They had been caught at the house where suspected informant Sandy Lynch had been interrogated by the IRA's 'nutting squad' [the IRA's much-feared internal security team].

Sandy Lynch was a member of the Provisional IRA, but his comrades suspected he had become an informant working for the security forces. Lynch was living in Magherafelt at the time but, as a result of their suspicions, was summoned to a meeting in west Belfast [in January 1990]. To get there, he had to go to one location, where he was made to swap cars, and then was taken to a house, 124 Carrigart Avenue, for interrogation.

The HMSU [Headquarters Mobile Support Unit – a highly-trained specialist uniformed team] had stormed the house and arrested everyone in it and freed the captured interviewee, Sandy Lynch. Lynch was upstairs in a bedroom, in a chair, tied up with bandages. It transpired information had been passed via the military to Special Branch, who in turn tasked the HMSU to rescue the prisoner and secure the house. We in CID hadn't known a thing about the operation that was going on until we were called in.

We became aware that Lynch was working for Special Branch and our theory was that he may have had a tracking device on him, which enabled the Branch to be able to hit the house he was being held in. We couldn't see any other way that they would have known to hit that exact address (they certainly weren't going to tell us in CID who were investigating the whole incident!).

During the course of the investigation, we were able to determine what had happened inside the house that night. We found a cassette tape that someone had attempted to destroy. Fortunately, our technical department were able to salvage enough of the tape and pieced together the bulk of what was recorded on it: Lynch being made to confess to his captors that he was an informant for Special Branch.

The central interrogator was identified as Freddie Scappaticci, who was known to be in charge of the IRA's internal security team. It was subsequently alleged that he was also the informer known as Stakeknife, who was handled by the military. Scappaticci then left the scene but Danny Morrison – Sinn Féin's director of publicity, and a senior figure in the organisation – and Anto Murray subsequently arrived at the house. It is believed they were there to confirm the verdict following Lynch's interrogation. The two men had actually walked past the surveillance operatives, a courting couple, on their way to the house. A slight delay is always called to 'let it soak' once someone goes to an address. This ensures they are on the premises.

Anto Murray later claimed that he heard the vehicles arriving [the HMSU vans that contained the assault team] and alerted the house occupants. Morrison made a run for it and went out the back. The cut-off units did not engage, but gave good evidence that they had witnessed Morrison run from the target house and scale the fence into the neighbours' home. There he told the family to say he had been there for a meeting, which they declined to do.

When the house was hit, it was a full rapid entry. No

distraction devices [stun grenades, CS 'tear gas' shotgun rounds, etc.] were used, as these can destroy evidential material. Rapid entry allows for best preservation of evidence. Unlike US movies, we dominate all prisoners in an upright position, on their knees, to avoid them transferring potential evidence on to the floor until they are put in an evidence protection cape prior to removal.

Morrison, Murray and the remnants of the interrogation team were among those arrested. There were no weapons found in the house but there is no question that, within an hour or so, Lynch would have been nutted. A different team from that which carried out the interrogation would have arrived to carry out the execution. That would be why the storming of the house was triggered so quickly by the HMSU.

In the follow-up search, police recovered an electronic bug detector that was used by the IRA personnel in the house. It was powered by a small, square PP3 battery, upon which a thumb print had been left, presumably as the person fitting it had pushed it into the housing. The thumb print was Scappaticci's. We knew that Scappaticci was a senior PIRA member, and Lynch in his statement had identified him as his interrogator because he'd known the voice, having previously worked with him on the IRA internal security team [the nutting squad]. But when Scappaticci was eventually arrested, he refuted the evidence we had, tying him to the scene: 'Yes, I do a bit of handyman work for the woman in that house and she got me round a while ago to fit a smoke alarm … I also fitted the battery.'

My boss appeared one morning and said that we had to go to Oliver Kelly's office in Castle Street – Kelly was the householder's wife's solicitor. She was going to give a statement to confirm what Scappaticci had told me: that he was a friend of the family and she had asked him to come round to put up a smoke director and put a battery in it. Of course, we had to wonder how this battery had managed to get out of the smoke detector and into the IRA bug detector without any other fingerprints or marks being on it. It is only in the last couple of years that it has been discovered that her visit to Oliver Kelly's office was organised by a very senior police officer on behalf of the military.

Scappaticci had immediately gone on the run, down South, but we had an order issued around the province that he was 'Lift on Sight' if spotted by security force personnel. After a while, my boss was approached by a senior officer to ask that the 'Lift on Sight' order be rescinded, as certain people needed him back in the province operating freely. Scappaticci would have been OTR [on the run] for about three years when it became known to, I presume, Special Branch that he had returned to Belfast and was working in the GPO at Tomb Street, which is where he was ultimately arrested.

The others in number 124 that night were convicted of the unlawful imprisonment of Sandy Lynch, accused by police of taking part in his false imprisonment and in conspiring to murder him. Morrison was sentenced to eight years in prison – it was said he was preparing to sanction the IRA's killing of Lynch – and released in 1995. The appeal court in Belfast overturned the conviction for false imprisonment and conspiracy to murder in 2008, but withheld its reasons for doing so.

The householders of 124 Carrigart Avenue, James and Veronica Martin, were subsequently charged and convicted of two counts of making property available to terrorists. They made admissions in Castlereagh and received fairly short jail sentences [their convictions were overturned in 2012–13]. In addition to the Lynch interrogation, their house had been used for a similar purpose before when Joe Fenton, a thirty-five-year-old father of four and an estate agent in west Belfast, had been detained and interrogated in number 124. Fenton had sorted out 'safe houses' for use by the Provisional IRA by providing access to vacant premises he was selling but would then inform his Special Branch handlers that the IRA would be using these premises to store weapons or hold meetings. This gave the intelligence services time to bug the premises or place trackers in the now-tampered-with weapons before the IRA used them. The IRA eventually caught on to this and Fenton was forced to make a tape admitting all that he had done – a tape that was subsequently played to his father. Then with his confession secured he was taken out into a nearby street and shot in the back of the head.

A husband and wife, Gerard and Catherine Mahon, had been shot dead [on 8 September 1985] after being interrogated by the IRA. What happened to those three people left us in no doubt as to what would have happened to Lynch.

15:08 – Central Ticket Office, Belfast.

I used to be attached to the central ticket office in Belfast. It was my job to deal with the letters of complaint we got from members of the public who had been given parking tickets that they felt had been issued in error. It was certainly a very busy job trying to keep on top of everything, and some of the excuses people used to explain why they should not have received a ticket were minters.

One letter that always springs to mind was from a lady who was adamant that she had parked her car on one side of the road, but in her absence the car had magically transferred to the other side of the road, where she was now illegally parked. Correspondence on this unusual phenomenon of the flying car went back and forth for quite some time.

The woman was unbending in her statement, no matter how many times or how many ways we pointed out to her how ridiculous her argument sounded, but she persisted so much I eventually got fed up writing to her and decided to end it once and for all. I put in a request for a copy of the CCTV for the appropriate times, intending to sit her down and have her watch herself parking the car in a spot where it would remain until she came back. That, I thought would put the matter to bed.

After a week or so, I received a tape with the relevant footage and sat down to watch, confident this would bring the matter to a close. To my astonishment this big crane drove into the street to carry out some work, but her vehicle was in the way. The driver got out, threw a few straps underneath her car, lifted it up and fired it across the street.

The woman had been completely correct, but I can tell you, if I hadn't seen it for myself, I would not have believed it in a hundred years.

15:10 – MSU, Cliftonville FC, North Belfast

Tension in republican areas was always high during August, with anti-internment bonfires and Orange parades close to interfaces happening on almost a daily basis. In August 1984, north and west Belfast experienced a series of anti-internment parades and events, many of which turned violent and led to rioting that lasted long after the events had passed.

The mobile support unit I was with was based in the north of the city, and we would spend afternoons patrolling, incurring the wrath of many groups of youths gathered at the interfaces. Such hostility was nothing new, but it had taken on a greater venom, with several references to the late Sean Downes, a native of west Belfast who [on 12 August 1984] had been hit by a plastic bullet when he was seen running with a stick towards police officers during an anti-internment rally. He subsequently died. It was made clear to us that we were not welcome in many parts of north Belfast.

It was against this background that Cliftonville Football Club played a long-standing friendly match against Glasgow Celtic at Solitude in north Belfast. Initially our unit was not involved in this event and were deployed to a different part of the city, but in the build-up to the game, several attacks were carried out on police patrolling the Antrim and Cliftonville Roads and our unit was diverted to this part of the city to be part of a regional reserve. We had not been involved in the planning for this match or attended any briefings beforehand and were amazed to discover that police were not only monitoring the match, but several were being deployed on foot inside the stadium.

The match attracted large numbers of fans who supported both Cliftonville and Celtic and who were not deemed to be high risk in terms of public disorder. Initially, the local officers in the ground were subjected to abuse but most fans focused on the game. However, many of us feared what would happen at half-time when there was nothing other than the police to attract their attention.

As predicted, the abuse towards the officers intensified and they tried to secure a safer location nearer the exits. Some of the hostile fans realised this and moved in large numbers to block the exit. Offers of assistance by the police units in reserve were rejected by senior police who felt our presence would make a bad situation worse. The situation developed quickly and police in the ground feared their exits were being deliberately blocked and they could be trapped inside the ground. The most vulnerable were a small group of officers in the Cage Stand and the adjoining Waterworks section of terracing.

Eventually we were given the orders to enter the stadium from behind the Cage Stand. The first unit went immediately left into the Cage Stand and our role was to create a sterile area at the Waterworks side to facilitate their exit along with the local officers trapped in the Cage Stand. Once the hostile element in the crowd realised what was happening, they surged towards the Cage Stand end of the ground and we took a severe hammering from bottles, stones and debris. The attacks intensified and a series of scuffles broke out. At the same time the other unit had battled their way into the Cage Stand and retrieved the local officers. A warning was given to the attackers that baton rounds would be fired if the rioting did not stop. However it just got worse, and I think we would have been overrun had a round not been discharged. The firing of the baton round created the sterile area needed to facilitate the exit of the other unit and we also were able to leave the stadium.

In the immediate aftermath of the incident it became apparent how precarious the situation had been for the local officers inside the ground – many said they did not think they would get out alive. For our part, nearly two thirds of the unit suffered injuries to arms and legs, as the only protective equipment then was a flak jacket and a riot helmet. We also learned later that an officer had lost his personal firearm in the melee and despite a search the next day it was not located. We often wondered if it had been used in a subsequent terrorist attack on the police or army.

But the biggest mystery of all was why on earth police were deployed to a friendly football match in north Belfast given the tension in the area and the risks this subjected them to, and when clearly there was no need for them to be there.

15:11 – VIP Escort Training, East Belfast

I was a sergeant in the force training department for a while in east Belfast. I was based in the old Belfast Rope Works, a large redbrick building that the police authority had rented. It was known back in the day as Connswater because it sat next to the Connswater River. There were different training facilities that went on there: weapon training and ranges out the back; and force training for probationer constables and full-time reserve men downstairs.

I always got on well with the firearms training boys. My father used to shoot for the RUC, and every year he went over to Bisley in England, representing the force at target shooting [the Imperial Meeting is a famous shooting competition held at the National Shooting Centre in Bisley]. I used to go down to both the Connswater and Sprucefield ranges with my dad when he was doing firearms training/practice. As a result, I knew some of the weapons instructors before I arrived to work in Connswater.

One day a couple of the firearms guys approached me to say they were doing a close protection course and two of the guys that were on it thought they were the bees knees – wise guys who couldn't be taught anything. The firearms instructors really wanted them brought down a peg or two and to be given a dose of reality. They had told the two smart arses that they would be doing an exercise that day where they would be assigned to a VIP – he would be their principal for the day, and they should accompany him as he went about his business. They had been taught a drill in which one of them should always be in front of the principal with the second of them behind, covering any

116

potential attack from the rear or side.

I was told that I would recognise the two minders as they would be alert and looking all round them as the principal came down the stairs. The principal himself was also to be very recognisable, wearing a distinctive tweed jacket and tie with a porkpie hat – the type people sometimes have fishing flies on out in the country. They had asked me to spring out from a side entrance and attack the VIP so that the instructors could see how the minders would react to the threat. I had been asked because they knew me and because I was fairly big, but more importantly I wasn't in firearms branch so the two minders would not think of me as being part of the training set up.

I was standing in a doorway, waiting on this gentleman when, all of a sudden, I saw him coming down the stairs, taking his time. He was wearing a tweed jacket and porkpie hat, as described, so I jumped him and put him down, all the time waiting for somebody to pull me off him, but it didn't happen. I got a set of handcuffs out but still nothing happened, so I carried on and managed to get his arms round his back and handcuffed him. I was feeling rather pleased with myself but, as I looked up to see where his minders were, another gentleman came down the stairs with a tweed jacket and porkpie hat.

I looked at the man I had just thrown to the ground and just then the training officer Chief Superintendent McCulloch, or Paddy Mary as he was known, came over and said, 'Ah, Professor Stevenson, I see you've met Sergeant Thompson.' Of course, the firearms boys took off, leaving me to it. I started to stutter my explanation but, fortunately for me, the professor took it all on the chin and actually thought it was hilarious that we had given him a good story to tell when he got back to England.

15:15 – Lisnaskea Police Station, County Fermanagh

I was transferred from Belleek RUC station to Lisnaskea, in which there was a more normalised type of policing compared to Belleek, where you had to act more like a soldier than a police officer. Lisnaskea was a mixed town and we had two vehicles on patrol at all times. One of the vehicles stayed in the town permanently, keeping a twenty-four-hour presence in and around Lisnaskea Main Street. The other vehicle covered the outlying rural area. We also had a vehicle covering Newtownbutler and one in Rosslea that was also part of our sub-division. If something happened anywhere there – police needing assistance or a terrorist attack against them – we would have backed each other up.

The threat from the terrorists was still very severe, though, which resulted in the public being very afraid. It started off with the shops refusing to serve soldiers, though they would still have served the police. We would go into the shop and get the soldiers what they wanted and give it to them. Then the IRA decided, no, we will stop them serving the police as well.

There was one shop in the town run by an elderly woman and her daughter, and they would still have served us, for which we were very grateful. The IRA told them to stop serving us and they said no. They told us that they'd not just been warned but threatened to make sure they would stop serving us but that they had refused. We thanked them but said that we couldn't put them at risk. They said, 'But we want to serve you, and you give us a lot of business.' We ended up making an arrangement with them in which we would give them an order by phone, and they would bring whatever it was we needed into Enniskillen and leave the stuff at an address we had provided. The arrangement worked very well. We left the money when we went to pick it up, so they still got the business and lived to tell the tale.

15:30 – Police Cadets

I left school at sixteen years of age and joined the police cadets. I had always wanted to be a police officer. In the cadets you were involved in many activities, one of which sticks in my memory. One year we were going to camp and the kids who were coming with us had had a parent from the police – or a few were from the UDR – murdered.

I remember thinking before we went that there would only be a few, maybe six to seven, kids there that we'd take out canoeing and hillwalking, do outdoor pursuits, things like that. The day the kids arrived was a day I'll never forget – there were at least thirty of them. I was only seventeen myself, horrified that some of them were only three or four years younger than me. That was the first thing that really hit me, the age of these kids who had lost a parent.

As we got to know them, it became apparent that this was something they looked forward to every year: getting away from the normal surroundings and meeting up together. There were lots of tears, lots of stories, but they had a bond because of what had happened to them all. At times you would have seen two or three of them just sitting crying in a group and whenever you went over to see how they were, it turned out they'd been talking about what had happened to their parents. Dreadful things that children shouldn't have to discuss, like their father being shot dead, blown up, or whatever. I just hoped that the trip helped them, and I was glad that, in some small part, it may have temporarily cheered them up.

There was one young girl in particular. She was from Randalstown and her father had been murdered. Every time we went out to do something, she would have been with me. One of the days we'd been at the beach at Runkerry. We had all been out along the length of the beach and by the time we came back the tide had come in – the water was up to my waist. She was scared to go through the water, and I had to put her on my shoulders and carry her. It was through doing stuff like that with them that you really got to know them well, and when at eighteen I went into the training centre in Enniskillen as a regular policeman, she sent me a congratulations card.

I took some photographs while we were at the camp, which would have been in 1981, so about forty years ago. I put them up on a social media group that has a police connection. I was subsequently contacted by a lady who said that she remembered going to some of these camps. We got in touch through private message, and I sent her the group photographs. She was able to point to herself in the photos, and I remembered her from the time we were all away. She had been quite hard on the cadets because she was really struggling to come to terms with what had happened to her father. She felt that we were the lucky ones; that we were still alive and her father, who she described as her hero, was dead.

We exchanged many messages, which were very emotional. She said, 'You've no idea how much those weeks in Runkerry meant to us all. Those were the happy memories of those difficult years.' She talked about memories she had of myself and another guy, Stephen, carrying her on one of the walks. We'd been out on the hills and she just refused to walk any further; she'd had enough. On that occasion Stephen and I had given her piggybacks, alternating with each other for about two and a half miles. She apologised for her behaviour but told me that, at that stage, her father had recently been murdered and she'd really struggled to cope. To this day, she still talks about our being the connection to her dad and the force.

I suppose the people in the camp trip with us didn't

realise we weren't that old ourselves and as a seventeen-year-old, it had a really big impact on how I felt. It seemed to make the reality of the job I was going into more apparent, although it didn't change my mind. Over the years, particularly on days that I was having a really crap time myself – when one of my colleagues had maybe been murdered, or after the difficult things I'd witnessed – I would have looked at those photographs. The kids that we had were fantastic, but I always felt they deserved better. When you look at a photograph with all of those kids altogether it's heartbreaking. In many ways it's children like that, in the circumstances they found themselves in, who are forgotten.

15:37 – Army Observation Post, West Belfast

I was asked to interview two guys who had been brought in for the attempted burglary of a disused factory in west Belfast. Our would-be burglars were from a different part of the city and had actually been caught on the premises. Their plan was to steal lead and copper from the building. Now, this was a very large factory that they had broken into, and they were making their way around, checking out which parts had the best pickings and seeing if they could manage to get the stuff out.

They turned a corner and suddenly they saw two teams of men playing football. All the players had proper football strips on and were two organised teams. They said that the players 'ran at them' (or attacked them as they would put it later). They described how the men had got hold of them and held them down; they complained that there were large puddles on the floor of the factory and one of the burglars said, 'I was drowning in the puddle.'

They were held there for a while by the footballers and eventually the police were sent for. When the cops turned up, they brought them down to the station for interview. What none of the people involved knew was that they could not have picked a worse place in the country to break into. Let's just say an observation post had been set up by a particular branch of the army up in the roof area of the factory where all the lead and copper was. The post was fully operational and full of all sorts of equipment that could have proved disastrous if these two burglars had stumbled upon everything. So while I was interviewing them at the station, the army lifted all their equipment, cleared out unseen and left no trace of ever having been there. I have no idea what army operation had been compromised, but I'm sure there were a few lucky terrorists who did not realise how close they were to having their day ruined.

Obviously, we did not want to make too big a fuss about what had happened, so the two guys left police custody thinking that I had been a really nice and understanding detective when I'd told them, 'Listen, you're not bad lads. I'll just give you a caution this time, but don't be coming back into this area with the intention of stealing anything.' The two of them left the station blissfully unaware of what just happened, but very happy.

15.44 – Special Branch

I was working in Special Branch and we had organised and set up an observation post [OP] on a house that terrorists were using. We had been watching the house closely for some time to see who showed up as we knew there was a rifle being stored there, though we had taken measures to ensure the rifle couldn't hurt anyone.

We waited and waited and decided we had been watching it long enough – obviously nothing had been planned by the terrorists – but we had to wait for the right opportunity to recover the weapon. At this time the peace process had kicked in, so we were sensitive to outside developments and being very cautious about what we were doing. One day, out of the blue, information came in that the department were conducting a series of house searches in the area concerned. Seeing this as a golden opportunity, we decided to search the house and recover the rifle. We gave the briefing, CID took over the operation and the search teams went into the premises. The weapon was recovered, along with a number of detonators and other terrorist paraphernalia.

Next morning, at about 7 a.m., I opened my office door and the phone is ringing. It's the chief constable. I was thinking, here comes the pat on the back for a good job well done and I bid him a cheery, 'Good morning, sir.' He greeted me with, 'I've had Mo fucking Mowlam [secretary of state] on the phone to me several times overnight. Are you trying to destroy the peace process all on your own or what?' 'What are you talking about?' I protested, 'I spoke with the chief of staff; he knew that search was going ahead.'

What had happened was, CID had got back to me and asked, 'Have you got any problem with us showing the press the haul for a photo opportunity?' I had said, 'No problem, just let command centre know,' which they did. Unfortunately, whenever they laid the haul out for the media it created havoc. As the camera panned along, the detonators were shown, and you could see quite clearly that they were date stamped. The problem was they had been manufactured during the peace process, indicating that the IRA had bought them while apparently in peace negotiations.

I remember saying to the chief constable, 'So you're telling me I have snatched defeat from the jaws of victory?' I will not repeat his response!

15:45 – Warrenpoint Police Station, County Down

I was on duty one afternoon when we received a call telling us that people were acting suspiciously around a telegraph pole near the village of Killowen, which sits between Rostrevor and Kilkeel on the Shore Road. We had to go and check it out, despite being quite apprehensive as to what the call might mean. A sergeant and I were the only crew available to deal with this, so we drove out to the area and were able from a distance to identify the pole that was being talked about. Of course, by the time we arrived there was no one to be seen anywhere near it.

We parked up on the far side of the road and took to the fields. The sergeant had a rifle and I had a Sterling sub-machine gun. We walked around the field to get to the nearest hedgerow to the pole, as it would offer us some sort of cover. It came as no great surprise when we discovered a command wire running along the bottom of the hedge. We realised the best way to make this safe was to walk away from the pole, towards the end of the command wire, which would have a battery on it for detonation.

We proceeded on either side of the hedge, going uphill and were quite concealed until we got higher up. Both of us were wearing caps because we wanted to make sure we were identifiable to any military personnel staking out the area. The drawback to this was that we were identifiable to any terrorist waiting to detonate the bomb. Obviously, these guys saw our caps before they saw us and, before we got eye contact with them, we heard a motorbike engine start, and begin to rev up. We immediately ran up to the top of the hill just in time to see the motorbike disappearing with two males on the back of it.

Sure enough, we found a battery beside the command wire and already connected waiting for another wire to be attached when the target was on site, allowing it to detonate. A device – a milk churn filled with explosives – was recovered, buried beside the telegraph pole. A few days later we received intelligence from Special Branch to say that the IRA had planted the bomb and the terrorists were intending to target a passing army patrol.

15:47 – Uniform Patrol, Belfast City Centre

A colleague and I were in an armoured Cortina in Belfast city centre. As we drove past the city hall, we saw a crowd of about thirty or forty DUP members having some form of protest about something, as they do. We were both in full uniform and I pretended I recognised someone in the group and asked my mate to take a run round the city hall again and bring us back down past them so I could check.

He readily agreed and, as he was driving round the block, I got the microphone for the public address system, which was built into the car. As we drew level with the protest I boomed, in my best Ian Paisley voice, 'I am telling you people now to get off the streets and make your way back to our headquarters immediately!'

Well my colleague nearly shit himself and said, 'For fuck's sake!' I said, 'Never worry about it,' while he took off at a high rate of knots down Chichester Street. I was killing myself laughing, and as I looked back, I saw all these DUP members standing with their placards looking very perplexed and generally skywards as they struggled to understand how their glorious leader's voice had appeared from nowhere, as if by divine intervention.

It was a silly thing I know, but we were bored and that's just what I do when I'm bored. John wasn't pleased because he didn't know it was going to happen, but after a few minutes, and after the initial shock faded, he was happy enough to take a fit of laughing himself.

16:00 – Oldpark Police Station, North Belfast

The Crumlin Road and surrounding area had a designated police patrol known as the Schools Patrol. Officers would man a fixed point at the beginning and end of the school day to protect the children of two local schools from attack and from each other. This was a dangerous patrol for the officers involved because of the set routine and officers would generally have been working it as overtime on their rest days as the section on duty couldn't have spared the manpower.

I was stationed in Oldpark RUC station in north Belfast from 1973 until 1976, when I was promoted to sergeant and transferred to Strabane RUC station. At 4 p.m. on 6 February 1976, I took the advanced driving test at Castlereagh RUC station in Belfast. I had just finished and was opening the car door, when I heard a conversation by two passing police officers, '… Jimmy Blakely and Willy Murdoch. Jimmy is dead, and Willie is seriously ill in hospital.' Time froze and my brain went into slow motion as I stepped out of the car. 'What did you just say?' I heard myself speak as if through a fog.

Jimmy was my section sergeant and Willy was one of two inspectors we had in Oldpark. They had been shot by the Ardoyne IRA outside my grandparents' house in the Cliftonville area. I drove immediately to the station to be with my colleagues. I can still see the scene of this senseless slaughter as if it had happened yesterday. I had driven past it on my way to the station. Two good gentle officers murdered while they protected Catholic school girls walking home after a day's studying.

Jimmy and Willy had just reached Cliftonville Circus when they were both shot at close range. Jimmy, who had twenty-three years' service, was hit five times and died almost immediately. Willie was shot three times in the back and died the next day in hospital. He never regained consciousness.

A twenty-two-year-old man from north Belfast was convicted of the killings and of four other murders, as well as the manslaughter of a fifteen-month-old baby, Graham Dougan, one of the youngest to be killed in the Troubles. Dougan had died when an IRA bomb exploded near his parents' home in Glengormley. Police were going house to house, warning people to get clear. The Dougan family were about to evacuate the area and were sitting in the family car when the hundred-pound bomb exploded. The debris struck the baby who was sitting in his mother's arms in the front seat of the car.

Jimmy's son could not live with the slaughter of his father and committed suicide a couple of years later.

I relive that day every night in flashbacks. It leads the list of murders, bombings, intimidation and other bloodthirsty terrorist acts I witnessed. Catastrophic PTSD, the psychiatrist called it, accompanied by traumatic amnesia. Much forgotten but not in the flashbacks. Forty-five years later, I do not hate, but I am still angry at the senseless slaughter by terrorists from both sides of Ulster's tribal divide.

16:15 – HMSU, Belfast

A lot of people are under the impression that the only time HMSU were deployed was in counter-terrorism, but that's not the case. One operation from around that period that stands out in my mind was not of a subversive nature, but criminally orientated.

There had been a spate of cowardly attacks on elderly people in the Downpatrick area, carried out by a particularly vicious criminal gang. One attack had involved an elderly homeowner being beaten quite severely and threatened with having his fingers cut off with pruning shears. We had firm intelligence that the gang was expanding its operation to more daring, and ultimately, profit-yielding activities. An off license in quite a salubrious part of Belfast was mentioned, with information indicating that the manager might be in on the plot. The intelligence had come through a Criminal Investigation Department source and due to the severity of the methods used by the gang, extra resources were to be thrown at it, including ourselves.

We were briefed by a rather portly inspector within the Criminal Investigation Department's surveillance agency, C12. The brief was all blood and thunder: 'This gang is ruthless and will show no mercy, if afforded the opportunity.' Needless to say, our team was hyped up, ready to go, just on the limit between being in control and unhinged. Once briefed on the personalities involved, we made our plan

It was a simple plan. Put a number of uniform vehicles in the surrounding area, place the area out of bounds to local police, despite the fact that it was extremely close to the local police station, place eight of us in a covert van, along with entry equipment to force open any door, whether fortified or not, then enter a short time after the bad guys had forced their way into the premises. C12 were to provide the surveillance, so there was no technical assistance and no chopper involved, just old-fashioned surveillance by a dedicated group of very professional men and women, holding the target by foot and backed up with vehicle passes. No mean feat, but they did it extremely well.

The readout came fast and furious. The personalities mentioned came together, loitered near the target, entered the premises, locked the door, and manhandled the manager into the rear store. The control room allowed a few minutes to pass before deploying us. It was a short drive from our lie-up position to the premises.

There was a side door that led into the store. We pulled

up just below the premises, quickly assembled in our order of entry, lined up, gave each other a firm squeeze on the arm to signify readiness to enter. The first guy nodded to the method of entry team, who had already conducted a survey of the door, identifying it as medium construction and inward opening. One firm blow with the heavily-weighted, hand-held ram and the door was open. Mayhem quickly ensued. The first thing I noticed as I entered was a guy, gagged and bound, face down in the middle of the stock room, looking up at us with abject terror in his eyes. Was he an innocent? Was he complicit, and this was the moment he realised things had gone pear shaped? I was number two of three in the line-up, and saw two of my team immediately take control of two would-be robbers in the confined space.

My gaze was quickly drawn to a young guy who was rooted to the spot in a doorway that led into a smaller store. I yelled at it him to stand still. He turned and bolted into the adjacent store. The only thing was, he had nowhere to go, but that did not deter him from trying. In that moment, I saw something I had never seen before or since: cartoon-like, he ran square into a wall. Fortunately for him he had not gathered much pace, but he still hit the wall with some force.

I was quickly on him, and without prompting, he started to give me every evidential detail I could have hoped for: when they had arrived; what his role was; what the others' roles were. Bingo. I would have needed to have been a short-hand typist to get it verbatim, but I got the gist of it. Then I noticed something was not quite right. He was hyperventilating, and I was worried that he would pass out. I tried to calm him, but being dressed head to toe in black tactical gear, and having just fucked up his day totally, I was possibly not the best person to try and placate someone.

Things were further exacerbated when the sergeant in charge came over and demanded to know my suspect's name. That set him off again and he was taking deep gulping breaths. Could this have been the ruthless criminal who had terrorized elderly residents during domestic robberies? The tables had been well and truly turned. The sergeant and I exchanged glances that said, 'What the fuck!' I ushered my supervisor away, and finally my detainee calmed down, only for him to flare up again as I handcuffed him then placed the forensic cape over him. Not so tough and ruthless!

The scene was quickly under control with four prisoners all forensically caped and a 'hostage' freed. We now had a short time to wait for our own saloon vehicles to arrive to transport the suspects the short distance to a nearby police station. The idea at this stage of any operation is to keep prisoners, who are essentially co-accused, separated, to prevent communication between them. As I mentioned earlier, the intelligence had originated from the Criminal Investigation Department, and as we were about to find out, had come from a human source, or a 'two legged', as we referred to them [as opposed to information obtained via surveillance equipment]. It was not always essential for us to know the source of the intelligence, particularly if it was human. However, if the source was involved in the operation, it was a different ball game altogether. Source protection was, and is, paramount. The source needed to be well versed and schooled by their handler to protect their own identity. The consequences of being found out would not be good. So, you can imagine the collective surprise of the arrest party and the suspects when one of them started firing out wild suggestions that he was supposed to get away and demanding to see his handlers.

I was flabbergasted … this idiot, if he were a source,

had no regard for his own safety but he seemed extremely well informed, pointing out, for reasons known only to himself, the identity of one of the surveillance operators who was still driving around the immediate area. It was clear this 'suspect' had been well briefed by his handlers, as he claimed. He even knew details of the surveillance operators, something that would never have been disclosed to him in a Special Branch operation. The stupidest informant in the world aside, they were bang to rights, and ended up with jail sentences after entering pleas.

I am not sure how the pantomime of the source and his handlers played out, but the last I heard his legal team had issued subpoenas to have the handlers attend court. A fuck-up of monumental proportions for sure, but shit happened from time to time.

16:20 – Newry Police Station

A new police station was built in Newry, but one of the concessions made to those who didn't want the police there was that it would not have any cells: prisoners wouldn't be brought into Newry town, they would have to be shipped up to Banbridge instead. A no-expense-spared station costing millions, with a gym and squash courts, every modern facility for an up-to-date state-of-the-art police station that had the best of everything, but no cells. It was appeasement gone mad.

There were some really nice people in Newry who were very supportive of the police but couldn't necessarily have been seen to be. They genuinely wanted a police service to work with. They didn't want gangsters to be running the place they lived. Nevertheless, I remember Archie Hayes, an assistant chief constable, asking me, 'Is it right that there are three police forces in Northern Ireland? There's Belfast, there's the country and then there is Newry.'

A quarter of all the soldiers murdered in Northern Ireland and a sixth of all the police officers murdered in Northern Ireland were killed in Newry subdivisions.

There were a couple of memorial tablets in the old Key Square RUC station in remembrance of police officers who had been killed in the area. When they moved us to the brand-new, purpose-built police station at Ardmore, they decided to move these tablets too, and rededicate once they were in place.

A service was held one Sunday morning and the families of all the officers whose names were on the tablet were invited to attend. The sub-divisional commander read out the names of over fifty police officers. It was absolutely heartbreaking; you could have heard a pin drop as the names were read out in a most respectful and dignified quiet way. When you hear all the names read out together, it brings home to you what sacrifice has been made.

16:40 – Warrenpoint Police Station, County Down

The 27 August 1979 is a day I will never forget. I was on duty in the Warrenpoint RUC station when news began to filter through that Lord Mountbatten had been murdered while lobster fishing off of Mullaghmore, County Sligo, along with three other people, two of them children. At that stage, I didn't think the day could get any worse.

I was sitting in the enquiry office of the station when the first of the Narrow Water bombs went off. The station was a mile away, but I was actually blown off my chair from the sheer impact of the shockwaves. I'm not quite sure whether it was my reaction or it was the blast, but I ended up on the floor. The IRA had planted two roadside bombs, the first of which had been concealed by bales of hay on a tractor trailer parked at the side of the dual carriageway. It had been detonated as an army convoy passed the trailer.

I was at the scene shortly after the first explosion, though I was in the second car at the scene as the Warrenpoint mobile patrol vehicle, a soft skin Ford escort, had arrived before us. They were wearing caps, uniforms and carrying firearms, rifles and the like. We had arrived in a civilian car because there weren't any more police cars attached to Warrenpoint and we made a point of getting out with long arms and our caps on to identify ourselves to the other personnel who were there.

A lorry there was on fire but the thing I distinctly remember was the smell in the air. That smell of burning human flesh is something I have never forgotten. Some ammunition was exploding from the heat from the lorry. We were also coming under fire from the direction of the Republic of Ireland – I have no doubt about that whatsoever due to the direction the rounds were coming from. The dual carriageway runs parallel to Carlingford Lough and forms part of the border between the two countries that are only a few hundred yards apart. Consequently, the soldiers were firing into the South, as were we. It was more an attempt to provide cover for people trying to help the injured and make the terrorists keep their heads down than anything else.

A follow-up operation was swinging into place and reinforcements were arriving constantly by helicopter and in vehicles. During the course of the commotion, we saw a hand waving out of the long grass in the central reservation. We ran down, leaving our long arms behind us, and found this guy lying in the grass. It was only when I was beside him on my knees trying to help that I realised he had no legs. He couldn't stay where he was as he was totally exposed to the gunmen across the lough. We had to move him.

We picked him up between us, one arm over each

133

shoulder, and started back towards the car where we could provide cover and first aid. We were aware of a Wessex helicopter coming in, as it was raising a lot of dust and causing us to keep our heads down to protect our eyes as we moved forward. It was just at this point that the second bomb went off and a stone came out of the gate lodge wall and hit our soldier in the head. His head was completely removed, and the blast knocked us off our feet. We realised there was nothing more we could do, so we left him there to get back under cover ourselves.

Six soldiers died in the first explosion, immediately after which reinforcements and medics had begun to arrive at the scene. The surviving paratroopers and soldiers who came to their assistance established a defensive position behind the nearby gates and wall of Narrow Water Castle, not realising that the IRA had anticipated they would do so. A secondary device had been planted at the wall and was detonated half an hour after the first explosion, killing another twelve soldiers, including Lieutenant-Colonel Blair who had gone to the scene by helicopter after the initial attack. So close was Blair to the explosion that his remains were never found. Throughout this time, shots continued to be exchanged across the lough with the terrorists responsible. Sixteen of the eighteen soldiers killed in the attack were from the Parachute Regiment. More than twenty other soldiers were seriously injured and one civilian, Michael Hudson from London, was killed when soldiers returned fire at the terrorists that had detonated the bombs – he had been birdwatching in the Republic of Ireland. A scene of carnage in the most picturesque of settings. When I eventually got back to the station the night of the attack, I smoked sixty cigarettes in an hour and drank a forty-ounce bottle of vodka.

A colossal number of RUC turned up to preserve and

clear the scene [to confirm no more secondary bombs had been planted] so the investigation could begin. The next morning there were 1,200 police in Warrenpoint, and a lot of them were there for quite a number of days. A divisional mobile support unit [DMSU] arrived from Armagh, guarding our station in case of further attack. There was also a chuck wagon parked out on the street as there was no room in the station. The extra guards were in place for two weeks so that it was safe for the guys who were cleaning up to come in for a rest.

Despite the intensity of the follow-up operation, we got calls at the station for weeks on end to come and pick up human remains found by wildfowlers who would regularly operate in the area.

RUC detectives who were investigating the murders of the soldiers established that the firing point for detonation of the bombs was across the border in the Irish Republic, on the other side of the lough. They were denied access to the firing point for some time and when they did eventually get there, the grass had just been cut and the area tidied up. A forensic report was requested of the area where the detonation occurred, and the prolonged gun attack launched. It appears they are still waiting for it. One of the IRA men said to be involved was Brendan Burns. He was stopped by Gardaí as he and another republican were driving away on a motorcycle on the road opposite Narrow Water just after the explosion. He died in 1988 when a bomb he was handling exploded prematurely.

At the inquest in 1980, an army doctor gave harrowing details of the scene where he said he found dead and injured men, scattered limbs and decapitated bodies. Female members of the jury were excluded by the coroner from examining photographs taken at the scene.

One injured paratrooper said, 'For ... about seven days I

had no recollection of anything. The left side of my skull is plastic. I lost my left eye. I've got the greater part of my left forearm missing and there's a steel nail through the bone in my forearm.'

Another stated, 'As we accelerated away on to a type of dual carriageway there was a rumble and I got a flash of lightning, then a sensation of flying and I knew automatically that we'd been involved in an explosion. As I looked to my left, I noticed my legs were on fire and I could hear voices – "He's dead, he's dead" – and the voices kept getting stronger coming towards me, and I sat up and said, "I'm not dead." I was put on the helicopter. The helicopter was just taking off when it happened all over again: the rumble, the flash.'

16:45 – Narrow Water Castle, County Down

A dear friend of mine called to see me one afternoon and, somehow, we ended up talking about the Narrow Water bomb. I'd been there but I had never talked about it before – I have always tried to put it out of my mind. We had to pick up body parts and put them into black bin bags. There was no mapping it all out, it was just really a cleaning-up exercise. There was no attempt to identify what parts went where, nor could you have done so anyway. It was just carnage. I was barely twenty years old when I walked out of Lisburn Road police station. I should have been going home but was told to get into a transit van to go and help at Warrenpoint. I didn't even know what had happened and now I can't forget.

16:50 – Special Branch Office, Newry Police Station

The attack in Warrenpoint at Narrow Water Castle was hailed as a great victory for the IRA: they'd inflicted the highest number of deaths on the British army in a single atrocity and made headlines worldwide. I subsequently learned from intelligence that came across my desk in relation to the Warrenpoint attack that the Parachute Regiment were not the target and that confirmed that what had occurred that day had been a fluke.

It had always been a bit of a mystery for us how the IRA would know there was a company changeover taking place in the military. It's very easy for their propaganda people to infer and allege that they had a super intelligent system, but we in Special Branch don't believe it, nor ever saw that depth of intelligence ever being gathered by them.

The real targets were Royal Marine and Royal Navy personnel who used a boat permanently anchored in Carlingford Lough as a base. They used to attract the odd shot from a sniper across the lough in the Republic of Ireland. They were there as a deterrent to any terrorists who would use Carlingford Lough as a resupply route for the IRA as they tried to bring in weapons and explosives from arms dumps in the south, or who would use the lough as an escape route after carrying out murders or similar attacks in Northern Ireland. The personnel on the boat were changed over quite frequently – every seven to ten days – but they also needed food and provisions to be resupplied, which is what the IRA had been waiting for.

What happened that day actually led to a change in procedure. As it was the second bomb that had done the bulk of the damage, from then on the military decreed that, where possible, the incident control point would be set up in the crater of the first bomb, as that was the one place that there wouldn't be a second explosion. In the years to come the lessons learned following the Warrenpoint attack saved more lives than I could even guess, not just in Northern Ireland but in Iraq, Afghanistan and other theatres as well.

16:55 – CID Office, Newry Police Station

For a few years, a maracycle from Belfast to Dublin and back again was a very popular and well-supported feature on the sporting calendar. It ticked a lot of boxes and was hailed as a very cross-community event. At any given time there would have been a lot of cyclists travelling in either direction on the roads between Dublin and Belfast. The occasion also attracted a lot of sightseers and tourists as the event grew in popularity.

During one maracycle the Provisional IRA attached a bomb to the railings on the Dublin Road just outside Newry. It is impossible to tell who their intended target was given the large number of civilians present in the area – there would only have only been an intermittent police presence and not for long periods. Information had been received by Special Branch about the intended attack and an observation post was mounted in the appropriate area. Sean Mathers, the O/C Newry IRA, and Michael Hillen were arrested after they were found at the end of the command wire which would detonate the bomb. Police were able to forensically link both terrorists to the device. They were sentenced in court to twenty years and twenty-one years imprisonment respectively. Hillen had previously been sentenced to twenty-five years for another terrorist offence and became the longest-serving prisoner on either part of the island.

There is no doubt the operation saved many lives as a bomb of that sort would have been a very indiscriminate weapon in a very crowded area but, in the eyes of the terrorist, preferable to having the two sides of the community come together to build relations.

17:00 – Coffee-time Reflections

Obviously, being in the police in the 1980s and 1990s was a very dangerous job. Security was a constant theme in your life, whether you were at work or off duty and in your own home. While you were at work was bad enough, but in some ways easier because your senses were heightened as the chances of an attack were greater. Of course, you also had your colleagues whose senses were equally heightened, and collectively you were well armed and felt you had a chance of surviving whatever happened. At home, you ended up very suspicious of people, particularly strangers, coming into your social scene. Which was difficult with your kids, and indeed your wife, mixing in different groups connected to schools … what most people would just call normal life.

I was living in north Down and while trying not to be paranoid about security, I did take sensible precautions. One of the things I did was tell my neighbours that I was an electrician – my wife did the same if anyone asked her what I did. This worked very well for quite some time until eventually, a neighbour asked me to give him a quote for some electrical work. It was a bit of a quandary as I didn't want to be rude, but equally couldn't do it. I tried to say that I was busy and that he would really be better off getting someone else who could tend to his problem much more quickly. Unfortunately, he was completely undeterred and said he was happy to wait to give me the business.

It was becoming increasingly difficult to sustain the pretence, but the straw that broke the camel's back was when he walked into the enquiry office at the station I was working in. There was no way to avoid him. I was standing there at the front desk in full uniform as the SDO. To make matters worse, it turned out he was in to sign bail in connection with some fraud he had been charged with through his business. Embarrassment all round, but it did solve the problem of the quotation for electrical work. He has never spoken to me from that day to this!

17:10 – Andersonstown Police Station, West Belfast

People talk about the victims in the RUC. There is no doubt some of our colleagues suffered terrible injuries and we know all too well that we've been to too many funerals. But sometimes the victims aren't seen.

I was a young constable, stationed in Andersonstown barracks in the heart of west Belfast. While based there, we had to park in the military section of Musgrave Park Hospital then were ferried in and out of the station in armoured military vehicles [Pigs] as it was not safe to drive our own vehicles into work. I was just married, and my wife, who was twenty-one at the time, was at Queen's University doing her final exams. We only had the one car, so quite often she would drive into Musgrave Park to the helipad, either to drop me off in the morning, or to pick me up after an early shift.

It was 24 May 1983 and I was on the early shift. We were doing the bank patrol, which involved following a cash delivery vehicle that was visiting local banks – we were to provide a degree of lateral protection against robbery. We got a radio call from Andersonstown to say that a vehicle had been abandoned at the station with a proxy bomb inside. It was a massive Volkswagen Combi vehicle and it was parked outside the station. It had been one of those 'takeovers', friendly or not, in which the driver said, 'They forced me to drive it here.'

We returned to base immediately. When we got there, even the sub-divisional commander was out helping to move people back from the station. I remember one guy who was up a ladder refused to come down when we asked. He was in what was going to be the blast zone. 'Fuck off, you black bastards,' was his response – a phrase I was all too familiar with [this was a name used in some areas for the police].

We knew we did not have a lot of time, so we deployed immediately and began moving people back from their houses, those that were in proximity to the station. As we were doing that, the vehicle exploded, showering shrapnel everywhere. I was blown off my feet. I remember in the immediate aftermath of the blast, thinking as I lay on the ground, that I had pissed myself – I was soaking. It turned out, the bomb had been so big, and the blast so devastating, that it had ruptured the water mains. My dignity was intact. In the heated aftermath of the explosion someone had a negligent discharge from their firearm, causing further confusion.

We thought, first of all, that we had been caught in a primary explosion and that a secondary attack was still to come, so our level of anxiety was massive. One of the guys, Alan, had been wearing one of the turtle-shell flak jackets, which was completely blown off him. Shrapnel from the blast had hit him straight in the face and was embedded in his eye. At that moment, I was in shock. I was carrying one of those army first-aid packs that you take out. You know, you're shaking, you're afraid, and you're trying to apply first aid to an injured colleague. He had dropped his radio and he kept saying, 'Jim, Jim, my radio, my radio.' The shock was such that he thought he could pick it up and carry on working – that was his only concern. We put him in the back of one of the Land Rovers and, with the doors flapping wildly, drove him straight to the Royal Victoria Hospital. He was in a bad way and sadly lost his eye.

Back at the scene, we continued to clear through the rubble. There was a sergeant called Willie, a real character and a classic station sergeant. He appeared, coughing and spluttering and completely covered in white dust, then looked at me and said, 'For fuck's sake, every member of your family has been on the phone to see if you're okay!'

The place was decimated. We continued trying to clear the scene and doing what we could for the injured. We found the guy that had been on the ladder; he had a broken leg.

Later, just after five o'clock, the station sergeant came out of what remained of the station and shouted, 'Has anybody got a wife or girlfriend at Musgrave Park Hospital?' I said, 'I have.' 'Well, she's just thrown a fit at the helipad.' They took me in a Land Rover to the helipad where my wife had been sitting, waiting for me since three o'clock. I hadn't turned up, so she'd switched on the radio and the first reports on the five o'clock news had stated that Andersonstown RUC station had been devastated by a huge explosion, one police officer had been killed and there were multiple injuries.

She listened to the news and thought, 'I'm here, it's two hours later, I have heard nothing.' Fearing the worst she got out of the car, threw a fit, and was put into a hut by the army guys at the hospital. I was driven up there from Andersonstown, got out of the back of the Land Rover covered in the remnants of the first aid I had been administering and plastered in blood.

You take on the risk yourself when you join the job, but you don't take time to reflect on the impact this has on your family. What occurred that day was devastating for her; the trauma impacted her greatly. She was very much an innocent, whose only connection was that she'd happened to marry someone involved in that world. We had to move house three times over the years, under threat from terrorists. Every time, she had to give up a home she had built. I suppose you would write two of them off because we'd had information in advance of a pending attack. On the other occasion, though, two males were arrested in our front garden waiting for me to come out of the house to go to work. They had intended to kill me. I cannot help but think sometimes about those people in the margins of the police family. They had a very direct horror, thinking the most awful things had happened to their loved ones. This has an impact on you as well.

17:19 – CID Office, Grosvenor Road Police Station, Belfast City Centre

When I was in Grosvenor Road CID, I was instructed to attend a house search in the area. It proved to be an interesting lesson in how the Provisional IRA operated.

In the couple of days immediately preceding the house search there had been a whole lot of covert police and the army activity concentrated in the Beechmount area of west Belfast. The whole area was out of bounds: there was surveillance going on, there was a lot of toing and froing from police and army. It was very clear, we thought, that there was something major going on – they were up to something.

I subsequently learned that surveillance teams had been watching IRA members, who would move around together, then split up, go their separate ways, then be joined by another person. They would split up, get into a taxi, go into a house, come out the back door into the alleyway, go into another house through the back alleyway and come out the front door of another house across the alley. They were doing lots of back and forth, back and forth.

Eventually the TCG [the Tasking Coordinating Group is a secure net for operatives – all radio communication and control during an operation goes through here] made a decision to search a particular house in Beechmount. I was at the scene. In the house were really well-known IRA players who had been heavily involved in the explosives end of their campaign. This was the most effective bombing team in Belfast, responsible for the big city-centre bombs that were wiping out the commercial heart of Belfast. Their recent behaviour led us to conclude that these IRA personnel had come together because they were planning a major bombing attack. Now, with catching these people together in the house you'd think it was time for champagne and cigars but, as they were being led out of the house, one of the Provisionals spoke to me. I hadn't expected him to speak – these people never spoke to police – but he obviously saw me as being the detective in charge of the search. He said, 'I hope you know what you're doing, because we do.' That was all he said before he was taken to Castlereagh holding centre for interrogation. It was only when I thought about it later that I realised what he was really saying.

Over at Castlereagh, forensic examination of him for traces of explosives proved negative and he never spoke once throughout his entire detention in the holding centre. The same applied to the four other IRA members who were arrested in the house at the same time. A search of the house they had been in also proved negative. Searches were also carried out in every house, street and alleyway they had been in while under surveillance, including the taxi they had used, which police had located and seized. Every search proved negative.

It was a few months before we realised that what they were doing that day was deliberately trying to flush out an informant. They had been moving in and around the area, particularly the Beechmount area, until they were satisfied that the only people who knew where they were was themselves and thirty-four-year-old mother of three, Caroline Moreland from Beechmount Grove who, for whatever reason, had come under suspicion. In July 1994, Caroline was abducted, taken down to the County Fermanagh border and shot dead as an alleged informant.

She had been missing for fifteen days before her body was found

Now I don't know whether Caroline Moreland was an informant – I never met the woman, I never had any dealings with her – but if that were true, if she was involved in passing information about the location of the bombing team then what the Provos did was tactically sound. It was a reminder that the terrorists were very much alive to our habits and tactics. They could calculate how we thought, displaying the level of sophistication that they had reached as an organisation. They knew we would have to respond if that number of high-ranking terrorists were seen to be active in an area – it underscored the lengths to which they would go to thwart us.

17:40 – CID Office, Lisburn Police Station, County Antrim

When I was in CID, Lisburn RUC station, an explosion took place on the Portadown train near Moira in which people were injured. I had been sitting in the house watching the news when I heard and, as it happened in my area, I knew it was only a matter of time before I got the phone call calling me into work. I rang the office to see what was going on, then left the house. I arrived at the station quite quickly (I lived nearby) and was told to make my way to the railway station and the scene. At this time, we were in the early stages of establishing exactly what had happened.

I now know that the train had started its journey at Bangor, where two bombs had been brought on and placed under seats. The train left Bangor at 5.40 p.m. and was due to carry on as far as Portadown. The bombers had apparently believed that the service terminated at Central Station, Belfast, where they got off. A phone call was made to the local newspaper warning of a bomb in Central Station, which was searched but nothing was found.

The train, meanwhile, had left Central Station and, just after it had passed through the Botanic area, one of the bombs was discovered. It had been in a haversack, and one of the staff placed it on an embankment near Sandy Row. The railway authorities were informed, as were the police and military, but it was felt that the threat in relation to the bomb had been concluded. The train continued on its journey. The second bomb exploded on the train as it passed through open countryside near Moira; it too had been contained in a haversack.

A number of passengers were injured and taken to Lagan Valley Hospital but Roberta Bartholomew, a twenty-two-year-old civil servant, was not so lucky. She was killed when the bomb exploded. She had been on her way home from work in the Department of Agriculture in Belfast to spend the weekend with her family.

I took her father to identify her body but I hadn't the heart to show him her face and head because of the extent of her injuries. Instead I showed him her hand as there was an identifiable ring on it, to save him having the memory of that sight. Her arm, the one with the hand that had the ring, wasn't actually attached to her body but I held it tight against her and blocked his view.

He identified her and while I was doing some form-filling he said to me, 'Will this take long?' I said, 'No, why?' He explained to me that he was in a bit of a hurry. I couldn't understand what he could have to do that was so important, having just identified his daughter's body so I asked him, 'What is it that you need to do? Is there anything that we can help you with?' He told me that he had to get to the station to collect his daughter. It was the saddest thing and it affected me very greatly; to the extent that I left the police over it. I'd had enough.

Roberta had been a prominent member of the Young

Farmers' Club and they established a cup which was awarded annually in her memory. She was buried from her local church in Richhill, where she had been a Sunday School teacher at the time of her death.

The local press speculated that she had been transporting the bomb for the IRA when it exploded, which was utter nonsense. A teenager from the Short Strand area of east Belfast was detained after admitting that he'd left the two bombs on the train. He was one of the two-man bombing team responsible.

17:42 – Lisburn Road Police Station, Belfast

The radio crackled into life: 'Foxtrot 4, pickup Sierra Foxtrot Romeo, usual location.' I said, 'Roger' and I went to our favourite local Chinese (they gave us discount) and picked up a special fried rice. I dropped it off to the SDO back at base, who thanked me and then said, 'By the way, the sergeant is still waiting in the sangar at Dunmurry station. Better get your skates on!'

Sierra: Sergeant

Foxtrot Romeo: Dunmurry station

Usual location: for pickup was the sangar at the front of the station.

Severe communication breakdown, and several years of abuse!

17:45 – Boucher Road, Belfast

I think we found some of the incidents that occurred funny because they were so dangerous and we just didn't know what else to do.

We had a short-wheelbase Hotspur [a bulletproof Land Rover] and one day, as we were going along the Boucher Road in Belfast, we heard shots pinging off the side of it. Fortunately for us the armour held up and none of the shots penetrated the vehicle. We drove on to get out of the killing zone and, once we felt we were in a safe area, we got out to have a look around the truck to see if there were any strike marks on it. Everyone was punch-drunk with euphoria and laughing uncontrollably. We had just been shot at – it was a fairly serious attempt to murder police – but the weird thing was that everybody was just laughing and falling about. That was how we handled it.

17:49 – Stewartstown Police Station, County Tyrone

The attacks by the IRA in the country area were far more sophisticated than those around the cities. In the city, attacks were planned methodically and all the rest of it, but there was a marked difference between the two, particularly when it came to manpower, as shown by an attack on Stewartstown station.

The IRA had managed to block every road into Stewartstown village and had at least four gunmen placed on each of those roads – that's over twenty terrorists deployed just to set up roadblocks so they could mount their attack. They had a slurry tanker filled with diesel fuel to spray over the wall at the front of the station, after which they would detonate a device to ignite the fuel. They had ten heavily-armed people looking after that phase of the attack. There was then a team of six at the back of the station, standing by the emergency gate, which served as an escape route in the event a proxy bomb or something was left at the front of the station. The IRA team at the rear were armed with heavy machine guns, expecting that if and when the station went up in the fire, and personnel tried to escape out the back, they would be waiting to wipe them out.

By a complete fluke there were no police officers in the station. While the IRA were making ready their plans for the attack, the officers had left to do a run to Cookstown RUC station. Had that not happened, there would have been only three officers present to defend the station and themselves.

But that was the type of thing we were dealing with; that level of intensity. The IRA had mounted a massive operation and that high threat level was constantly there. We daren't have dropped our guard for a second.

17:50 – Sion Mills Police Station, County Tyrone

I was tasked to attend a sudden death in a staunchly nationalist area. I was the observer in the patrol vehicle, which meant that I would be dealing with the paperwork involved. We believed that the household we had to visit was firmly in the republican branch of nationalism, but there had been a death in the family, and it had to be dealt with just like any other. However, as we were making our way to the house, our section sergeant radioed and told us to return to base.

I had been wondering why we had been called back when the sergeant approached me and said, 'Go and put your tunic on. Lose the gun belt and take off your flak jacket – it will make a vast amount of difference going into that house.' I couldn't see it when he told me, but I have to say he was right. By appearing in a tunic, it took away that hard-line appearance. They could see immediately that I'd made the effort, which was seen for what it was, a token of respect. I explained we were not there as police officers investigating a crime, we were simply there on behalf of the coroner to carry out initial enquiries on his behalf. [The role of the police in these instances is to rule out foul play and establish if the deceased had seen their doctor within twenty-eight days, and who could then issue a death certificate. Failing that, a post-mortem would have to take place and an inquest held to establish cause of death.]

I was doing what I could to help the family given the circumstances and they were very appreciative of it. Before I left that house, I was offered a cup of tea, which wasn't a commonplace occurrence. I declined in case someone else arrived at the house and saw me taking tea, as I knew there would be severe repercussions for the family who had enough on their plate. Before I opened the front door, and as we shook hands, I was thanked for attending the wake house and for my help in dealing with the death.

18:12 – Brookeborough Police Station, County Fermanagh

On 21 January 1991, the IRA murdered Cullen Stephenson, a sixty-three-year-old retired RUC reservist, in Brookeborough, County Fermanagh. Stephenson, who had left the police reserve two years prior to the attack, was returning home at around 6 p.m. from his work in a nearby creamery, in which he had worked for over forty years. Eyewitnesses would later tell the inquest that four or five gunmen, dressed in combat-style clothing, had been seen gathered round his car, firing shots inside. Mrs Stephenson narrowly missed death as two of the bullets came through a window in the house, which she was sitting beside, waiting on her husband's return from work.

I was off duty and lying on my bed in the station when the inspector came running in to tell me about a shooting. He said we were to make our way there immediately. We arrived on the scene to find a man lying in his car, obviously dead. They had just blasted him at close range with automatic weapons and he had had no chance. A member of the public shouted to me that the gunmen had run up the hill towards the nearby Catholic church, so I set off in pursuit. I checked around the junction, the church itself and the graveyard, but they were long gone. It was a while afterwards that I found out that the IRA had left a timed explosive device at the junction by the church in anticipation of the ICP [Incident

Control Point] or a roadblock being set up there as police dealt with the crime scene.

Back at the scene, the forensic examination was under way and, once they had finished, the undertaker started to remove the body. As he was having difficulty, a colleague and I assisted in lifting the body from the car. Then I took a silver kidney-shaped dish from the undertaker, climbed back into the car and scraped skull, brains and hair from off the seat into the dish. I was an experienced police officer, professional, and he was one of us – he deserved nothing less than professionalism and respect.

A few days later we went out to do searches in the local area. I was always the detailed log-keeper, and this time was no exception. Expecting the searches to be a dirty, grimy affair I had put on an old Dartex coat with no epaulettes. The inspector and another senior officer arrived during the proceedings in full uniform, with pips and braid. Every time one of the search teams found anything, or finished a task, they informed me as log-keeper, and I then noted the details, entering timings for the record and assigning them their next task in the search.

In one of the houses there was an elderly man sitting in a corner and he suddenly piped up, 'I want to know who you are.' I told him that the details would be on the search record, which he would be given, but he shook his head. 'No,' he said, 'that man there' – he pointed to the inspector – 'he has all the regalia, but you have none at all and you're giving all the orders. I want to know who you are.' He received the same answer as before, but a week or two later I was amazed to read in one of the Sunday newspapers that 'Agents of British Intelligence in RUC uniform had directed searches in the Lisnaskea area.'

Of such are rumours born …

18:57 – MSU, Enniskillen

Every year, during the build-up to Christmas, there was an increased threat of a bomb in the town, so we initiated what they called 'Op Arnhem', which involved sealing off the three bridges into Enniskillen and checking all traffic coming into the town. The operation usually commenced in November for the expected rush in Christmas shoppers, many of whom travelled up from the Republic, and lasted until the holiday period had passed. We started at 7 a.m., went out to an allocated point, and stopped cars all day until the town was sealed off at 7 p.m.

It was Christmastime 1992, and for a time, the operation was a novelty. Then it became amazingly boring: day after day, standing in the same spot, stopping cars for twelve hours. We tried to vary the location between the crews, we even tried to send a few crew members back to the station for short breaks, but the powers-that-be chased them out again.

As the weeks passed and Christmas loomed ever closer the threat level got ever higher. We actually had shopkeepers who would deliberately leave unattended cars in the town centre, and then complain that the police had not checked them, that a bomb had got through, and the bosses were in a panic. Everyone was watching us, ready to blame us for any inadequacy. But finally the big day passed, and the town was sealed to traffic for two days. Imagine our frustration when some bright spark reckoned that the IRA would just bring a bomb in after Christmas and decided the VCPs should continue. No one was the slightest bit concerned about the danger the people carrying out the VCPs were exposed to. We stood in the same spot, twelve hours a day, day after day, for weeks: January, February, March; snow, rain or sunshine. I'd had enough and I applied for leave, but it was turned down because, 'We were too stretched.'

We all started to get very short-tempered and suspicious:

who was skiving? who was nipping in for two-hour toilet breaks? who was making urgent phone calls that went on for hours. Some of the more experienced 'slippy' men got themselves moved into little 'urgent' jobs, which left the rest of us even more short-staffed. The final straw came when one of my colleagues applied for leave at short notice and it was granted. Why him and not me? I stood on the bridge in the pouring rain, and the tears streamed out of me. I just couldn't face any more. I really was at the point of throwing the rifle over the bridge and walking off.

I went to my GP and he put me on immediate sick leave, and shortly afterwards I was transferred out of the unit. Four months of non-stop, permanent VCPs, twelve hours per day, to the exclusion of all else. Not quite what I joined for.

19:07 – CID Office, Armagh Police Station

I had to attend the post-mortem of someone who had been murdered and I was accompanied by a girl who had just arrived into SOCO. She was a great girl and very keen but of course new. Ted said to me, 'Would you have any spare rounds of ammunition with you?' I said, 'Actually, I have a spare magazine,' which he asked me to give to him. I handed it over and he removed six bullets from it and carried on rummaging in the stomach cavity of the body.

Now the victim had actually been shot, and he produced a bullet and called me over: 'Look at this.' I said, 'Sure that's a live round,' and he said, 'Get the scenes of crime officer quick'. She came over and I handed her the bullet: 'Hang on, how did this person get shot by a live round?' Ted, meanwhile, was still appearing to rummage and one after the other, he comes out with six bullets in total. She was carefully labelling and bagging them as if they were evidence. She said, 'That's the first time I've ever seen anyone shot with live rounds.'

20:03 – Oldpark Police Station, North Belfast

I was an inspector in Oldpark RUC station in north Belfast, one of the most dangerous places in Europe to be a policeman. In our very small sub-division we had 168 civilians, 22 soldiers and 14 policemen killed in the space of just five years.

On 12 March 1975, around eight o'clock, I was out on patrol in our Land Rover. We – that is, a driver, two men, a policewoman in the rear and me beside the driver – were driving down Cliftonville Road approaching a street to our right. It was dark with no street lighting thanks to the nightly rioting. As we approached the adjoining street, Orient Gardens, I saw two flashes and heard what appeared to be two gunshots. We turned into the street and saw light coming from an open doorway, which opened out directly on to the pavement. We made our way towards it.

We could see no one in the street so we stopped at the open door to see what was going on. There was a man lying there with his head on the doorstep and his body lying within the hallway. He had a head wound which had caused a lot of blood loss. His head was lying in the pool of blood. I knew he was dead because the blood was already congealing, indicating it was no longer pumping out of his body as his heart had stopped beating.

I learned later that it had been another sectarian murder carried out by the INLA. The victim was Raymond Carrothers, a Protestant. The gunman had knocked the door and when Raymond's son had answered, he'd asked the boy, 'Is your daddy in?' The child shouted 'Daddy' and returned to the living room. When he'd heard the shots he'd rushed back to the hall and found his father lying in a pool of blood.

I looked up from the body and down the hallway. At the base of the stairs, I saw three children huddled together, the oldest about twelve and the youngest about five. The oldest was holding the other two. They were staring in silent shock, not moving, or uttering a sound. I stepped over the body that I assumed was their father, careful not to step in the blood. I ushered them into the adjacent living room and had the policewoman who had followed me, take care of them. I left them there to carry out a search around the area for the perpetrators.

The sight of those three waifs is one I will never forget. It remains clearly imprinted in my memory and will do so until I die.

20:08 – Border, County Fermanagh

The part-time reserve members who worked near the border were magic. A lot of the members were farmers who were more than happy to serve – they also got a personal protection weapon given to them, which they were glad of because the IRA were targeting Protestant people living at the border then, particularly the farmers. The area was known as the killing fields of Fermanagh.

I remember being out with one of the reserve members – I won't mention his name – and he was pointing out to me where everyone lived and who they were: 'He's in Sinn Féin, he's an Ulster Unionist councillor, but every year they come together to do the harvest, but one of them is actively targeting the other.' Weird and wonderful stories like that. He told me about his grandfather who'd had a problem with some of the land he owned. His farm had straddled the border but one of the fields was prone to flooding because of an old culvert. His solution was simple. He diverted the stream and moved the culvert 200 yards further along. He didn't realise that in the course of his land management programme he'd caused Northern Ireland to gain 200 yards because the culvert had always been regarded as the border. It didn't go unnoticed – the

155

next time the Department of the Environment came out to do work in the area, they just resurfaced the road up to the culvert and the border was confirmed.

20:17 – CID Office, Andersonstown Police Station, West Belfast

I was stationed in Andersonstown in west Belfast when I got a case I will never forget. It was on the same night that the office had its annual Christmas function. My partner and I had left the office to go and deal with an incident involving a girl who had recently given birth. She was from one of the housing estates in the area. She had gone to do some shopping – it was the first time she'd left the house since coming home from hospital with the baby. She had left the child with her husband, but the baby ended up having to be brought to the local hospital [RVH]. The staff there had called the police as their suspicions had been aroused. We found out that the baby had been crying, much to the annoyance of the husband, who had picked the child up by the ankles and subsequently shook it to death. We arrested the guy and, when we interviewed him, he eventually admitted what he had done.

We had to see the child for ourselves as part of our investigation, but going down to the morgue to see that wee baby was a harrowing experience.

Later on, when we'd finished the paperwork on the case, we made our way to the office Christmas function. It was in a place in Bangor and obviously we were late getting to it. When we arrived, I looked around the room at everybody enjoying themselves, then my partner and I looked at each other and, without speaking to anyone, she and I walked out and went home. We just didn't have the heart for it.

We actually went to this wee baby's funeral and the sight

of the little white coffin has always stuck with me. Through all the horrendous shootings and bombings and things that I have seen and dealt with, that coffin haunts me.

The father got four years for manslaughter – the child wasn't a month old. He couldn't deal with his child crying and that was his way to stop it.

20:37 – HMSU, Belfast

The 1990s were busy for the unit. When we were not covering routine surveillance operations, or more complex surveillance operations on specific locations and people, we were generally deployed on intelligence-driven, reactive operations. The mainstay were anti-terrorist operations, though even the operations that appeared criminally-driven invariably had a subversive element to them.

I was relishing the role, and in a short period had arrested a number of terrorist suspects from both sides of the political divide: loyalists with an under-car booby trap on the upper Shankill Road; a republican sympathiser in Poleglass who was keeping a coffee grinder with traces of explosives in it; loyalist paramilitaries planning a robbery with fake police uniforms near the reservoirs in the hills above Carrickfergus. It was constant. One operation stands out, though – not because it was particularly dangerous, but more because of the comic value to it.

Intelligence had come in that loyalist paramilitaries had identified a postmistress living in a rural location, only twenty minutes from Belfast, who had the keys to a busy post office in Belfast. They had identified when the unemployment and pension funds were delivered and had decided to take the postmistress hostage, detain her family in their own home, and force her to open the post office and make off with the spoils. They would then release her and her family – a son and daughter-in-law.

Once the intelligence had been verified, we set about doing a covert survey of her house. It was an imposing, detached residence set in some land with stables attached. The stables were to prove invaluable. The plan was simple. The tech boys inserted covert cameras in the house directly relayed to monitors in the stable. Then we'd substitute her son and daughter-in-law with police officers and covertly drop off a full team of eight to occupy the stable. Deployment was for four days at a time. Simple.

The drop off went smoothly: insertion complete. We soon made ourselves comfortable in the stable, where we had a couple of direct vantage points, including an overview of the approach to the driveway and the doors of the house. Then the waiting began. Maintaining professionalism in such a small environment with seven other men, who have to eat, sleep and shit in front of each other, is challenging to say the least. Silence has to be 100 per cent. Again, not easy, but if compromised, so invariably was the job.

Two days passed and we were into the third evening when we heard movement at the driveway entrance, which was set back about forty metres from the house. Voices, distant at first, with thick Belfast accents, were suddenly very close. The order of 'Stand to!' was given, quickly followed by, 'Stand by!' I was on watch at the time from the vantage point, and had identified three heavy-set males in dark clothing in discussion. It was clear this was our team, which I was relaying as quietly as possible to a colleague at the base of my vantage point. I struggled to contain my laughter when I heard one say to another, 'It's my turn to hold the gun!', which I could now see.

The three then quickly made their way to the side door of the house and knocked on the door. This was answered by Bob, the officer playing the postmistress' son, as was the plan. They manhandled him, pointed the pistol in his face, and pushed him into the living room, where the postmistress and her bogus daughter-in-law were.

The video link to the stable was good, although a little grainy. By this time the entry team had assembled, ready to go in, on the say so from the operations room in Belfast, or from the commander of the house party if he felt the entry needed to be instant. It appeared to be getting quite heated, at which point the commander in the stable took the decision to enter via the same back door used by the criminals. We'd planned in advance that Bob would leave the door unlocked.

The team assembled, squeezes were given to signify readiness, then *bang!* In they went and pandemonium ensued. The would-be kidnappers saw their plan evaporating – the tables had been turned in quite a dramatic fashion. A few scuffles followed, a few blows were traded, but all three were soon arrested, searched and forensically 'caped'. Job done. Result.

One comment made in the aftermath will stick with me forever: Bob, who was not the biggest physical specimen commented, 'It's a good job you lot came in when you did, because I was about to cut up rough!' Needless to say this was repeated to him regularly during the ensuing piss-up, and many times in the weeks and months that followed. It was typical of the camaraderie and sense of humour that prevailed in the job, no matter the circumstances. A very important safety valve.

20:45 – Belfast Regional Control Centre, Castlereagh Police Station

Belfast Regional Control centre is based in Castlereagh RUC station, the home of the 'uniform' call sign, and is responsible for deploying police resources in the greater Belfast area as and where they are required. Calls for assistance, or incidents being reported by the public via telephone, would all be received there, including emergency 999 phone calls.

As you might imagine, a vast array of information is received at the centre on a daily basis. This can vary from a report of a lost dog to an incident with multiple murders having taken place. Every call coming in has to be assessed, after which the appropriate response is instigated from the police in the area concerned. At peak times, the number of calls being handled can be colossal. During such busy times not every obviously-hoax 999 call was being logged, nor the 'action taken' section completed by the receiving officer. Word of this practice filtered its way up to the officers in charge and as a result, the order came down from on high that all 999 calls must be fully logged, irrespective of their content.

One night shortly after this edict was received a 999 call came in, 'There's a bomb under your seat, you black bastard.'

Call details duly logged. Action taken: 'changed seats'.

20.49 – Coalisland Police Station, County Tyrone

I joined the RUC in September 1974 and went to my first station, Coalisland, in January 1975. One Sunday evening, in the summer of that year, I was detailed driver of one of our mobiles, a mustard-coloured Austin Maxi from what was known as the 'hire fleet'. From memory, we only had the vehicle a few days. I had a full-time reserve constable as observer and two part-timers as crew with me.

I drove out along Washingbay Road, turned right along Coole Road and, while I would normally have turned left on to Doone Avenue, for no good reason I decided on this occasion to carry on straight. A few seconds later we heard bullets striking the road all around us. I immediately accelerated but unfortunately there was nowhere to escape to. The road was fifteen feet or so above the surrounding fields and dead straight at that point. The full-time reserve constable opened fire from the front passenger seat, and we were very lucky we all escaped without injury.

Had I turned left that Sunday we would have been side-on to where the terrorists were lying in wait. We'd have been less than fifty metres from the ambush point, which was at an old, abandoned house just a few metres from the road. I've no doubt someone would have been killed or injured. The terrorists had seen the car coming down Washingbay Road and, when we went on by, they took up a position at the end of a short driveway to open fire from there instead. When all the agencies had been tasked, it became apparent that three different rifles had been used in the attack but thankfully none of the bullets struck the vehicle.

Some years later, when I was a detective constable, we were interviewing members of east Tyrone PIRA about a number of terrorist crimes when it became apparent that the person I was interviewing was one of the gunmen who had tried to murder us that afternoon. The really strange thing was, I felt no animosity towards him. Maybe if someone had been injured or killed it would have been different, but I knew he was going to face a long prison sentence and maybe that was consolation enough.

It was interesting to hear from him how they went to a local bar every Sunday, had a few drinks, and then went to their rifle hide. They took out what weapons they'd need and laid out an ambush, waiting for a police or army vehicle to come along. We used to carry out VCPs in that area regularly but had developed a habit of stopping a number of vehicles and driving off in the middle of them. This had saved lives on a number of occasions as he told me they hadn't been sure which one was the police car, so they hadn't opened fire.

The admission that he had been one of the ones who'd shot at us caused me a slight problem, however. He was to be charged with my attempted murder (he would later be convicted of it) but I had never told my parents that I'd been ambushed as I hadn't wanted them to worry unduly about me. Now I had to make a phone call to my father and tell him that someone was about to be charged with my attempted murder. I explained my thinking in the circumstances to him as best I could but was more than happy to let him explain to my mother why I had never told them about it!

20.50 – Antrim Police Station, County Antrim

When I was stationed in Antrim, I was the first policeman in the RUC to become a canoeing instructor. For two summers I was the only trained canoeist in community relations who could teach the people we were trying to help. As a result, I had to do all the summer camps the branch were involved in. I went to them all and took the kids canoeing. Then I trained another three police officers to do it so there were four of us in total.

It was a good project. The camps were always mixed, with both Protestant and Catholic kids, and they went on them for at least a week … occasionally two weeks. I found that the kids always got on really well and mixed together. But then you'd drop them off home. With the best will in the world, even if they wanted to stay in touch, they just couldn't do it, which meant the previous two weeks were gone.

We did bus trips, discos – all the usual attempts were made to bring the children in the communities together. We also did lectures in schools, and not just drop-ins. I went to school for twelve weeks and talked about the police: what we were doing to make life better for residents and what our objectives were. The strongest sign that I had to let me know we were making headway was when one of the schools in Antrim got a message delivered via their parents' association that said, 'Stop the police coming up to the school. Stop these lectures happening.' Obviously, we were making inroads that didn't suit some people's agenda. The headmaster was forced to tell us, 'I'm sorry, but you have to stop.'

Maybe we managed to steer some of them away from joining UDA, UVF, IRA or whatever – I'd certainly like to think so – but for the most part, community relations was an uphill battle with ingrained problems in its path.

20:52 – MSU, Londonderry

On the night of 23 March 1987, just before 9 p.m., Leslie Jarvis, a sixty-two-year-old lecturer at Magilligan prison was murdered by the IRA. Jarvis taught crafts and was attending night classes at Magee college. He always parked close to the college and that night, when class was finished, he got into his Skoda car. Three masked IRA gunman opened fire on him with a low-velocity rifle. Up to six shots went through the windscreen, hitting Jarvis in the head and killing him instantly. Before they left, they placed a bomb on the back seat of the car, turning the scene of his murder into a come on.

Two detectives, Austin Wilson and John Bennison, two real characters, responded to the scene at the car and tried to give Leslie first aid. When they were within sufficient proximity, the device was detonated, and they were killed by the resulting explosion.

I was an MSU sergeant in Strand Road at the time and was getting ready to go on shift when I heard the bomb at Magee college go off. We were deployed on to the scene. It turned out that Martin McGuinness had been in close proximity. I'm not saying he carried out the attack, but he was certainly able to see what happened. Such was the severity of the explosion that parts of the bodies were stuck to the wall and we couldn't get the fire brigade to hose down the walls of human matter – they simply refused to do it. We sealed the area and remained there for most of the night.

Incidents like that can be very difficult to deal with and people often ask, 'How do you respond?' The fact is, you don't go out seeking vengeance, you just get on with your job. The following night, when we were on patrol outside one of the bars in the city, people were chanting the names of those who had died, asking which one of us had had to scrape them off the walls. The horror of all that, yet we didn't drive people off the street, we didn't respond in anger or violence, just continued with what we were doing. I remember one young guy, a real troublemaker from Strabane, leaning out, chanting, calling us all the names under the sun and I felt like responding. It was the utmost vulgar provocation but you have to take it on the chin, you have to move on. We got back in the vehicle and left. But we were angry and emotional.

I was the sergeant on the bearer party at Austin's funeral, and the wails of his wife as the coffin came out haunted me for a very long time.

The following Christmas, two men were killed while carrying a bomb towards Strand Road police station. As they turned a corner into Strand Road, the bomb had exploded. There was nothing left of them. They were the two guys suspected of killing Austin, John and Leslie Jarvis. They were in the IRA team from the Bogside/ Creggan area.

20.56 – Oldpark Police Station, North Belfast

On 27 March 1976, while I was an inspector in Oldpark, Belfast, we received a report of an explosion at the Junction of Oldpark Road and Mountview Street. It was approximately 8.50 p.m. The building concerned was a shop with an apartment above. The apartment had been taken over by the army as an observation post, manned by four members of the Royal Horse Artillery.

The military presence had been noted by the local IRA and a bomb had been placed in the shop portion of the building, directly underneath the observation post. The explosion blew out the outside walls of the shop, lifted the floors and roof, which then collapsed into the ground floor as a mass of rubble and splintered timber. One soldier was blown out of the building, but the other three were trapped under the rubble.

The first vehicle to arrive was the district mobile patrol unit, crewed by a sergeant and three constables and closely followed by my unit and two special patrol vehicles. Arrival time after the explosion would have been about five minutes. Ambulances and fire appliances followed minutes later.

The scene when we arrived was chaotic, with civilian residents climbing over the rubble attempting a rescue. These well-meaning people were trying to lever a portion of the collapsed floor to get at the men underneath. They had lifted one end of a concrete beam about twelve feet long and eight by eight inches in width. The other end was embedded in the rubble. But as the location of the trapped soldiers was unknown, police had to stop the civilians from moving the beam.

I meanwhile was told by the soldier who had been blown out of the building that three of his comrades were trapped inside. This soldier was walking but in shock and I had him placed in the first ambulance with a police member to escort him to hospital. Police, firemen, and some locals located two of the trapped soldiers, who were then taken to the hospital. This was excellent work, but it was the rescue of the third trapped soldier where exceptional work was done.

The remaining trapped soldier was not located until thirty minutes after the rescue operation had begun, indicating the volume of debris under which he was trapped. Had the initial rescue operation by the civilians gone ahead, the large beam would have pivoted over the spot where the soldier was subsequently found, no doubt with disastrous results. His legs were trapped underneath rubble and a wooden beam. His torso was trapped between rubble and a portion of a reinforced wall. The rubble was supported by other debris, which if moved without consideration would have caused the trapped man to be crushed. It was necessary to support the weight of the roof which was lying on top of the rubble. This support work was carried out by five SPG members who used a large beam as a lever. They had to hold this in place as four other SPG members built a retaining wall of bricks to compensate for any load bearing rubble the roof was losing by being shifted. The local crew maintained voice contact with the trapped soldier and continued to carefully clear rubble away from him as the SPG men continued their work.

When the floor was raised enough and with the retaining wall in position, a tunnel was formed and one of the local crew, a full-time reserve member, crawled through. This meant he was right underneath and deep inside the rubble, depending upon the SPG to maintain the hastily-constructed wall. It was a brave action on his part. He was placing himself in no little danger and into harm's way. Without his courageous work there would have been no way of telling how intricately the soldier was trapped and therefore no way of knowing the best way to get him out. Only the reserve constable was in a position to see the actual pieces of debris that were trapping the man. He directed the firemen and other police, telling them what clearing was necessary while he dealt with some pieces of angle iron and bricks, all from his place in the tunnel, underneath the roof of a collapsed building with tons of rubble overhead. Only when the trapped soldier was freed did the reserve constable climb out of the rubble. The good news was none of the soldiers was seriously injured but it could so easily have ended very differently.

It was my privilege as the officer in charge of the operation to recommend the members involved for favourable records. The reserve constable I recommended for special recommendation. This had been an exceptional situation, but similar actions by police, who placed themselves in harm's way on a daily basis, took place throughout Northern Ireland then. I believe proper recognition was not often given when it was duly deserved because it was so commonplace and therefore considered 'run of the mill'!

21:00 – Coffee-time Reflections

Over the years a vast number of people, from both sides of the divide, worked as informants and many lives were saved because of them. Just one little snippet of information could make a difference and enable us to put all the pieces of a picture together – especially if we had several different sources talking about something seemingly useless. That one bit of information could complete the picture and put us in a position to act.

I remember one person who got summoned to Dundalk to be interrogated by the IRA. Quite often suspected informants were tortured and would have confessed to anything to get it over with, so they didn't always get it right either. This person in Dundalk underwent a fairly intense interrogation for some hours but held up and refused to admit anything.

The IRA team eventually said, 'Okay, we believe you. We'll get you home.' He got out into the car with them and, as they were driving north, they were stopped at a Garda checkpoint. The officer went round with his torch checking the passengers. The person who had been interrogated may have had a few marks on him as a result of his ordeal, and the officer asked if everything was all right. He said, 'Fine, thanks,' and the Garda let them go.

The temptation of course was to say to the guard, 'Thank God you're here. No, it's not all right,' and tell them what had happened. Had he done so he would have been dead – the checkpoint wasn't real. It was Provisional IRA members in Garda uniforms pretending to do a VCP. It was his final test.

21:05 – Strabane Police Station, County Tyrone

Strabane was a hotbed of activity in the late eighties, and the town was too dangerous to live in. Consequently, I lived in a room in the station, as did a few of my colleagues. One night, some of the others nipped out to get a bag of chips in nearby Sion Mills. They parked up at the bottom of the Melmount Road, which had a clear line of sight out to the checkpoint on Lifford Road, known locally as the Camel's Hump. They were sitting in their shorts and T-shirts in a civilian car, eating their chips when two IRA gunman came out of the Ballycolman estate. In a sporadic burst that emptied the magazine, the gunmen opened fire towards the security check at the Camel's Hump. They then casually walked across the road in front of the car with four unarmed cops staring at them with their mouths open, eating their chips.

The four of them came back into the station and said, 'Thank God we didn't have our guns on us because we would have felt obliged to engage the terrorists,' but I can tell you they were as white as sheets when they came in.

21:14 – Oldpark Police Station, North Belfast

I was in Oldpark one evening when we got a late call, it was probably around nine or ten o'clock. It was a winter's night and the caller reported a suspicious device in the doorway of a Co-op shop down the Oldpark Road. I was the observer in Charlie three, the vehicle tasked [to attend the call], and the logical way for us to approach it would have been from the north, down the Oldpark Road. However, I told the driver to go the long way round, down the Cliftonville Road and up Rosapenna Street and then stop about a hundred yards short of the Oldpark Road junction.

I got out and went up in the dark to look across. I didn't even cross the street to the Co-op as I could quite clearly see the box and there did appear to be wires coming out of it. It turned out to be what the ATO call 'an elaborate hoax' – it had been constructed to look like the real thing. It certainly wasn't put there by kids messing around. I went back down to the truck and said to the boys that I was going to call the army. The drill was that the army would come out and sanitise the whole area. They would put out maybe two platoons of soldiers in four-man bricks, which meant at least six, and maybe more to ensure the area was sterile. If there were any gunmen about the place they wouldn't know if there was another patrol just behind them or in front of them, or where they were, and of course, that was the whole idea. You effectively neuter the IRA team because they have no idea how many bricks are circulating around them. What they do know is that they aren't alone.

The boys weren't keen on getting the army out because

it usually took at least an hour for them to arrive, then the ATO, and by the time he got out it could be the guts of two hours. From our point of view, that would keep us there until well after midnight. The ATO did come out but it must have been an hour and a half at least before he was able to move on the device.

One of the bricks now circulating the area intercepted a top, very well-known IRA gunman leaving the top of the Oldpark Road about 150 yards from where the incident was centred. We were in the Ardoyne Road, further down past the device, staying far back from what would be the kill zone, when about fifteen minutes later another IRA man from the same team came from exactly the same direction.

It was subsequently confirmed by Special Branch that the gunmen had been lying in wait, waiting for a patrol to walk over and examine the device. If we had, they would have had a clear shot at us. Instead, I had looked over from a distance, effectively foiling their attack. Also, if we'd gone the shorter way, as they might have expected us to do, they could have shot the vehicle up as we passed them. But once the terrorists saw we didn't fit into their plan, and the army started appearing on the scene around them, they cached the weapons and went off home to bed.

It wasn't a *lucky* escape – if you do the drills properly and exercise common sense you will be all right. I was ex-military and always did. But when you take shortcuts and take the easiest way, that's when you get into trouble – you play into the gunman's hands. Instead, our crew's main concern was, will we get finished on time?

21:19 – MSU, Border, County Fermanagh

The IRA lured the local dog warden, a part-time UDR member, to a remote farmhouse near Belleek on the Fermanagh border with Donegal. The dog warden had received a report that a dog had been worrying sheep in the area and had gone to investigate. The call was bogus. A four-man team of terrorists had taken over the farmhouse the previous night, holding the elderly owner captive as they lay in wait.

A number of shots were fired by the gunmen at the warden's easily identifiable council van as he approached the house. Although wounded, he managed to fire back with his personal protection firearm and succeeded in killing Joseph McManus, one of the terrorists. McManus, age twenty-one and from Sligo in the Irish Republic, was known to police as an active IRA man who came from a well-established republican family. His father, Sean McManus, had been chairman of Sinn Féin, even visiting Libya on their behalf.

I was in the MSU at the time, and we went to the scene for follow-up searches and to provide security for personnel on the ground. We remained at the scene until it became too dark to continue but then, as everyone was packing up to leave, I was informed that a colleague and I would have to hold the scene overnight. We had military personnel dug in all around us so we thought it would be a safe, but long, boring and hungry shift. I had been married for only six months by this stage, and we were in the days before mobile phones, so I asked one of the departing constables if he would telephone my wife on return to the station and tell her of my extended duty.

Like all police wives in those days, my wife was sitting at home watching the news on television, and worrying about the shooting while trying to pretend not to – the victims had not been named and nothing had been released to the press. When the phone rang at such a late hour she had some trepidation, made even worse by the fact that my colleague got straight to the point. 'Hello, Susan, I've got some bad news for you, Jonathan won't be coming home tonight.' There was quite a long silence, during which my wife was thinking: 'Surely that's not the way they tell you? Don't they send someone round or something?'

Eventually, realising his lack of tact, my colleague explained the situation. Even then it took some reassurance from him before she accepted that I was indeed all right and unharmed. The everyday stress of waiting for the phone to ring or the knock at the door was always there, day and night, not too far under the surface. All it required was the wrong word, or a thoughtless remark, to trigger the nightmares.

21:22 – Sion Mills Police Station, County Tyrone

There was an old Alsatian dog that used to live in the grounds of the station. It wasn't a police dog or anything; I think it was a stray that the guys just adopted and fed so it stayed there. Sion Mills was a limited opening station; we just opened for the early and late shift.

We called in one night for a bit of a break and I noticed the dog had got itself a football from somewhere and was pushing it all round the station. We didn't pay too much attention to it at first. We even played football with the dog and though I remember remarking that the ball was quite heavy, again not much attention was paid. When those old leather balls got wet they were heavy.

I was at home on a rest day when Marty, a fella I worked with, rang me and said, 'Do you remember the ball out in the yard that we played football with, when messing about with the dog the other night? Well, the army came in here for a break from foot patrol yesterday and one of the guys was messing about with the dog, kicking the ball for it. At one point when the ball landed it fell open into two halves. The whole inside of it was packed with explosives.'

The IRA had thrown the ball over the fence one night and the dog had found it. They must have seen our entry and exit pattern as we had pretty good procedures that we stuck to. We would have the dog section out with us on occasion, and men would have always walked out with rifles first to cover any vehicles leaving the station. The IRA must have been watching us and decided to go down a different avenue to attack and decided to throw the ball over.

It was a good reminder that the IRA were always looking for new and inventive ways to attack you. The army sergeant said that there was a mechanism in it that should have armed itself when it landed, but on this occasion, it hadn't worked.

22:00 – Lisnaskea Police Station, County Fermanagh

It was November and the weather was very cold and frosty. The border campaign was underway and the IRA were busy at night laying culvert bombs and other devices to catch both the police and army unawares. This was at the same time as the terrorists were targeting and murdering farmers in the border area, most of whom would have also been part-time members of the Ulster Defence Regiment.

We had just had our evening meal in Lisnaskea station and we – me and three others – were detailed for the evening patrol. We were to carry out VCPs on the Derrylin Road out as far as our boundary, which was the New Bridge a few miles out on the shore of Lough Erne. We began our VCPs at the farthest point from Lisnaskea and worked inwards. By about 10 p.m. we were close to the town and had set up a VCP at the point where the railway had once crossed the road. Our driver had concealed our vehicle up a laneway. By this time a hard frost had developed, and we tried our best to keep warm without showing our presence on the road, only appearing on the approach of a vehicle.

Suddenly a car could be heard in the distance with the distinctive noise of its exhaust being carried in the crisp frosty air. In those days and in rural areas you could identify whose car it was by the sound. I said to my crew, 'That sounds like old Charlie, which is a bit odd as we spoke to him when he was going home nearly two hours ago.' Anyway, along he comes in his old Singer car, which had seen better days but nevertheless suited his needs. 'That's a cold one tonight, Charlie. Where are you off too now as I thought you would have been tucked up by this time?' 'Yer right there, constable, but I got a call a wee while ago to go and see a man in Maguiresbridge as he had a wee pup for me.' 'Okay, on your way and mind the roads.'

About half an hour passes and a call came through on the radio to go to the scene of a damage-only accident at Maguiresbridge, where the bypass was being built. Off we head to the scene and what should we find but old Charlie's car resting, and very sorry looking for itself, on a traffic island which was under construction. The car had suffered some damage, but no sign of Charlie. There was some blood on the dash on the driver's side and it transpired that Charlie had a cut on the head and a local had taken him to A & E at the Erne Hospital.

Nothing remained but to get the local recovery man to remove the vehicle, but before doing so I wanted to check and see if there was anything of value in the car that should be removed. Nothing of any significance was found until I opened the boot and found a crate full of lemonade bottles. 'This has got to be good,' I thought to myself. A bit strange that old Charlie would have a crate of lemonade. I suspected that these bottles might contain a certain liquid that could be made in that part of Fermanagh. True enough it transpired that it was a crateful of poteen. I seized the crate for further investigation. Old Charlie's car was recovered from the scene and we returned to the station for a well-earned break. The content of the bottles was duly examined and destroyed by emptying it down the drain.

One evening a week later I called out with Charlie to check his driving licence and insurance, and to get an explanation as to what had happened on the night in question. That was that, but just before I left Charlie asked me, 'Did you find anything in the car?' I told him that there was a crate of poteen in the boot. He was not too happy at this and said that they had been bottles of distilled water for the lorries at work. I told Charlie that I knew the difference between distilled water and poteen and that he should count himself lucky that he was not being prosecuted for having it. I had to laugh as his final question was, 'And what did you do with it?' To which I replied, 'Poured it down the drain.'

It was a costly night for Charlie – his car was a write-off, he lost the profit from a crate of poteen and he had a nasty bump on the head!

22:34 – CID Office, Newry Police Station

In August 1991 there was a murder in Newry. We were at a retirement do for our detective chief superintendent when the call came in. I received a message that there was a report of a body found at a house about 400 yards from the border, at Ferry Hill Road to be precise.

The deceased was Rose-Marie Moran, a thirty-two-year-old mother who had been stabbed thirty-seven times. When I arrived at the scene, I noticed there was also a gun beside the badly mutilated body. It turned out the wee gun was a Lone Star plastic pistol that belonged to her four-year-old son. Her white Mercedes car had been stolen from the house and this was recovered the next day in Dundalk in the Irish Republic.

The next day, myself and a colleague from Newry CID went to Dundalk to see where the car had been found and because the deceased's husband was from Dundalk and had a home there. The Garda showed me where the car was recovered and took me round to the husband's family home. While we were there, we saw two fellas sitting in a car close by and the guard who was showing me round said, 'I'll just go over and chat to them. I don't know who they are.' He had a bit of a chat with them, came back over to me and said, 'Those two fellas are from about here.'

We had a lot of fingerprints from the car and the house where the murder had happened so I asked the Garda to get elimination fingerprints from the family members and anybody who could be connected to the house or indeed the car. It turned out the guard I got speaking to, Denis Compton, was the same one who had been showing me around the day after the murder and he remembered the names of the two boys he had gone over to speak to. He thought, 'I'll just get their fingerprints while I'm at it, just in case.' I got a call from him and he said, 'Just to let you know, we have identified these two sets of fingerprints and he gave me two names, Philip Quigley and Daniel Larkin. While he was telling me I was thinking to myself, who are these people and what is he talking about? It only clicked when he said, 'That's the two boys from the day you came down. We saw them when I was showing you around.' It was just one of those moments in an inquiry that you never forget. Their fingerprints were a match for those found on adhesive tape round the handle of the knife that had been the murder weapon. It had been recovered in the victim's car, along with a note they had taken from the house as well.

This case ended up being the first time the RUC ever used an offender profiler. It turned out the husband, Joseph

Moran, was having an affair with his wife's niece, Anita McKeown, and she had wanted the wife to be killed. She'd realised that he would never leave his wife to be with her.

Eventually, almost a year later, the husband admitted his involvement in the murder. He made a seven-page statement outlining his part in the crime and all that he had done. He had approached these two eighteen-year-olds who had never been in trouble before and asked them, 'Do you know anybody that could kill someone in the north?' The two lads had agreed to carry out the murder themselves and a fee of £10,000 was agreed, although in the end they never got anything. The husband drove the two would-be assassins to his house before his wife arrived home from work. When Mrs Moran arrived, they stabbed her thirty-seven times and stole her white Mercedes car.

Moran's girlfriend, who was in Northern Ireland, was arrested and admitted her part in the conspiracy. Initially while she was being interviewed, she wasn't going to admit her involvement, but we brought her down to Dundalk to confront her 'lover' and when she got back up to the north, she admitted it.

In 1999, eight years after the murder, Joseph Moran was finally convicted in Northern Ireland of his wife's murder and sentenced to life imprisonment. Anita McKeown was sentenced to eight years imprisonment for conspiracy to murder, though would only serve four. She joined the scheme in which female prisoners could write to male prisoners, and ended up with a fella from the INLA who was doing life for the murder of three police officers: Snowdon Corkey and Ronnie Irwin from Markethill (local councillor Seamus Mallon knew the officers and was first on the scene having been sitting nearby in his car when he heard the shots), and Johnny Wasson from Armagh, who never carried a gun and was the second-longest serving police officer in Northern Ireland. The father of five was shot six times in the head and chest as he got out of his car outside his home, just five weeks before he was due to retire after serving the community for forty-two years. His wife, who heard the shots, was first on the scene.

Philip Quigley was arrested in Dundalk and extradited. He was found to have had a borderline intellectual disability but was subsequently convicted of manslaughter and sentenced to eight years. The final twist in the story was that while Daniel Larkin, the guy who had done most of the stabbing, eventually admitted it – though he tried to explain it away as a burglary gone wrong. The Garda told the judge exactly what happened and informed him that there was new evidence (they didn't specify what that evidence was, but it would have been disclosed in time), but the southern courts still refused to extradite him. I even got myself into trouble for talking about it to the Secretary of State for Northern Ireland, Patrick Mayhew, when he visited Crossmaglen RUC station. I accompanied him and we chatted during the flight in the helicopter. He said to me, 'Is there anything I can do for you?' and I brought up this case, 'Well, funny you should mention that.' I got a rocket from headquarters for my trouble: 'What are you doing contacting the secretary of state?'

So there's a guy down south who literally got away with murder and is still wanted in Northern Ireland to this day. There is nothing worse than knowing who committed a crime and not being able to bring them before the court to answer for it.

22:40 – Neighbourhood Policing

I found that working with young people had its own rewards. I found the best thing you could ever do was to build trust so that they wouldn't run away when you approached. I often turned a blind eye to drinking, smoking and other shenanigans young people get involved in – I always drew the line at drugs though – but they were just children with nothing to do, nowhere to go, and who needed an authority figure in their lives. I took a young lad home one night, rolling, paralytic drunk, and when we got there I asked his father when he had last seen him. The father replied that he had given him a tenner for a bottle of vodka and kicked him out of the house. That was home life for many. A lot of them just wanted to be somewhere warm, to have someone to talk to and someone who cared, who would help if they could. In return I got a lot of gossip, intelligence, and tips from them – who was doing what in the area, what was hidden where, and who was supplying. I never betrayed their trust, but fed a lot of good intel into the system, or else acted on it myself, and often fed them a lot of chips in return.

In one town I covered we had three young persons who were always together, one girl in her mid-teens, one older male and one younger. They were inseparable. I would meet them round the streets or standing in dark alleys and they were a good laugh, very pro-police. They were a mixture of Protestant and Catholic and didn't care about politics. They just had no money and no home life. The older guy was heavily into cannabis: he was a very intelligent lad, but just lost to the drug and when he got high would do silly things like lying down in front of cars or attacking them on the road and smashing them up. The younger one was gay, a great wee guy, and the girl used to dye his hair and put make-up on him. They were always together with a bottle of cheap cider and I discreetly kept an eye on them when I could.

One night we got an emergency call to the house of the older guy, the drug user. His father had reported that someone was being murdered. The son lived in an annex off the main house – it was painted black inside, walls, doors, ceiling, the lot, and the windows were all boarded up. We arrived, blue lights and sirens wailing, and put the door in only to find the three friends sitting in the bedroom and all as well as could be.

The story was, they had been hitting the drink in the bedroom, maybe a bit of blow as well, and the older male and the girl started to have sex in the bed. Afterwards the two of them reckoned that the younger male was feeling left out, so they decided that both he and the older male would do it. The young guy was having none of it, so when the older male advanced menacingly on him he panicked and ran for the door, only to find it locked. In his panic he pulled the door handle clean off. The older male was still approaching slowly and menacingly, the girl was in hysterics, and he was so afraid that he started to scream for help and kick the door. The father, hearing the noise, assumed his son had crossed the line again and this time was killing someone, so he called 999. It was a relief once we had established no one was in any danger and had sorted the mess out. There were a lot of diplomatic updates via the radio in order to have the matter kept quiet and written off.

Sadly though, the older male died from drug misuse just a few years later, and the younger guy committed suicide only last year. I've no idea where the girl is. It's such a tragic waste of life, but they could see no future and no hope. It happened time and again, and still goes on today.

22:46 – Armagh Police Station, County Armagh

In a little village called Milford, just south of Armagh city, an under-car booby-trap bomb was placed on a vehicle belonging to a former member of the UDR. The bomb exploded one Sunday night as he was driving out of the car park at Milford Everton Amateur Football Club, where he served on the committee and worked as a caretaker.

My colleague and I happened to be first on the scene. We stopped our car a little way away off then got out and walked towards it. We could see the wreckage of the car, which still had smoke coming from it. As I got nearer the car, I noticed something on the ground, up against the kerb – it turned out to be a severed hand. To this day I don't know why I did it, but I just lifted it and brought it with me to the car. The victim was still alive when I got there and appeared to be conscious. I started to talk to him; just talking, trying to reassure him. I remember saying, 'The ambulance is on its way. I have your hand here, they can do wonders these days. We'll get it into a bucket of ice – we will be able to save your hand for you.' It was only then that I looked at the rest of him and saw that he didn't exist from the waist down. Within seconds, he was dead.

The victim, Wilfred McIlveen, was just thirty-seven and married with four children. The club had a mixed membership, and the well-respected victim was married to a Catholic. His daughter appealed for no retaliation and said, 'God will deal with those responsible when the time comes.' His brother had been a part-time police officer who was murdered by the IRA in 1973.

Not long after this I went on a CID course to England where we were talking in one of the classes about our experiences and I mentioned this murder explaining it had just been me and a fella who had been seconded to CID for six months. The English cops could not believe what I was telling them, and I had to explain that we just didn't have the manpower. That was just the way it was because of the number of murders and serious crimes we were dealing with day to day.

22:50 – Mountpottinger Police Station, East Belfast

I always said we were a third religion: I never asked anybody whether they were Protestant or Catholic, you were a police officer.

There was a policewoman in Mountpottinger who came to my unit for a while. She happened to be a Roman Catholic whose brother was a top IRA man in Toomebridge. He'd told her when she joined the police, 'If you go ahead with your plan and join, never come back near us because you'd not be welcome. If you do come back and I see you, I'll kill you.' This had obviously been a massive decision for her, knowing that she would be cutting all ties with her family; she also had to almost prove herself with her colleagues, because, being suspicious by nature, they all suspected something.

She came over to Mountpottinger's sister station, Willowfield, when I was the inspector there. I received a phone call telling me her mother had died; it was from the parish priest in Toomebridge. He told me this lady had died and quite bluntly said, 'The sons have told me to pass on that Fiona isn't to come anywhere near the funeral. I know the feeling that we have here.' I told him that I would contact Fiona and tell her what their position was.

I brought her into my office and told her about the phone call from the priest. It turned out that she didn't even know her mother had died. I said, 'The priest has made an offer for you if you wish to take it up. Your mother's remains are going to be in the chapel tonight and he is prepared to go with you and let you come in around two or three in the morning, if you want.'

She was keen to say goodbye to her mother, so I took her up to Toomebridge and we went in to the church. I stayed outside to let her go in the place in private and she was able to spend about an hour there. I think she had a bit of a service with the priest, so at least she got something to console her at such a time. That was good. She got closure. But she daren't have gone anywhere near the funeral, it would just have been too dangerous. She now lives somewhere out of the country because the threat from her brother still exists.

22:53 – CID Office, Woodbourne Police Station, West Belfast

Way back in what was a lifetime ago, I was based in Bravo Whiskey [(BW), Woodbourne police station] as a detective. West Belfast was embroiled in the hunger strikes and was a cauldron of terrorism and street violence. Such was the level of activity that all B Division CID were assigned to late or night shifts, centrally located at Bravo Oscar [BO] in Springfield Parade, to react to the more serious incidents. We still had to cover our own areas during the day: just like our uniform colleagues we were working seemingly endless double shifts and sometimes more.

One such evening I had completed a late shift at BW, attending to various call-outs and catching up on the accompanying paperwork, as well as being scheduled to work a week's nightshift at BO with other CID from around the division. I had been so engrossed in paperwork that I had let the clock tick by my intended departure time and missed my lift [in an army Saracen armoured vehicle] to the night briefing.

Worried about being late, I jumped into my private car with the 'usual' accessories, and made the quick decision to drive over the top end of the division, which would take me though Andersonstown – a quicker, more direct route. Not once did I give any thought to the very real risk from the ongoing rioting, burning buses or widespread hijacking of vehicles throughout the area.

It was not long before I encountered the debris from many days of rioting all over the road. It was everywhere; you couldn't really avoid it. My senses were at an elevated level, constantly looking around for activity or anything out of place. There was debris everywhere and it wasn't always easy to see. On top of that, I was trying not to bring my car under notice despite being well over the speed limit to make up time. There wasn't another car on the road – why would there be in the middle of the worst street disorder Northern Ireland's ever seen!

I realise with hindsight now that it was only a matter of time before the inevitable happened: my rear offside tyre blew. I pulled over to see the extent of the blowout. I knew my spare was in good order so I waited for a couple of minutes to appraise the situation. No human activity around that I could see, so I made the decision to change the tyre as fast as I could and get the hell out of Dodge to avoid further damage to me or the car.

There I was in the middle of west Belfast during the hunger strikes, hunkered over the wheel of my car and trying desperately to wind the jack up, when I heard voices coming from my nearside. I looked through the windows of the car and in the dim street lighting I could make out a group of male and female teenagers coming towards me. It seemed as though they were beside me within seconds.

A couple of the young lads engaged me in a casual conversation about my predicament and even offered to help as I hunkered at the side of the car, now trying to work twice as fast as I had been. I was also acutely aware that the butt of my gun was possibly sticking out from the side of the pleats in my jacket. Knowing that if I was identified or even suspected of being a cop I would be in serious trouble, I stood up and related a story that I had just dropped my girlfriend off at a local address and was in a hurry to get to the Royal Victoria Hospital to begin my shift as a new doctor in the emergency department.

'Leave it to us.' Then three of them took over the task and speedily changed the wheel while I engaged in casual chat with the others. They told me they were coming from a disco in nearby Taughmonagh hence they were in high spirits, with the girls commenting admiringly at the lads completing my tyre change. When it came to lowering the car off the jack, they gathered round the car and, with one coordinated heave, manually hoisted the rear of the car to enable a quick jack removal. It had become more like a Formula One pitstop!

I jumped into the car, thanked them profusely and sped away. My relief was palpable and I berated myself as I thought what might have been had they noticed my gun or if someone had recognised me. I remember calling myself all the 'stupid fuckers' under the sun but was just so completely relieved that I had pulled it off.

I had only driven a few hundred yards when, with a bang and a shudder, my offside front tyre blew. I was so engaged with my previous good fortune that I hadn't noticed more smouldering debris and had driven right through it. Fuck it, no spare now. So there I was, driving at speed on a puncture that was very quickly deteriorating to the rim and throwing up loads of attention-grabbing sparks. I thought, 'I am not stopping for anything; my luck has been used up.'

I arrived at the gate of Springfield Parade and the squaddie took a look at my wheel. 'Hey mate, do you know you have no tyre?' All I could do was laugh with relief and acknowledge that I was aware of it but cracking up at his obvious understatement.

Next day I arranged to get the car to the garage. It was then that I realised how expensive Saab parts were. One wheel, two tyres, some wheel arch damage and they had to realign my rear bumper. A very expensive shortcut, but I was still alive and able to laugh about it.

A few years later I was stationed at Belfast Regional Crime Squad (BRC) in 1988 when Corporals Howes and Wood were murdered at the same place in the most savage and brutal way – I watched it on Heli-telly and although the circumstances were totally different, I couldn't stop thinking about my 'lucky' ordeal.

Here we are forty years on, and I still think about what might have been, and how fortunate it was that I had encountered some decent kids willing to help. Something or somebody was looking after me that night.

22:58 – Life in an RUC Family

It started as just another day, but the events of 29 November 1993 became the reason I would come to say, 'Now I don't live, I exist.'

I awoke around 7.30 a.m. and started to plan the day ahead in my mind. The weather outside was dull, cold and snowy. After breakfast the boys and I headed off for school: Mark and David to the further education college, where they were studying to qualify for university; Iain and Tim to the local grammar school; and me to the local primary school where I worked as a classroom assistant in the reception class.

School was warm and the sound of excited children greeted me on my arrival. Christmas was on the horizon – there were decorations to make, practice for the carol service and school nativity play. Busy time. What had I to do today? Ah yes, shopping. Buy and post a Christmas present to Colin, a friend who had gone off to work in a school in Jamaica. He wasn't getting home for Christmas. We wanted him to know that our thoughts were with him at this special time of the year. I lifted Mark at the end of school to help me choose a present for Colin. The weather hadn't improved any, so we ran in and out of shops trying to avoid getting too wet. Shopping done, the rest of the boys were collected from school and ... home. I was glad we had installed oil-fired central heating, as the house was warm. A fire was soon glowing in the grate and I had a hot cup of tea, just the job.

Arthur was up getting showered to go out on duty with the RUC. His shift was from 3 p.m. until 11 p.m. When Arthur had joined the force he'd only enjoyed two years of normal policing – he always said that he joined to be a policeman, not a soldier. All of our married life has had to be lived out carefully – can't go there ... check the car for explosive devices ... don't answer the door before finding out who is there ... don't set regular patterns ... and so on.

After supper I headed off to bed, about 10.30 p.m., with the intention of reading for a while. I had just settled down and put off the bedroom light when I heard a loud noise. I thought that it was Iain as he was in the room next to mine. I shouted, asking was he out of bed, but the reply came, 'No, but I heard it too!' Immediately there was a terrifyingly loud noise that I couldn't figure out. We all congregated in the hallway in the middle of the house, the four boys and myself. David, the second eldest, said, 'That's shooting.' 'No,' I said, 'it must be the back boiler.' Then another series of noises – yes, it was shooting. The older boys shouted for us to lie down, and Timothy, the youngest, was crouched in the foetal position by his bedroom door. He was in hysterics. I watched my hand shaking as I reached for the telephone to dial the station. I used the direct line into the control room, and it was Arthur's voice that answered. He was bright and breezy when he heard my voice and said, 'How's it going, my dear?' and as calmly as I could, I told him that our home was under attack. He was so distressed at the call that someone else had to take over and deal with the situation.

The minutes after the shooting, before the police arrived, seemed like hours. The deafening silence was overpowering, and I had to crawl into the dining room to look out the window. I did this very carefully. The main road never looked so deserted before. Where were the police? Was our dog shot? – I couldn't wait. At the first sight of a police car I went out into the garden and started to look for Bracken, our dog. He was in his kennel and unharmed. Then people, people everywhere. I didn't want them here – army, police, all running through the house and garden shouting orders, telling us what we must do. I was standing in my nightclothes, as were the boys. I wondered, 'Is this a nightmare? Will I wake up soon?' I thought that nothing else could happen that night, so I said, 'We will stay at home.' I was told that we couldn't as forensic people would be in and out of the house all night. We were advised to go. I phoned my sister, who lived in a village about eight miles away and while I was speaking to her there was an almighty explosion that ripped through the house. I was so frightened. I dropped the phone and ran to see what had happened. The terrorists had left a bomb in the garden as well.

It turned out that my youngest boy had called the security forces searching outside in for tea, which he had made – a miracle – but the real miracle is that no one was injured in the blast. The explosion caused a lot of structural damage to the front of the house. No hesitation now, we were bundled into police cars and driven off at great speed in the direction of the police station. There we were able to make phone calls to family and explain the situation before it was put out on the media. Then, to my sister's house where we couldn't take in what had happened to us. For several days we lived in a state of limbo.

We were moved to St Andrew's police convalescent home in Yorkshire where the staff greeted us with tears in their eyes. We must have looked a sorry sight: mum, dad and four boys homeless because the IRA didn't like the RUC.

Nights
23:00—07:00 hours

23:00 – Uniform Patrol, Armagh

I got promoted to uniform sergeant while in Armagh RUC station. On my first shift, I was on night duty and the patrol car I was in was attacked with drogue bombs and automatic gunfire. To add to the problem, I hadn't a clue where I was. I reported that the car was under attack and asked the boys with me, 'Where are we?' They said Barrack Hill, so I transmitted 'Barrack Hill. No injuries.'

Various other police patrols made their way to Barrack Hill, which is just outside Gough, but could find no sign of anything untoward. They drove around the area but there was nothing apparent. It turned out we were in Banbrook Hill, which was on the other side of Armagh completely, down near the Shambles. Thankfully nobody was hurt but I did feel a total fool, and a bit embarrassed that I didn't even know where I was. In my defence, I'd only ever been in Armagh once before, but of course that didn't stop the banter. Mind you, lesson learned: after that, any time a patrol car I was in turned a corner I would glance up to see the name of the street. Can you imagine needing immediate assistance and not knowing where you were to request it?

23:05 – Andersonstown Police Station, West Belfast

When I was in Andersonstown, there was a young hood called McCabe who was a bit of a local character – his nickname was Didilo for some reason. He was a habitual car thief, and he arrived in to sign bail one evening when I was on the front desk. There happened to be a man in front of him who was reporting that his car had been stolen – he was telling me that it was his pride and joy and the first car he had bought from new. Didilo was sitting on the seat beside him, waiting to sign bail.

I took details about the car from the man, filled in the

forms and asked if anything else had been stolen. The whole time, he kept looking around at Didilo. The man told me about the radio and a number of cassette tapes being stolen, but the next thing, he grabbed Didilo by the throat and shouted, 'That's my fucking scarf!' He then started to beat the living crap out of Didilo in the enquiry office. What were the odds on him coming in to sign bail at the same time the person whose car he had stolen is giving police the relevant details?

Didilo was an interesting character. He had been kneecapped several times by the IRA and ended up dying the way he lived, in a road traffic accident in a stolen car. He had stolen a 2.8i Ford Capri and hit a concrete roundabout while being chased by the police. On impact he had flown out of his seat – he was not wearing a seatbelt – crashed through the glass sunroof and completely severed his head.

23:17 – Border, County Fermangh

The Fermanagh border was a very difficult place to police because from Belleek to Belcoo there were dozens of concession roads that crossed [the border] from north to south. A lot of them weren't meant to be driven along but quite often you had to. All the actual border crossings had been cratered by the military, though the locals would fill them in as quickly as they were blown up. It went round in circles for a while: the IRA would come down into the area to operate; the army blew up the roads to hinder them; the next day they were filled in again.

At the bottom of the main street in Belleek was the Hotel Carlton. The back of the hotel faced the river and on the other side of the water was the Republic of Ireland. There was a weir across the river that you could actually walk along as it was a fairly substantial structure, and the Provisional IRA would often come across the walkway at the weir from the south and lie in wait for any of us to come along.

We were still driving in and out of the station in our private cars at the time, which, in hindsight, is unbelievable given the threat levels. A colleague of mine, Bertie, had a blue Ford Escort with a defective exhaust and one time, it just so happened that a blue Ford Escort with a defective exhaust came down the road, but it turned out it wasn't Bertie. It was actually a Provisional IRA member from Belcoo who happened to be driving down the road in an almost identical car. His colleagues opened fire on the car and shot him. They didn't manage to kill him, but a good bit of his hand was blown off.

The station was manned by eight police officers and forty soldiers at that time and one of the sergeants stationed with us, he just liked to drink. I was station duty officer one night and everybody else was in bed. The phone rang and it was the pub at the corner of the street, right on the border. I was happy enough it was a genuine call as I knew the man who ran the pub. He said, 'Your sergeant's here and he's blocked. You'd better come and get him.'

There were a few of us who would have gone right down the street to get him – we certainly couldn't leave him there – but there was no way you could go out alone. Because this bloody man was sitting in a pub drunk, I had to get everybody up out of bed to be able to go and get him back safely. Six policemen and an army team had to go down to the pub to rescue the sergeant. He came back armed with two bottles of whiskey and sat down in the enquiry office, totally oblivious to the fuss he had caused, and said to his rescue posse, 'Right boys, that was good work. Let's have a drink.' He fed the soldiers drink like there was no tomorrow. When their officer in charge came in, he went ballistic – I've never heard a bollocking like it!

23:27 – Cookstown Police Station, County Tyrone

When I was an inspector in Cookstown we had a strange incident occur when the IRA took a car from a house but, unusually, also took the owner, who they made drive the car. He was accompanied by the two IRA men – one sat in the passenger seat and the other one was in the back with a barrel they had placed in the back seat. This barrel had wires and all the attendant look of a bomb.

There were driving in from Ardboe towards Coagh, but about a mile out of Coagh, the terrorist in the back of the car started shouting, 'This fucking thing has started ticking. Stop, stop!' So they stopped the car and bailed out. They told the owner, 'You go and report to the police that there's a bomb in this car.' The owner of the car took off towards Coagh village and the terrorists went in the other direction. But the vehicle owner saw them being picked up quite quickly.

I was the duty inspector, so this was all relayed through to me. I said, 'This doesn't smell right at all, there's something not right there.' The police on duty from Coagh were in the station at Cookstown, about to make their way out to the now-abandoned car. I instructed them by radio to contact me by telephone as they didn't have a secure radio.

They stopped at the station to phone me and I asked, 'Have you seen the car?'

'Yes, but we haven't gone up to it yet.'

'Well don't go up to it,' I instructed, then I asked them to describe for me where it was. I also asked them, 'If you had been going out there to set up a VCP, is there anywhere that you would have pulled in?'

'Aye, the car park of the Orange Hall.'

'How far is that from the car?'

'About three hundred yards.'

I told them to stay in the village and set up their diversion point there and let nobody get in or out. I then told the Moneymore police to go to the area on the Ardboe side, set up a VCP and put a diversion in place, but under no circumstances were they to go anywhere near the car. Next, I contacted the local parish priest and told him that I thought there was a strong possibility of a bomb and asked if he would he let his parishioners know. [With a few well-placed calls, local priests would inform the community, and people who used the nearby fields, about the danger, preventing anyone from stumbling accidentally into the area.]

It was quite late in the evening; the weather was terrible – it was pouring out of the heavens – so I liaised with our colleagues in the military, and we arranged to go out the next day to do a route clearance. The route clearance began at first light and was completed right up to where the car sat. The ATO then examined the vehicle and declared that there was no bomb, it was an empty barrel with some wires connected – an elaborate hoax. I still wasn't happy and said, 'It's a lot of trouble to go to for a hoax; it must be to draw us in. There's something in the area.'

The sub-divisional commander (SDC) was back at the station by this stage. He said, 'Well, we've cleared it, there's nothing there.' I held my ground and said, 'No, there's something: they didn't do all this for no reason. There's definitely something there. I think the clearance will have to be done again tomorrow before you reopen this.' He wasn't happy about it but reluctantly said, 'Okay, we'll keep it closed for one more day.'

We went out the following morning and again did a complete route clearance. They were going through the gravel car park at the Orange Hall, just at the side of the road, when I saw one of the soldiers start to lean forward to pick something up. As I saw him, I shouted, 'Stop, what are you doing?' Just as I was saying it, he lifted a girlie magazine, a porn mag. There was a fishing line attached inside it, but because it had rained so heavily, the paper was soaked, and the fishing line came through it and tore it from the magazine.

When I had been stationed in Belleek RUC station, three police officers were blown up in Belcoo at the border in Fermanagh. The IRA had opened fire on the station in the middle of the night, at around 3 a.m., as some UDR members were leaving. At the time, it had seemed like madness because they were unlikely to hit anyone as the barracks were secure. The next day at first light, police came out to carry out an examination of the area around the firing point, to look for any empty cases or other evidence. There were four of them in total, searching a section of the old derelict Sligo–Leitrim railway line, about two hundred yards from the police station. There was a girlie magazine lying on the ground and one of the boys lifted it. A fishing line had been attached to it, and when the magazine was picked up, the line was pulled, detonating a bomb that had been buried in the ground just yards from the firing point. It killed three of them. The fourth officer was left blinded by the blast – he had actually gone through the depot with me. Eyewitnesses spoke of the gruesome scenes following the explosion. A local Catholic priest said, 'It was a horrible sight which made me feel quite sick. All I could do was say some prayers and try to comfort people.'

So, when I saw the soldier bend down that's why I shouted 'Stop.' The ATO who was with us, plus a dog handler and his four-legged friend, had already gone over it. I told the ATO what had happened in Belcoo and suggested he have a good look round where the magazine was found. They cleared away the gravel to discover a plastic sealed box with about 1.5lb of Semtex explosives in it, which is odourless. Contained as it was, within a sealed plastic box, the dog would have had no chance of finding it. There was a wooden dowel attached to the fishing line, but again, the rain had done its work and the wood had swollen, making it jam.

It was a gut feeling that you get that something is just not right.

23:30 – Tennent Street Police Station, North Belfast

I joined the RUC Part-Time Reserve on its formation in 1970. There were 112 men in that first batch of recruits, and I was number R111. As I lived in the Woodvale area of Belfast, my first station was Tennent Street which, even then, was in the thick of the Troubles!

Lord Hunt and his committee had disarmed the RUC, hoping to make it into an English-type police service (clearly PIRA didn't get the memo!) but some officers were still armed when doing protection duties, such as patrols around the High Court on the Crumlin Road in Belfast. However, on many nights, from 21:00 hours until 01:00 hours the following morning, two part-time reserve officers carried out the same duty armed only with their batons and, if they were lucky, a radio with which to summon assistance when required.

On one such night towards the end of 1970, a colleague and I were patrolling down Florence Place alongside the courthouse. We were about halfway down the street when we heard a loud burst of gunfire from further up the Crumlin Road, towards Ardoyne. We both turned to go back up to the main road to see if we could see anything when a bullet struck the road beside me. A gunman had been waiting for us at the bottom of the street but had taken a 'pot shot' when we turned away from him.

We got ourselves up to the main road in double quick

time and radioed for assistance. A Land Rover arrived about forty-five minutes later (it was a busy night) and the sergeant asked if we had any blood showing. I told him no, to which he replied, 'No problem then,' leaving us to make our own way back to Tennent Street station.

Not long after, on Friday 26 February 1971, I was detailed for station security (complete with baton) at the front gates of the station from 21:00 hours until 01:00 hours. My role was to watch for anything untoward in Tennent Street and facilitate vehicles and personnel arriving and leaving the base. Later that night, I opened the barrier and said goodnight to Detective Inspector Cecil Patterson and Constable Robert Buckley who were heading out to help deal with rioting at Ardoyne. A short time later both were shot dead by an IRA gunman.

One night in June 1971 I was the 'third' man in Charlie 1, our local mobile patrol car, when we got a report that men were seen acting suspiciously at a house close to the Tennent Street/Crumlin Road junction. We responded and our driver parked the police car opposite the house in question. The driver and observer jumped out of the car drawing their guns and the observer said to me, 'You cover us.' Of course, I wasn't armed and all I could say was, 'What with?' to which the observer exclaimed, 'You're not much fucking use,' and headed off across the road to investigate the report. Fortunately, it was a false alarm, but it made me question my practical use as a police officer.

Having served for a year since joining the reserve – a year in which I had been deployed as station duty officer, station security, foot patrols, mobile patrols and transit duty (when we drove around the area in a transit van acting as support for any police requesting assistance) – I resigned at the end of July 1971. It was partly because of this feeling of little use, but also because my wife and I were relocating to live in Hillsborough, County Down, where I rejoined in 1974.

23.32 – MSU, Strand Road Police Station, Londonderry

I was a young sergeant in the 'purples' mobile support unit in Strand Road RUC station, Londonderry. It was a very busy time with serious incidents seemingly incessant.

One night we were coming out of Strand Road barracks when we heard a lot of automatic gunfire. It sounded as though it was being fired from the Shantallow area, which was confirmed by a contact report coming over the radio from the sanger at Fort George army barracks: 'Contact, contact, we are under fire.' The shots were coming from around the petrol station on the Culmore Road, just above the barracks.

What had happened was that two young IRA recruits, Tony Gough and John Doherty, were being blooded, one more than the other, as it turned out. The two had pulled up in a car adjacent to the garage, intending to attack police coming out of Strand Road. They sat in the car and waited for the shift changeover to take place but there was no sign of the police personnel moving, no one had started coming out, and they were becoming increasingly impatient. They were feeling very vulnerable because of where they were. They decided to open fire on the sanger at the army camp instead so they could tell their bosses they had done the best they could in the circumstances before they sped off.

Now, just up behind them, across the main road, was a wall and little did they know that behind that wall was a three-brick army foot patrol made up of twelve soldiers on their way back to Fort George. The soldiers had stopped for a pee break (because once they passed the wall they would be exposed on open ground and their normal operational procedure was to run up and zigzag their way back into the barracks). When they'd heard the sound of gunfire, they immediately looked over the wall. Across the road they could see this Datsun car with a male leaning out the window firing the shots. In keeping with their training, they then charged across the road, opening fire as they did so. In the heat of the moment, with the fear and adrenalin pumping, the army advanced to engage the gunmen, managing to actually reload on the way over and continuing to fire into the vehicle. From memory, the vehicle was hit seventy-six times.

The gunmen's car veered across the road before coming to a stop. The driver, Tony Gough, who was wearing a balaclava and gloves, had been hit five times and was found slumped over the steering wheel. His accomplice had been wounded but not fatally.

As the incident was happening, we were coming out of Strand Road and were first responders at the scene. When we got there, the army had already taken Doherty from the vehicle and he was lying spreadeagled on the ground under arrest. Gough with his balaclava still on, was leaning over towards the side of the window – he had been fatally wounded in the head.

I remember that when we arrived at the vehicle, the first thing we wanted to do was get the army away from Doherty. This man had just been involved in trying to murder members of the security forces, probably friends of the soldiers at the scene. I just wanted to be sure that nothing happened that shouldn't happen.

We placed Doherty in our Land Rover and brought him back to Strand Road RUC station, under arrest. On the way back he remained in a state of heightened anxiety and had a degree of verbal diarrhoea. He talked about what he had just done and how he and Gough had met, things like that. When we got back to the station he was processed and put in a cell. I then had to get changed as I was being sent to carry out a search of Tony Gough's home. It was not something I was looking forward to doing because my instructions were to carry out the search, but not to tell his parents what had happened until we had finished. Only then could we deliver the death message.

Because of what had just happened, in that moment you have got fixed in your mind that these are bad, bad, people who have just tried to kill your colleagues. Doherty had already spilled his guts about his mate's involvement. Gough had been killed in an act of attempted murder. All this was running through my mind as I drove up to and prepared to enter Gough's family home. I went up to the front door and said, 'We are here to search your house under section such-and-such of the Emergency Provisions Act.' I brought in the search team and introduced them to Gough's father and mother. I then searched his parents in front of the rest of the team, which was the normal procedure in those circumstances. There were also three daughters in the house.

You cannot help but expect confrontation when going into that sort of environment: you're entering the privacy of someone's home, coming in with a whole load of police officers to carry out what will be a fairly invasive search, and they genuinely have no idea about what is going on.

The first thing I did when I went into the house was say to one of the guys with me, 'Unplug the phone and make sure the television is switched off.' I didn't want them finding out what had happened by word of mouth. I also gave instructions to the police officer guarding the door: 'Do not let anyone into the house. I don't care who they are, do not let them up the path.' I was very conscious of retaining a high level of isolation and keeping the crucial information about the death of the young fella from his parents. As the team began to search the house, I stood chatting with the mum and dad. I'd seen a photograph of their son on the mantelpiece, so I said, 'I know that young fella, who is that?' 'Oh, that's our son, Tony.' 'Where would I have seen him?' 'You might have seen him down at Fanny Wiley's,' which is a border crossing into Donegal.

The conversation develops with these lovely people, genuinely decent people, who are just ordinary parents, and the next thing I'm saying is, 'Do you know what, you're right.' Then one of his sisters says, 'He walks the dog down there, you might have met then.' As if I'm trying to place him, I say, 'Who do you think he would have been with?' Then they all begin to talk about who his friends are and who he hung about with, which of course has all been noted.

We finish conducting the search of the house but not a single thing was found that would be remotely incriminating. We brought the team down and did our exit procedure, which involved searching them again and talking to the family. Then I got the team to go outside and said, 'Get into the Land Rover as soon as I come out, we're going to drive straight off.'

I then closed the front door. Now it was just me and the family in the house. I asked the father if he'd step into the porch area, just at the bottom of the stairs and I said, 'You might want to sit on the stairs, I've got some bad news for you.' He sat on the stairs and I said, 'I'm so sorry, but your son was involved in a shooting incident with the army tonight and he's been killed.'

The man was obviously shattered, and I was bracing myself for the onslaught, expecting him to call for the family or become aggressive. He did neither, he was just bereft. He asked me, 'Would you come in to tell my wife?' I took my flak jacket and everything off and went in and sat in the lounge with them to explain as much as I could. They were completely shocked: 'I just don't believe it. Our Tony is not like that. He would never do anything like that.' It was very obvious they genuinely believed what they were saying. They were just in a complete state of shock from what had happened.

This may not be what people want to hear but I have often felt ashamed when I have reflected back on this, not because it was the wrong thing to do – at the time it was undoubtedly the right thing to do – but because of the surreptitious way that I'd had to engage with them. Because of my stereotypical view about where we had to go to carry out the search. I'd assumed it was going to be hostile, with a battle to get in to the house and a battle to get out again, when to tell you the truth it was a lesson learned for me: you cannot judge. People have different views and aspirations, but we all love our children. They loved their son and were totally blindsided that he had been involved in any way. They were as much a victim of radicalisation by the IRA as he was, a young guy out on active service for the first time being drawn into something by his associates. Not only is it a tragedy that his life had been lost, or that others could have been lost by his action, but tragic too for his family who were dignified and decent people.

00:00 – Mobile Patrol, North Antrim

At around midnight the mobile patrol on night duty would visit a local fish and chip shop at closing time and get a generous helping of what hadn't been sold to share with the rest of the party. The all-female staff welcomed us as we would disperse the drunks and see the ladies safely off the premises.

Standing outside the shop while my colleague was inside,

my attention was drawn to the intermittent sound of a car horn. It was a clear dry summer's evening, and the main road was brightly lit. Stopped about twenty feet from the traffic lights was a car straddling the centre white line. There were no other vehicles or other road users around. As I approached the car, I could see a lone male sitting upright in the driver's seat with both hands on the steering wheel sounding the car horn, his vision fixed on the road in front.

I rapped on the driver's window. Instantly the driver wound it down, and I asked, 'Is there something wrong, sir?' To which he replied, 'I can't get past those bloody elephants.' 'Elephants?' I asked, and he snapped, 'Those bloody elephants on the road!' Now we are all guilty at one time or another of being made out to be stupid and I was about to be that stupid person. Foolishly I stepped back from the car and looked up the road. As soon as I did, I heard the rear tyres of the car spinning on the road and, with the smell of burning rubber, I stood spellbound as the car disappeared at speed into the darkness.

My colleagues didn't come to me to find out what had happened. It was only on the journey back to the station that one remarked, 'You certainly upset your man. What did you say to him?' I was not going to mention the non-existent elephants blocking the road as I would have been the butt of station humour for weeks, if not months. Instead I answered, 'Ah, just a mate of mine trying to be funny!'

I might have been stupid, but I wasn't daft!

00:11 – Lurgan Police Station, County Armagh

I was stationed in the Craigavon/Lurgan area. The demarcation line between Lurgan station and Craigavon station was a place called Centrepoint, an entertainment complex in a predominantly nationalist area – although it was used by people from all sides – that stayed open late at night and always had lots of people milling about. There were always a lot of cars and taxis around.

I was on night duty, and we got a call to say that there was a house on fire, just within the Lurgan area. The fire brigade had requested that we attend to support them. The crews were all busy and, as the call had come directly from the fire brigade, I decided to answer it myself and took a full-time reserve officer with me; a really nice guy, Alan, who drove me.

The closer I got to where the fire was supposed to be – a cul-de-sac down an old country lane off the main carriageway – the more concerned I became about the call. We were being asked to support the fire brigade, but they hadn't arrived yet. I thought, no, I'm just going to hold back and wait beside the main carriageway where I can see more of what was going on. I sat and watched the traffic going past, but I kept seeing this same car going up and down the road. I got a check done on the vehicle and asked for police to have it stopped. It turned out the car was being driven by three well-known republican players. They and their vehicle were searched but they had nothing on them they shouldn't have, and they were let go. But they still kept appearing up and down the road. Of course, this was really very unusual, especially having already been stopped – there was no point in stopping them again, but it was strange for them to have stayed in the area.

The fire brigade had still not arrived, and I said to Alan, 'Listen, we're stuck out in the middle of the road here, go across to the other side of the carriageway,' which was the side where the laneway leading down to the house was. It had originally been a lane that intercepted the main road but was now a dead end. We reversed into it a little bit to wait on the fire brigade but still had a good view of vehicles approaching us.

Having reversed in, we sat close to the junction on the left-hand side of the laneway. It was a summer night, so I opened the door and, for no particular reason, I asked Alan to turn the engine off. He turned the engine off, the lights off and the place went deadly quiet. We sat there for about five or ten minutes looking out across the road towards the four-lane carriageway. Suddenly a head popped up from the ditch beside the laneway where we had been parked earlier. I shook my head thinking, no I didn't see that, but peeler's curiosity got to me and I said, 'Drive me back over there.'

My senses were immediately heightened, and I remember distinctly cocking my rifle because I just knew there was something not right about it all. When we got across to where I'd seen the man's head stick up, we saw these two fellas lying in a ditch. I got out of the vehicle. I was in full combat mode, holding my rifle.

One of the guys, who wasn't the fella who'd stuck his head up, stood up. He was white with shock and shaking from head to toe. He pointed at the other guy, who hadn't yet moved a muscle, and said, 'He's abducted me. I'm in the UDR.' It turned out the other person was Damien Duffy, the brother of Colin Duffy, who has been charged with many murders and is an extremely well-known republican terrorist from Lurgan.

This fella in the ditch, who I will call Paul, was identified as a UDR soldier. He had gone to Centrepoint to play ten pin bowling and been recognised by Duffy and his mates, who had then grabbed him and taken him to the ditch I'd found them in. The car that I'd seen driving up and down had been waiting for us to leave so that they could take him away to meet his fate. When we'd pulled across the street and turned the engine off, Duffy must have thought we had left so he stuck his head up to look. By the grace of

God, I happened to be looking in that direction and saw him. If we had not happened to stop where we did, and the other vehicle had picked the UDR man up, I have no doubt he would have been taken away and given an awful death. Duffy was arrested, handcuffed, taken away and got ten years in prison for his trouble.

I felt very pleased with myself: I'd just rescued a UDR soldier who would have been brutally murdered and I'd arrested a well-known IRA man in the act of committing a terrorist crime. I had used the handcuffs I'd bought (this had been before handcuffs were issued to us) and had put Duffy in a forensic cape (I had been stationed in west Belfast and that was what we did there) – all was looking good. Then, on our way down to the holding centre in Gough barracks, Armagh, Alan took a wrong turn. I had been to Gough many times, and Damien Duffy had been there as many times as I had, but unfortunately our driver had not. The only thing Damien Duffy said for the next seven days was, 'You missed your turning, you have to go back up there to the left.'

My great day collapsed when the terrorist had to tell the driver how to get to the police station.

00:16 – Border, County Fermanagh

I was the border inspector for Rosslea–Newtownbutler, and the sub-divisional commander there was a very easy-going man; he liked to let the inspectors run everything. I was then ops planning inspector [the operational planning inspector would organise manpower to deal with tasks in the area] and, when the chief was off, I was the acting sub-divisional commander, effectively running the show.

We had to travel by helicopter. The RAF were fairly straitlaced – they did everything properly and by the book – but if it was the army air cover taking us into Rosslea, one of the boys would only have to say, 'We've got a new inspector with us and he hates flying,' and they would go in so low. They would almost take the backs of cars as they flew through the trees, or hedge hopped … anything to scare the life out of the new guy. It was good fun; they were a great bunch of lads. I remember one time the alarm went off and we had to do an emergency landing. The alarm had detected a surface-to-air missile, which fortunately turned out to be a fault. The adrenalin rush was mad – the crew were split fairly evenly between those who wanted to walk back and those who wanted to fly. I have to admit, I said to the sergeant, 'You fly back, and I'll walk!'

We had thirty-six Provisional IRA men from the Rosslea and Donegal area who were on the run. Every single one of them was Lift on Sight. All that did was force them to move across the border to Clones in County Monaghan, where they all became full-time terrorists instead of part-time. This helped them become more sophisticated and the threat levels and terrorist activity increased greatly. For instance, they started military-style robberies: they'd set up an illegal checkpoint on either side of a garage and, with all the camouflage gear, they certainly looked the part.

They'd also leave bombs: one of the biggest ever car bombs was left at the permanent checkpoint in Rosslea on the Fermanagh border; it was in the region of 3000lb of explosives. They got a local man – the son of the cook that lived locally – tied him to the seat of his van and started smashing his legs with batons to make him drive to the vehicle checkpoint. When he arrived, he very bravely shouted a warning to the troops: 'There's a bomb in the back of the van. Let me out.' A squaddie cut him out of the seat – where he got a knife from so quickly, I don't know, but get him out he did – and they all ran off in a scattering match. The high-tech solution for such an occurrence was to shelter in a large hole in the ground, which they ran towards and jumped into. Fortunately, the bomb did not go off – it would have levelled everything over a massive area.

The problem was, the terrorists were able to cross the border at will, no matter how many main roads were set with checkpoints or unapproved roads were cratered. They still had local knowledge across fields and lane ways. We ran several operations to target them, and we had quite some success in recovery of firearms and caches of explosives, but word eventually reached the terrorists that the person behind all these operations was the ops planning inspector … that is, me.

The result of this, unfortunately, was that I was targeted specifically. I got a call [from Special Branch] to that effect. I went to their office to find out what was going on and was told that they had been speaking to their counterparts from Monaghan Garda station. My name had been mentioned in information they had received from an IRA source. I had to change my car and have secure plates put on it. The false plates were changed every two or three days. Then I got a call from Branch to tell me I was not to leave the station. They had received information from the Garda, who said the IRA had set up an ambush on the main Street of Lisnaskea and that if I was to go up that estate I would be attacked, and from the terrorists' point of view, hopefully murdered.

A week later I got another call to say that an emergency operation was to be planned and, 'You have to make your way to Clogher straightaway.' So, I went immediately, but there wasn't an operation; it was really a reason to get me out of the station without causing alarm. I was told on arrival, 'We've sent another car to get your wife and children from your home. We have information to say that the Provisionals are on their way to your home as we speak, and the SAS are moving in.' My family and I were taken to Belfast; we had just the clothes that we were wearing. Talk about a moonlight flit.

The SAS lay in ambush at the house, but the IRA did not turn up. Sources said that they had heard the Puma helicopter PB 3. This was matte black, had a special noise-reducing engine and flew with no lights, but the IRA must have seen something of it or heard something. Whatever happened while they were on their way to my home, it made them call off the attack. The Garda were even able to tell us where the IRA team had crossed the border in both directions on their way to my house.

00:20 – Clogher Police Station, County Tyrone

In 1967, in a definite step up for me, I was transferred from Mountfield, a hamlet with some eighteen street lights, to Clogher, a village of some forty street lights and a main street that was largely inhabited on one side only. In those days, Clogher station was a sub-district headquarters, run by District Inspector Gilchrist (3rd class), later officer in charge of the Reserve Force in Belfast. We had Head Constable Jack McConnell, later superintendent SPG, who lived in the attached married quarters, a sergeant from Crime Special (forerunner of Special Branch), a sergeant from CID and approximately eighteen constables, of which I was the junior by quite a few years.

The first apparatus I had to get the hang of in the station was an antiquated telephone switchboard. It consisted of several rows of wee holes that I would fill with what looked like table tennis balls, each of which had a number painted on the front. Each office had its own line and numbered table tennis ball. When a call came in for a certain office I had to crank furiously at a winding handle on the side of the switchboard, wait until the – hopefully correct – ball fell into its 'nest', and then plug in what looked like a .303 pull through [a length of thick cord attached to a piece of metal that would be pulled through a rifle barrel in order to clean it] into another smaller hole below the nest. It was easy ... after about six months.

I was out on patrol one night duty. I was driving a [Ford] Zephyr Six along one of the many narrow country roads that surround Clogher, when I hit a bird that had, unfortunately for it, carried out a rather sluggish take off. I braked through a flurry of feathers and strange noises then dismounted to see if I'd caused any damage to the car. The bird, which was draped over the verge, was dead but didn't display any outward signs of injury. The observer, who obviously hadn't been doing his job properly, now took an interest and excitedly declared, 'That's a pheasant, Victor, and better than that, it's a hen pheasant. There's good eating in them. Throw it in the boot. I take it you know what to do with it?' I was a townie, I hadn't a clue what to do with the poor bird, so on the way back to base he gave me a quick rundown on how to prepare a dead game fowl.

Back at the station I threw the bird into one of the sheds in the yard until I was off duty. After changeover I chopped the pheasant's head off with an old hatchet and tied it upside down from a rafter over an old empty paint tin. Apparently, I had to let the blood drain from it before the gutting could take place. I wasn't sure what gutting actually meant, though: I didn't know what came out and what stayed in.

I suppose it must have been around 9.00 a.m. and I was standing in the kitchen having a well-earned mug of tea when the head constable came in from the yard. 'Right, there's a dead bird hanging in one of the sheds. Anybody know anything about it?' I nodded tentatively over my mug and explained what had happened. I hadn't been driving recklessly and the poor bird had just been a bit slow in getting itself airborne. He looked at me, 'Fallers, do you not know that this is close season for hen pheasants? It is a serious offence to kill one and you have committed that offence. I won't allow this bird to remain on RUC property because if I do, I'll be guilty of aiding and abetting you.'

I started to splutter a reply, not really knowing what I was going to say apart from the fact I hadn't a clue what close season he was talking about, which probably wouldn't have done me any favours. Fortunately, he cut me short: 'There's one thing about me, I look after my men. Put your mind at rest, I'll take the responsibility of getting rid of the evidence. I want that paint tin emptied, though. Not a trace of blood is to be seen in it. Right?'

'Yes, sir,' I replied gratefully, 'it won't happen again.'

Night duty was finished, and I happily went off on two day's short leave, as it was called then. I ran into the head constable shortly after I returned to the station and he gave me a little smile and quietly said, 'The wife thought that was the tastiest pheasant we have had for a long time. Tell me, where exactly was it you accidentally ran into it?'

Huh! Naive or what?

00:38 – Witness Protection, CID

In the 1980s there had been a spate of so-called 'supergrass trials' involving both loyalist and republican terrorists who had decided to turn Queen's evidence and name their colleagues in court and give evidence against them for crimes named.

As a result, police ended up having to take the supergrasses out of the country as their lives were in danger from their former colleagues. We needed to keep them happy and alive to give evidence to the courts, after which they would be resettled somewhere. We became known in police circles as 'the minders'.

I was babysitting a loyalist supergrass across the water [in England] and one day he decided he wanted to go for a swim. I went with him to the local swimming baths. He got changed into his swimming trunks and his chest, arms and back – every bit of him – was covered in huge loyalist tattoos. As you can imagine, the English people were staring at him as they had never seen anything like it. The laugh was he couldn't swim a stroke and pottered about at the shallow end like a beached whale. I pretended not to know him and stayed down at the deep end.

Then he decided he wanted to watch a football match, and me being a Spurs fan I thought, well, we can go and watch Spurs. The other fella from the RUC who was with me had served for a while in the Met police force and knew his way around. More importantly, he knew who to speak to about getting us tickets. He contacted Tottenham Hotspur local CID and we got tickets for the match. All went well and the supergrass enjoyed the day out.

After the game we went for a few beers, and eventually the supergrass got talking to one of the detectives from the Met that was with us. The detective turned out to be a fanatical Rangers fan who was originally from Glasgow. With drink on board, the truth eventually came out to the Scottish detective as to who the supergrass was. The evening ended with the two of them on a karaoke stage in London singing 'The Sash'!

00:40 – Sion Mills Police Station, County Tyrone

Sion Mills, Northern Ireland, Saturday 28 January 1989. It was a long time ago, and as the years trundle on I have always expected, or more accurately hoped, that my memories of the horrible incident that unfolded on that day would fade to an acceptable recollection of a sequence of events. However, I can say for sure, some things never change.

Sion Mills is a pretty village known for a famous cricket match many decades ago. The village is approximately three miles outside Strabane and, as Sion was a limited opening station and our hardware and valuables needed to be secured elsewhere, our station officers had to start and finish their shifts in Strabane station.

Friday, 27 January 1989, late shift: 15:00 to 23:00 with overtime meant I was scheduled to be on duty until 02:00. Pretty standard start to the weekend late shift, with the Friday overtime to pay passing attention to the pub/disco in the village as it had seen its fair share of problems with drunken brawls and serious assaults over the years. The pub's clientele was less than savoury and very republican, with the majority coming from the head of the town in Strabane and a nearby area called the Glebe.

Monty and I covered the early evening opening time at the station and probably completed a few FAC [firearm certificate/licence] applications or renewals from village residents – the usual stuff in the station. After closing the station, we headed out on mobile patrol. We were usually paired together, however on this occasion, for whatever reason, he drove the main vehicle, NI70, with two others – the observer and rear cover (who would carry a longarm) – and I drove NI71 with one other, the observer. While on patrol, we had the usual array of VCPs along with some community policing: stopping and chatting with locals and visitors.

I remember the community policing attempts being met with a varied response depending on the recipient. Occasionally, a good brisk foot patrol was called for and we'd utilize a piece of military equipment [an ECM (electronic countermeasures) backpack] that jammed radio signals and could be used to remotely detonate bombs intended for police and/or military. As I said, pretty standard stuff for a Friday late turn.

Typically, we'd stay out and see the patrons arrive at Mellon's pub for their evening of frivolity and get an idea of who was who. The pub was only a couple of hundred yards from the station – convenient. Anyway, we saw the folks into the pub and around 11 p.m. we went into the station for a cuppa with the obligatory milk chocolate digestives just to keep our strength up. We played a few hands of cards, a penny a point; Monty ended up owing me something like 26p. He took great delight in shouting out to me as we headed back out on patrol, 'You'll never get it from me.' We laughed and left the station yard, locking up the large steel gates behind us.

We had been out for a while when at around 00:40, a call came in for us to attend Mellon's – something about an assault to be investigated and information for us. We were on Melmount Road travelling in the direction of Strabane. My vehicle was in front of Monty's but he turned in at a nearby petrol station, closed at that time of night, on the Strabane side of the pub. The owner of that petrol station had asked us not to be on his premises because he didn't want to be thought of as being friendly to police – that could be dangerous for him and his business – and I remember thinking, 'He'll be at the pub before me.' As I arrived, I saw NI70 already pulled over beside the pub. That part of the building was single level with a flat roof, which I believe extended back to the rear area of the premises. I had stopped the vehicle in the lane for Victoria Bridge and signalled right to pull over behind Monty's vehicle. Billy, who was the observer in NI70, got out of the car and went to find out if there was a problem in the pub, to be told by the doorman, there wasn't one.

Suddenly there was a loud bang, the type you can both hear and feel, and the NI70 was engulfed in smoke. I remember pulling my vehicle across the road, blocking traffic and using the radio – 'Contact, contact, contact!' – and giving a brief description of what I could see and where we were. Then I got out and rushed over to NI70. Almost immediately the revellers had piled out of the pub, cheering, spitting on us and starting to throw pint glasses, bottles and anything else they could find at us. The rear passenger, Glen, had pulled himself out of the vehicle and was now slumped on the ground, leaning against the rear wheel on the passenger side. I immediately saw that he was seriously injured, needing urgent medical attention. I grabbed the first aid box. Almost straight away there was a lady beside me who said that she was a nurse and could attend to the injured officer, but she was soon driven away by the crowd.

Billy ran back to the car from the pub. It was very clear to him as well that Glen was very seriously injured; I think he lost an eye. The whole interior of the car was covered in human matter. Billy took the gun out of Glen's holster, gathered in the other gun, then lay on top of Glen's body to protect him at the back of the car as the crowd spat, kicked and threw pint glasses on top of him.

I went to Monty's door, opened it and could see he was gone. The explosion had done considerable damage and taken Monty's life. I had to retrieve Monty's side arm and long arm to stop them being stolen or used against me as the crowd closed in. To protect the scene, myself and my colleagues I had to draw my gun and that's when everything appeared to go into slow motion. I recall shouting, 'Get back, get back!' then I had a weird thought that reloading my gun will need to be fast if I'm to survive this. It felt like we were stranded there for ages before backup arrived.

Thankfully, there had been a military patrol nearby in the Glebe area plus several makeshift crews from the outgoing shift in Strabane had scrambled to come to our aid. The Strabane crews ended up toe to toe with the crowd to protect Glen and preserve Monty's remains.

The next thing I remember is being back at Strabane station and having to call my family as they had seen the incident reported on the TV: 'Police attacked in Sion Mills. One officer believed to be dead, another seriously injured.' It turned out that the call had been a 'come on' to give the IRA the opportunity to drop a drogue bomb from the flat roof of the bar on to Monty's vehicle: a direct hit above the driver's seat. The roof looked like someone had punched a huge hole in it.

Monty was married with a young child; he was twenty-six.

01:08 – Lurgan Police Station, County Armagh

I came back to Lurgan in 1997, a fortnight after two officers from my section, constables John Graham and Davy Johnston, had been shot dead by the IRA. They had been out on foot patrol in Church Walk, only yards from the station, when two terrorists ran up behind them and shot them both in the back of the head at point-blank range. They died instantly. You could really feel the sense of loss in the station, and feelings of grief and sorrow in the section itself were palpable.

Colin Duffy, a well-known republican from the Kilwilke estate in the town had been charged with the murders within days of the crime. The detectives involved had carried out a lot of work to ensure the case against Duffy was solid, and there was sufficient evidence to put him in front of the court. It was interesting to then see the defence's campaign immediately kick into life and undermine the evidence against him. For instance, there had been a positive identification of Duffy from a witness, known as witness D, who had lived and worked throughout Lurgan – including Kilwilke estate – for years. She had seen the murder take place and had provided a statement in which she named Duffy as the gunman. She had known him for ten years. Duffy was refused bail.

The campaign to discredit the evidence against Duffy was run by his solicitor, Rosemary Nelson. She had a whole series of people, all around Lurgan, saying that at the time the witness claimed Colin Duffy had carried out the murder he had been elsewhere. Her witnesses would pop up and say that, on this date and time I saw Colin Duffy and he was over here … he was over there, they effectively painted an alternative location for Duffy during the time that he was allegedly carrying out the murder.

This was what greeted my return to Lurgan RUC station. The charges against Duffy were subsequently withdrawn and I was the duty inspector on the day he was released from prison. I was told that there was going to be a republican cavalcade through the town centre to celebrate Duffy's release. Their intention was to collect Duffy at the prison, then come into the town from the motorway with their cavalcade of cars, waving Irish flags, beeping their horns and cheering Duffy like some returning hero – a show parade up and down Lurgan's main street near the police station.

I noticed that the old barriers for closing the town centre (from the days of car bombs) were still in place and I made the decision to close the town and redirect them to another estate. Tension in the town was extremely high, so I wasn't going to have police officers witnessing the spectacle of the person they believed had murdered two of their colleagues cheering and being driven past the very spot those colleagues had been slain just weeks before.

The next evening, my section was on night duty and I called out to Lurgan station to see a queue of people out the door, hordes of people, and I walked in thinking, 'What on earth has happened here?'. It turned out that the previous night, my section had stopped a car not far away from the police station and in the car was Colin Duffy and a few others. Unfortunately, they had stopped the car outside a pub at closing time. A crowd had come out and a bit of a disturbance began. They attempted to arrest Duffy for disorderly behaviour, or breach of the peace or something, but he pulls a young police officer into the back of the car and assaults him quite severely. The young police officer is now thinking, 'I'm in a car on my own with a guy who's just been released from prison for murdering two of my colleagues, my life is in real danger here.'

By the time I got in for the late shift, Duffy had been arrested for grievous bodily harm and was in the custody suite with Rosemary Nelson, his solicitor. The queue of people out the door were all there to make complaints against the police, claims of alleged brutality, and as the duty inspector I had to interview and record statements from all of them. I then go down to interview Duffy and his solicitor, who would make similar complaints.

By the time I got to them my temper was up. Duffy and his solicitor were sitting in an interview room which has a big sign saying 'No Smoking', but I walked in and the two of them were sitting smoking. I remember that I slammed down the bundle of papers I was carrying and said, 'It says no smoking, put the cigarettes out.' The two of them, like lambs, put their cigarettes out. It occurred to me afterwards, what was I going to do if they hadn't? I could hardly escort both of them off the premises.

I did find it really interesting to see the republican

machine kicking into operation. Before the night was over, I was taking phone calls from right across Europe and the United States, including New York. Some said they represented Amnesty International, or equivalent groups, and were demanding the release of Colin Duffy who they alleged was the victim of police brutality and police harassment. Groups were literally phoning in and sending faxes from all over the world. That was the level of campaigning that had started in such a short time. It reminded me of the campaign that kicked off during the Drumcree parade stand-off, the common denominator being Rosemary Nelson.

01:30 – Lisnaskea Police Station, County Fermanagh

In 1973, the Twelfth of July unfortunately fell on my section's night shift. It was normal practice for the night crew to begin their shift at 7 p.m. on 11 July, thus providing manpower for extra patrolling. The shift began well with everyone being in good form and nothing exceptional occurring. At 11 p.m. the duty sergeant told the night crew to take an hour's break, which enabled us to have a little refreshment and be ready again for briefing at changeover time.

Patrolling there at that time involved two vehicles: an armoured Cortina and a Land Rover. The station only had one Land Rover, a 'soft skinned' type, and it did not afford the occupants any protection. No such thing as Makrolon or any such luxuries. This Land Rover was the newest one in the RUC fleet and of course no one wished to be the first person to put a scrape on it. I drew the short straw as driver, but we always changed over the drivers halfway through the night.

We set off shortly after midnight for a general patrol around the town and its close vicinity – the bars were empty and the streets clear. At 1.30 a.m. we received a call to go to Newtownbutler to pick up a member coming off duty who was going home to Lisnaskea. On the way, as we approached the townland of Moorlough on a fairly straight stretch of road, our attention was drawn to a large Friesian cow standing at the roadside. I slowed down and the sergeant, George, who was sitting in the passenger seat, said that we should put it into the field. I looked at the cow and thought that it looked fairly settled as it was chewing its cud. I suggested that we head on up to Newtownbutler and that if it was still there on our return journey then we could put it into a field. Then the sergeant said that, when we'd been on our break, he'd had to go up to Newtownbutler in an unmarked car to deliver a dispatch and that there had been a cow in the very same spot. He'd stopped, opened a gate and put the cow into a field. When he told me that my suspicions were aroused, and I said that if he'd put it into the field, someone had purposely let it out again. So we proceeded to Newtownbutler and collected our passenger.

Back down the road to Moorlough and there is the cow, still at the side of the road. I stopped the Land Rover well short of where it was and the crew debussed from the rear. Two of them headed for the gate when I shouted to them to stop. There was a Fermanagh gate there at the corner of the field [strands of barbed wire on posts used to make a gateway]. The cow was driven through the gap and myself and the rest of the crew remounted to continue our journey to Lisnaskea. We had hardly travelled more than 20 yards and were level with the gateway to the field when all I saw was this almighty orange flash in front of me. I am alleged to have said, 'My God, the end of the world.' Someone shouted from the rear, 'Let me get them' and I felt an SMG [sub-machine gun] on my shoulder, ready to go. Instinct clicked into gear — I had been in situations such as this in other parts of the world – and as everyone on board appeared to be uninjured, I slammed the Rover into a lower gear and told the guys to hold on. I don't know how I did it, but the Land Rover jumped over the bomb crater and boulders that were littered across the road. Hearts were pumping, adrenalin was flowing, but we were alive.

With our headlights switched off, we proceeded for a short distance before stopping to assess the damage to the vehicle. Alas, the latest vehicle of the fleet resembled nothing more than a seagull with an engine – both sides of it were flapping loose. Suddenly a car sped out of the Donagh Road and headed off in the direction of Lisnaskea. The sergeant said to me, 'Jimmy, do you think you could catch that car?' So I put an inch to my step, despite knowing full well that, owing to the condition of the Land Rover, that would be an impossibility. I put the foot down and, getting as much speed out of the Rover that I could, we headed for Lisnaskea.

The sergeant gave an update of the situation over the radio and instructed the guard at the station to get out on the road with the .303 rifle and try to stop the car we were pursuing. By the time the guard got himself into a suitable position the car had already gone over the ramps at full speed. We remained in pursuit with our vehicle now resembling something out of *Smokey and the Bandit*. We reached Maguiresbridge and proceeded towards Lisbellaw where, before our very eyes, right in the centre of Lisbellaw, there was the car stopped by a UDR patrol.

The occupants were spreadeagled at the side of the road. One of them said to the sergeant, 'Boy, I am glad to see you here. I tried to tell these men who we were and where we were coming from, but they would not listen.' The two men were actually two respected businessmen from Enniskillen, though their clothing was somewhat dishevelled, and the fronts of their trousers were soaking wet. It turned out they had been returning from a night out in Clones and had taken the back road home. Just outside Donagh they had stopped to relieve themselves when, suddenly, there had been a loud explosion and they jumped into their car and left the area. They were completely innocent and had nothing to do with the incident. We thanked the UDR for being alert and for their quick response and allowed the two businessmen to proceed home.

A couple of weekends later our crew were summoned to a certain hotel where the chief constable, Sir Jamie Flanagan, was there to meet us. We had a great meeting and a party at which copious amounts of black and other liquids were consumed. In those days that was normal and what happened after incidents such as this – no such thing as Occupational Health then.

Lisnaskea RUC was one of the best places I was ever stationed, if not the best, and I am happy to say that, to the best of my knowledge, everyone in that crew is still with us today. I am sure that they still remember the cow on the road on the Twelfth.

01:35 – Oldpark Police Station, North Belfast

North Belfast was often described as a `patchwork quilt' as several loyalist and republican areas sat side by side with the interface often being a major road or junction. The army units deployed to support the police usually came on a three-month rotation that meant frequent turnovers and little ability to gather local knowledge. Every new regiment wanted to outdo the previous regiment, be it in stop and search, vehicle stops or even house searches for weapons and munitions. Part of our job as local neighbourhood police officers was to curtail their enthusiasm and direct their energies towards more productive outcomes. Some regiments were more receptive than others.

One of the Scottish regiments was commanded by a colonel with a very rich pedigree and considerable land in the north-west of Scotland. He was very 'old school': extremely polite and genuinely wanted to do his best for the local community. He was quite alarmed when I told him one day that we had received a number of complaints about his soldiers being abusive to a particular lady in the district whose husband was serving a jail sentence for republican terrorist activities.

The feedback he received from his senior NCOs [non-commissioned officers] disputed the woman's claims and suggested the soldiers' behaviour was impeccable. I was less confident in this assessment and suggested to the colonel that he might wish to meet the woman and judge for himself. This he quickly agreed to, and a 'chance' meeting was arranged at a quiet venue where the woman worked part-time. At the meeting he was his usual polite and charming self but was quickly taken aback by the nature of the verbal abuse allegations made, especially when it was revealed that many of these incidents occurred in front of her young daughter.

On the way back to the army base he confided in me that he believed the woman and was deeply shocked that any of his soldiers would behave in such a manner. He quickly gathered his officers and senior NCOs and made his feelings known to them – that is, that any such future behaviour was not acceptable.

Some time passed before I saw the woman again and she reassured me the verbal abuse had stopped and in fact the soldiers were very polite to her. I passed this on to the colonel and he was delighted by the change in behaviour.

Some weeks later I was shopping with my wife in an out-of-town shopping centre when we bumped into the lady concerned. She was gushing in her praise for me without going into the details of the incidents and my wife was greatly impressed. However, she was less impressed when I told her of the lady's husband and the litany of terrorist activities that resulted in his jail sentence.

01:38 – Strabane Police Station, County Tyrone

The Provos took another pop at the army in Bridge Street in Strabane one night and the army returned fire and clipped one of the IRA boys, Tommy Brogan. The IRA men managed to make their escape in a getaway car and the army scrambled a Wessex helicopter to try and tail them. Brogan got out of the car, realising there was army air cover and opened fire at the helicopter, with total disregard for anyone who lived in the densely populated estate had he managed to bring the Wessex down.

He was clearly wounded by that stage and went to ground in the estate. The bosses all knew he'd been clipped because of the blood found at the firing point and they sealed the entire estate off. They did nine hundred house searches in three days. Obviously whatever intelligence they got back from both the public and police sources was very good as they eventually got him – I think the people in the estate were phoning because they were pissed off that the helicopter might have crashed into their homes.

He was found in the base of a divan bed in the family home of a well-known IRA man. By the time they discovered and arrested him he had received professional medical treatment and was very well patched up.

The laugh was, one of the crews, I think it was M2 from Strabane, had searched that house three times. I remember the guys taking the piss out of the unit about their missing him initially. When any of that unit came into the station they would have done things like sit in a chair with a lampshade on their head and say, 'I'm Tommy Brogan and tonight, Matthew, I'm going to be a standard lamp!'

01:44 – Lisburn Road, South Belfast

It was the late seventies, just after I had finished at the training centre. I was working at Lisburn Road station in Belfast when we received a call about a girl being attacked on the Stranmillis Road. We made our way there and found her just at the junction. She was in a terrible state and said that she had been attacked by the Incredible Hulk.

We initially thought this must be a wind up – you wouldn't have put it past our colleagues with me being the new guy just out of training; it was nearly expected they would be taking the piss. But the thing was, we could see that this girl was not acting. We asked her where the Incredible Hulk had gone and she directed us towards a back entry. Ricky, who was with me, moved towards the entry, which was just off the Stranmillis Road. I had a Sterling sub-machine gun and walked towards the entry to cover Ricky, who only had his handgun, but I was also trying to keep an eye on the girl and didn't want to get too far from her.

All of a sudden, from one of those wee covered yards at the back of houses, out bursts the Incredible Hulk. He jumped on top of Ricky and quite a fight started between them. As they were fighting, this green monster was roaring, yelling, shouting and beating the crap out of Ricky who appeared to be in serious trouble. Being just out of the Depot, I had never experienced anything like this and to be honest didn't really know what to do, but I knew I had to protect my partner. I cocked the SMG and raised it to my shoulder and was very, very close to shooting him. Really, the only reason I didn't open fire was because I was worried about hitting Ricky.

Then all of a sudden, the Incredible Hulk stopped fighting and started giggling, adding to my confusion in the darkness. Well, it turned out that the guy was completely blocked and had been at a fancy-dress party nearby. His girlfriend had been with him and they'd had an argument. I was fit to be tied and also determined that he should be arrested and prosecuted. If truth be told, he had scared the shit out of me. Ricky of course was the senior man and I was the new guy. He was very pragmatic and just said, 'Look, a bit of hijinks, forget about it or you'll never hear the end of it.'

That fella did not realise how close he had come to being shot and if I had shot the Incredible Hulk, I have no doubt it would have been the end of my career before it had even started!

01:48 – CID Office, Woodbourne Police Station, West Belfast

One of the things about working in republican areas during the Troubles was that you couldn't just jump into the CID car and attend whatever scene you had been called to, or even go to someone's home for something simple like a burglary. All police personnel – uniform, CID, no matter what you were in – always had to be on their guard and expect the unexpected in terms of attack. The IRA spent their lives trying to work out new ways in which to kill you. They had concealed a booby-trap bomb inside a lamppost at one scene I was at. You would never in a thousand years have known there was anything wrong with that light, or how close to death you actually were. They were very sophisticated at times and in the way they chose to attack. There is no point in kidding yourself that they weren't, they were, and you'd forget that at your peril.

Consequently, we were taken out to the various scenes

we had to attend in the back of armoured Land Rovers, which were always accompanied by army personnel. Our colleagues in uniform branch were absolutely brilliant and great to work with. Not only did they keep us protected, but they would have reminded us, if they thought we needed it, of things they thought we should or should not do out on the street. For example, in such areas you would never have seen a uniformed police officer standing at someone's front door with his hat on. A hat would identify him as police to anyone on the other side of the door who may have been in a position to shoot him. I remember one of the uniform lads saying to me one day, 'Never go to a door that has a curtain on it and press the bell.' The fear was that the bell might be connected to an explosive device on the other side of the door, which would detonate when you pressed it. You might have stood to the side of the door and knocked, but you would never have pressed that bell because of that possibility.

I had two young kids at the time. My wife and I got a rare day out with them and we all went up to Portrush, a popular holiday resort on the Antrim coast. We left home early with the intention of spending the day there, and to get the full benefit of the time we had. We took the kids to the famous Barry's Amusements and they were loving it. However, I had noticed some people following us. It did not seem to matter where we went, they were there and when we went into Barry's they stayed behind us. I didn't say anything because I didn't want to upset the family but then my wife said to me, 'You know there are people following us,' and I said to her, 'I do,' but with the kids being small I didn't want to do anything to frighten them. I wasn't even armed as I'd thought I was just out for the day with the family. But then I thought, play it safe, we better leave. We actually had to leave Portrush, never mind leave Barry's and go somewhere else along the coast. It was much to the disappointment of my children who couldn't understand why they couldn't continue to play on the amusements and of course I couldn't tell them. I knew these people were from west Belfast, where I was stationed at the time, and I just couldn't take the risk, and I'm 6 foot 4! They could easily have sent for a gun to be brought there. In the end, they didn't do anything to me or say anything untoward, but the menace was there, and I couldn't risk it with the kids. These things can escalate out of control in seconds.

01:52 – Crime Squad, Ballinderry, County Antrim

Robert Black was a paedophile. He worked for a company in England that delivered advertisements and posters. Once the company had sold the advertising space, it was his job to put the posters up on the relevant sites, which meant he travelled absolutely anywhere and everywhere. He travelled all over the United Kingdom and Ireland, north and south, using the back roads as much as possible, which let him build up a great knowledge of local areas. He used to sleep in his van and despite the Troubles, he would have slept anywhere. But like most paedophiles, he was always on the lookout for a potential victim, no matter where he was. As he travelled around the country, his MO was to pick up any children he saw on their own and take them away in his van.

On 12 August 1981, Jennifer Cardy, a nine-year-old girl from Ballinderry, disappeared. She had gone out cycling but had sadly never returned. Her disappearance led to a search that involved police, army and hundreds of volunteers. They found her bicycle dumped over a hedge, but not her. Her body was eventually found in McKee's Dam near Hillsborough on 18 August. She had been abducted, sexually assaulted and then murdered.

Several years passed and one of my bosses read about Robert Black [who in 1990 was convicted of abducting and sexually assaulting a six-year-old girl in Stow, Scotland, and in 1994 was convicted of the murders of three other young girls – eleven-year-old Susan Maxwell, five-year-old Caroline Hogg, and ten-year-old Sarah Harper]. My boss realised that there were many similarities between the murders that had taken place in England and the Jennifer Cardy case and how she had disappeared. One girl that he had tried to lift in England had escaped from him – although she had looked much younger, she was, in fact, about fifteen and that little bit stronger, which helped her fight him off.

Black had been arrested in July 1990 in Stow, Scotland, after a massive investigation, for he had killed all over England. A man [David Herkes] had been out mowing his lawn, and saw his neighbour's little girl out on the street. Robert Black happened to be there in his van. When the little girl disappeared, the man thought that something was not right. He gave police a description of the van and registration. Unfortunately, he had given the wrong registration number, but police called out to speak to him. As they were speaking, the van came back and the gentleman was able to say, 'That's the same van.' The police officers went after the van and stopped it. One of the officers – it was his daughter that had been kidnapped – searched it but didn't see anything initially. He noticed what he thought was a bundle of rags lying over in the corner, but when he pulled it out, it was in fact a sleeping bag. He opened the sleeping bag and inside it was his own little girl. That's how Black came to be arrested. They said that if the girl had been in the sleeping bag for much longer, she would have suffocated, not that he would have cared.

From what was known of Black and the abductions he had been involved in, he fitted everything that had happened to Jennifer. The MO was exactly the same.

Added to this, we were able to establish that he had been in Belfast for work at the time of her murder. We could prove that he had been in the area – records we found showed that he had got petrol in Northern Ireland in a garage at a roundabout in the area that day.

So my boss arranged for me to go over to England to interview Black in prison (where he was known as Smelly Bob) and see what I thought. Black would have talked to you all day. He was very personable, spoke well but would never admit anything. We were very experienced detectives, and we interviewed him for a full day but learned nothing from him. He was clever and had a great way of turning the conversation round. Prior to interviewing Black, we were briefed by a psychiatrist to try and get an insight into the way he thought, which at the time was quite pioneering. But Black was evil. You just knew that he was evil by the excuses he made. For instance, at the time of his arrest, police found the biggest discovery of pornographic material that had ever been seized as a single collection from an individual. We put questions to him about being a paedophile and that it was children he liked. He said, 'No, when they took all my magazines away there were fully-developed women in them.' I countered with, 'But not one woman had pubic hair.' He did not reply. It all came back to prepubescent girls.

In 2009, Black was charged with the murder of Jennifer Cardy. At his trial in Armagh in 2011, he was found guilty and received a further sentence of life imprisonment. He ended up dying in prison in Northern Ireland. Most evil, evil man.

01:56 – Donagh, County Fermanagh

Fermanagh was a difficult place to police: you could never be sure where the danger was coming from until it arrived.

I remember one night I was out on patrol – our patrol consisted of two vehicles with seven cops – near the village of Donagh, which had a Gaelic Athletic Club in the middle of the town. You really had no way of knowing how big a crowd was in it because the locals tended to walk there since it was so central to the village. It was about two o'clock in the morning and, as we were driving past the club, we noticed the lights were still on. We decided to check out what was going on. Unfortunately, there was an event on at the premises and the place was absolutely rammed to the gills. The greeting we got reminded me of an old Western film, where the music would stop as the sheriff walked up to the door. We went into the hall, six young fresh-faced police officers now looking at a crowd of about four hundred who did not seem best pleased to see us. Everything just stopped.

We still had options at this point and needed to decide what to do. Do you turn and live to fight another day? Or do you do what I did, which is think, we are the police and we're in charge here. I walked on into the club, but what I didn't realise at the time was that the rest of my team had stayed at the door. I had walked about twenty-five yards and still hadn't realised I was on my own.

This person was looking at me so I said to him, 'Can I speak to the manager please?' 'That's me,' he said, but this fella was no more the manager than I was. I continued, 'It's now twenty minutes to three, and this place should be closed.' 'I wonder would you fuck away off,' he said, then he punched me in the face. He had about four hundred Gaelic supporters on his side and then there was me, by now thirty yards or so away from the five other cops. My colleagues were no doubt thinking that this is a bit like the two fellas on safari: they're taking photographs of a lion and one of them changes his shoes to Nike runners. The second guy says, 'Don't be thinking you're going to run

– you'll never be able to outrun that lion.' The first fella replies, 'It doesn't matter as long as I can outrun you!'

I had just been punched in the face, which is clearly an assault on police, but I knew if I arrested this fella there would be a full-scale riot and we would get lynched, probably me first! I picked up my hat, turned and walked away. You could feel the atmosphere in the place, which was just bitterness and anger. You could almost taste the hostility in the room and I knew that if I reacted badly, somebody would be killed. I had got a smack in the face, but I was alive and really the only thing that had been badly hurt was my pride. I turned and walked away but I was angry for the rest of the night.

Twenty-four hours later we were doing a road check between Donagh and Newtownbutler and guess who comes driving along? My new friend who had punched me in the mouth. It's dark, I'm out on the road wearing my shiny new sergeant's outfit at the side of the VCP. I clocked him immediately and walked purposefully to his vehicle, leaned down and explained to him very quietly, 'You and I have unfinished business.' Suffice to say, he was arrested and duly prosecuted and, as a bonus, he got to feel the working end of a police baton, which ended badly for him. He got himself a few clips round the ankles and a charge sheet for disorderly behaviour at the VCP, then was further charged with resisting arrest and assaulting a police officer at the Gaelic club. Though, this being Fermanagh he was probably fined tuppence ha'penny or something. We got him in the long grass.

Fermanagh was a beautiful part of the world, and I spent two and a half years there. It was just unfortunate that some of the residents were too keen on talking when they should have been listening!

02:07 – Tennent Street Police Station, North Belfast

A team, made up of detectives from all over the city, was formed and based out of Tennent Street RUC station in north Belfast. They knew I was good at writing files so I got called into the team. The goal was to look into the UFF [Ulster Freedom Fighters, an offshoot of the UDA], who had been involved in a lot of murders at the time. They had been on a fairly indiscriminate killing spree for around a decade and most of the murders were unsolved. They were murdering more people than all the other terrorist groups put together, and the squad was formed specifically to deal with them. Fortunately for the public, the police had many informants in place and were subsequently able to capture and disrupt members of the UFF en route to what would have been huge atrocity shootings. A carload of them was intercepted going to kill a top republican in west Belfast; they fired an RPG-7 rocket at Connolly House, Sinn Féin's centre. They did the Ardoyne centre as well, and where they got that sort of equipment I couldn't tell you, but they had so much money through drug dealing. They could have found someone to sell the stuff easily enough and they were definitely in cahoots with their republican counterparts in the west of the city.

In 1988, James Pratt Craig, a senior UDA figure on the Shankill, was murdered in the Bunch of Grapes pub. I interviewed UVF man Crazy Craig, the taxi driver that drove James Craig to the pub where he was murdered. Crazy Craig, along with a man called King, was shot dead on the Shankill shortly after. I never had a guy in for a seven-day lift in Castlereagh as close to tipping over the edge and confessing his sins as Crazy Craig. You could actually see that he wanted the truth to come out of him; he wanted it out to escape the world he was living in. The full loyalty he had to his bosses was too great, but his loyalty was rewarded with assassination. The UDA carried out the killing because he had driven the taxi to the pub and that was enough to put him in the frame for it.

I think our squad got going in earnest around the end of 1992. The turning point came with the IRA attack on the Shankill Road which became known as the Shankill bombing. It was either the day of the Shankill bomb, or the day after, that we were all called to a meeting and told that we were to take Johnny Adair off the streets. This had come directly from Number Ten [Downing Street]. The plan was to stop looking at all the individual or even multiple murders carried out by the UFF and concentrate specifically on him, as it was fairly widely known that he was the driving force behind it all. It made sense to concentrate on the common denominator rather than have dozens of murder inquiries going on. The first task we had was to decide how we were going to go after Adair.

Coincidentally, just at that time a new offence had come into British legislation: individuals could now be charged with directing terrorism, though no one had yet been convicted of it. The idea was to try and get the ringleaders of terror groups rather than the foot soldiers. After all, it seemed as though these foot soldiers were not just expendable to all the ringleaders in terrorist organisations, they also seemed to be easily replaceable, which meant that jailing them was not having the intended impact on the terrorist's ability to act.

To charge someone with directing terrorism required us to be very inventive, but we were very lucky with Adair because of his personality. His ego was such that he liked to bum and blow about the things he did. Even if he didn't admit them fully, he liked to imply that he had; he liked to be the man in the picture and was proud of his public persona, which he nurtured. All of these traits came across in the things he said to two policemen who, unbeknown to him, were recording him.

We had got some very good neighbourhood police officers in Tennent Street: good guys who were very good at their job. They had great local knowledge and they knew Adair extremely well. Maybe he just felt comfortable talking in front of them and let his guard down, but I really think he just couldn't help myself. We decided to wire one of them up and anytime he was speaking to Adair he was able to record him bumming and blowing about what was going on, particularly after there had been a terrorist incident which involved any of his guys. These conversations were all taped.

We also gathered all the sightings of him we had from different areas across the province. This included him driving through Ardoyne with a Celtic shirt on, to try and blend in when he was targeting people. The police who stopped him on these occasions knew who he was, yet he would give his name as that of the leading IRA man in the area. When they would ask him to confirm his address, he would change tactics and ask them if they knew where the IRA man lived and tell them he was a pest controller [a concealed reference to murders that his gang carried out].

Then we looked at the financial end of his operation and gathered information on over twenty cars that he had been able to buy, all with cash. This was to be able to prove he was living beyond his means, or certainly legitimate means.

We had several offshoots to this inquiry. We dealt with a guy who lived just off the Ravenhill Road in east Belfast. He worked in radio workshops for the police in Lislea Drive but had knocked off a lot of stuff, like cameras and monitors, and sold then to Adair at quite a discount in order to line his own pockets. Adair's house, and clubroom beside it, was equipped with all this police stuff, which also meant he could monitor police radios. There was a Royal Marine from Balmoral Avenue who came to our attention at this time. He was from a lovely family, but when he came back home on leave from the Marines, he had gone to meet one of Adair's right-hand men, Winkie Dodds, to give him information on IRA men that he had encountered in his last six months tour of duty up in west Belfast. There was a similar situation with a Greenfinch [a female member of the UDR], who was based at Girdwood army barracks behind the Crumlin Road Gaol. She was also bringing information to them about republican terrorists. Both of these people were prosecuted for these offences, which bursts the bubble somewhat on the republican narrative about collusion.

The thinking from the government was that if Adair was not removed from the streets, we were never going to get peace here. One of his regular sayings, recorded by the neighbourhood beat men, was 'Shove your dove.' When we charged him with directing terrorism, he turned to me and said, 'See these hands, these can do anything. They can press the button, pull a trigger, point a guy out, anything.' Of course, that was recorded and entered into the ever-growing evidence pile. Then when we hit his house, we were ready with our case and seized all the UFF paraphernalia.

The arrests were made and while Adair was being interviewed by other detectives, I was tasked with interviewing his wife, Gina. I had met her quite a few times at different searches of their home or when going to arrest Johnny, so we weren't strangers and had a bit of a rapport – I had even had a smoke with her outside while her house was being searched, so I knew the form with her. She had been in propaganda photographs, whether for [the UDA's] C Company or being filmed with Kalashnikovs, Armalites and handguns in videos they released as a show of strength.

You couldn't mistake her, being the only one in a skirt. Plus, her eyes were so distinctive even in a balaclava. Part of the plan was to keep her in custody away from Johnny, so I brought her to Gough barracks for interrogation in Armagh rather than Castlereagh. I remember saying to her, 'Gina, obviously you've got plenty of money, you must eat out quite a lot, what's your favourite sort of food?' 'Chinese,' came the reply. 'What's your favourite Chinese dish then?' 'Gravy chip,' she said. And, of course, that ended up in the interview notes that were given in evidence.

The report against Adair was four inches thick, and there were six volumes of evidence, each of which was eight inches thick. I remember going to his solicitors, Bogue and McNulty from Carlisle Circus, with a hand truck to serve the papers for Adair's trial. The solicitor looked at the truck with all the papers and said, 'Holy fuck, what's that?' 'That's your evidence,' I said, and he remarked, 'There could be a play in this one!'

We eventually land into the court for the trial, prepared for a very lengthy one because the case was the first with this new charge. Consequently, we had no guideline but after half an hour of toing and froing from the lawyers, Adair eventually got up, pled guilty, and was sentenced to sixteen years for all the murders that were committed on his orders, and there were many!

That said, there is only one person that I know he killed personally, Noel Cardwell. He was a young lad of twenty-six but would have had the mental age of a twelve-year-old. He loved people in uniform, and as a result, he was always in and out of the RUC station in Tennent Street, close to where he lived. The guys in the sanger or enquiry office would have spoken to him as they knew him from around the area. Unfortunately for him, Adair decided he must be a tout [informant] and as a result they brought him to the shebeen C Company were operating in the Hopewell area at the bottom of the Shankill. They beat the six foot four gentle giant, then moved him to a derelict flat in Boundary Walk, which was used by the gang for interrogations. Once they had him there, he was beaten further, and his knees were smashed while they waited for Adair to arrive.

Adair had got changed into a smart black jacket and black shoes before going to the flat, where the now badly beaten Cardwell was hooded and on his knees. Adair then quite dramatically announced that the Ulster Freedom Fighters had found him guilty of treason and as such, sentenced him to the ultimate penalty – death. Adair then lifted his magnum pistol, placed it against the man's head and squeezed the trigger. Despite all his previous boasts and the impression he gave of being a big-time killer and gunman, his big secret, which only his closest friends knew, was that he had never killed anybody up to that point, previously ordering others to do the dirty work. For moment or two after killing Cardwell, Adair didn't seem to know what to do then quickly left the flat, handing the gun to someone else as he left.

The following morning, a neighbour heard groans coming from the flat and pushed open the front door to reveal an appalling sight. More than twelve hours after he had been shot, Noel Cardwell lay in a pool of blood, still alive but only just. It had been so cold during the night that his blood had been prevented from flowing at a normal rate, delaying his death and prolonging his pain for some hours. After being rushed to hospital, his body started to heat up, increasing his blood flow and he died barely fifty minutes after being found. That's the only person I know for a fact that Adair did himself. But I don't think the fella would even have been capable of being an informant. He wasn't in the UDA; he wasn't even able to live on his own and stayed with one of his sisters

I know quite a lot about Johnny Adair: he used to be a punk rocker and played the drums in a band with his mates. There were four of them in the band: two of them were Catholics from Ardoyne, which is ironic given what he ended up doing. He was a skinhead then, a back-alley glue sniffer. He joined the UDA. Young lads then joined these organisations to stop themselves from getting kneecapped over their antisocial behaviour, which shows you how dangerous it was on a nightly basis back then – you could hear automatic gunfire coming from an AK47 and some of the people doing the shooting were glue sniffers who could have hit anyone.

One thing I will concede about Johnny Adair was that he did strike terror into people's hearts, particularly in Ardoyne and west Belfast, because they could not walk the streets for fear of his guys showing up. First preference Sinn Féin voters would come up to known republicans and scream at them, 'This is all your fault.' He genuinely had everyone in republican areas nervous. I don't in any way say that to commend him and his gang, but it is true.

02:09 – HMSU, Belfast

Johnny Adair was obviously a prolific terrorist. He liked to talk and he let you know that basically he was the main man. If we weren't working on Johnny for anything, we would always stop for a chat whenever we saw him, gave him his turn just to let him know that we were keeping an eye on him. We wouldn't stop him if there was an ongoing operation directed at him.

We were driving along one night and there was Johnny Adair coming down from the Falls area of Belfast, headed for the lower Falls, so we checked in, 'Johnny's on the move, can we give him a tug?' 'Yeah, give him a tug, no problem,' was the reply. This was at the stage where there was a bit of a feud going on between him and the nationalist INLA – I think his mate, Winkie Dodds, had just been shot. We pulled him in, and he was very chirpy as usual. Unbeknown to us he'd realised that we weren't the ordinary local police by the way we were dressed (and I think at that stage we had the fast cars with the big aerials).

I said, 'So, Johnny, where are you coming from?'

'Just up the road there.'

'What were you doing up there?'

'There's a guy up there' – and he named him – 'there's a guy up there, he's in the INLA. You know it's not a very safe organisation to be in these days.'

We ended up checking this guy out – he was fine.

So roll on another couple of days and one of the guys came into work. His wife was in CID in west Belfast, and she'd told him that Johnny had been scooped a couple of days later. He was in being interviewed about his movements on the same night we'd stopped him because something else had happened, but his alibi was, 'It couldn't have been me.'

'What do you mean it couldn't have been you?' the CID said.

'Well it couldn't have been me, sure I was stopped by the Weetabix men.'

They said, 'You were stopped by who?'

He said, 'The Weetabix men – you know, those boys that can eat three Weetabix in one go? The big stormtroopers.'

'What do you mean the big stormtroopers?'

'The boys with the big sexy guns and the big sexy cars and the big sexy uniforms.' This is how Johnny referred to HMSU. He was stupid but he wasn't daft – that was Johnny, he'd turned us into his alibi.

Roll on a few years and Johnny was arrested. There had been an operation in play to arrest him, but there's never been a more fortunate man to be arrested than he was that night. If we hadn't got hold of him, the other side of his battalion would have because there was a massive feud going on between them.

When Johnny was arrested the threat was so great that a helicopter was brought in to pick him up directly. On his arrest he was taken immediately to Maghaberry prison. Until that moment we hadn't realised that Johnny was scared of flying. The two guys who arrested him were tall – one was six foot seven, and the other one was about six foot five – and when they ran him across a nearby football pitch to put him in the helicopter, you'd never seen anyone look as insignificant as he did getting into that helicopter.

A while later Adair did an interview with the press – I think it was the *Sunday World* – about how his arrest was carried out by this very specialised secret unit that was so secret only their bosses knew their names, and they were all known to each other by nicknames. Indeed they were so secretive that in the back of the helicopter they only spoke in sign language. Johnny didn't realise you can't hear each other speaking in a helicopter so we had to communicate by sign language or headphones. But that was Johnny's story, told to show his cronies how important he was that these 'Super Troopers' had to be deployed to arrest him!

Like a lot of terrorists he lived in fear of assassination from either side and as a result, the doors and windows of his home were caged and reinforced with steel bars to prevent any would-be assassination team from gaining entry. He was not so quick to tell his chums about his reaction when he'd seen the HMSU coming towards his house: he'd panicked and shouted, 'Wait, wait, I'll open the door for you. Don't be breaking everything!' He well knew it would only take a short time for our assault team to gain entry. But admitting that didn't suit his image.

02:12 – Armagh Police Station, County Armagh

I was in Armagh and, for no particular reason, I became the post-mortem guy. I certainly didn't volunteer for the role! There was a particular mortuary attendant who worked in Craigavon Hospital who I will call Ted. He was a real ghoul. Local rumour had it that Ted did the PM on his own wife and while you really shouldn't be taking humour out of a place like a mortuary, Ted was a serious wee man.

It was one of the first times I had been to Craigavon mortuary and, of course, Ted was there. The pathologist had done what he had to, and I had been given my all-important piece of paper with the cause of death on, which was all I needed. The pathologist left to go wherever he was needed next and that left just Ted and me in the mortuary. The next thing out of Ted was, 'Do you fancy a drink, young fella?' I said, 'Well, if you insist, I'll not turn you down, Ted.'

Ted was still wearing his surgical gloves and they were covered with blood and bits of body. He went over to a large first aid cabinet on the wall, it was white with a big red cross on it – of all things to be on the wall in a mortuary, it's not like your customers are going to need it! – and lifted out two glasses with his blood-soaked gloves on. I watched in disbelief as he stuck his fingers inside the glasses to pick them up. Then he set them on the desk along with a bottle of whiskey. By a very welcome stroke of luck, I don't like whiskey, which gave me a ready-made excuse! I said to Ted, 'I'm sorry, mate, I don't like whiskey.' He replied, 'That's all right,' and as I breathed a sigh of relief, he put the glasses and the bottle back in the cabinet.

This was fine until he added, 'Come on with me.' We walked back through into the cutting room where the body was still lying on the slab and toward the fridges with the trays for the bodies. He pulled open one of the fridges and out glides this body with a shroud over it, along the sides of which he had packed tins of beer to keep them cold. His next announcement was, 'Help yourself, son.' He had me. I was stuck and, very hesitantly, I took a can of beer. He went back to the cabinet and got himself a whiskey as if this was all perfectly normal.

02:16 – CID, Londonderry City Centre

One day I went into Londonderry city centre with a colleague. We had parked the car, ready to do a call, when we received a radio message to say there was a car bomb in the street that we were parked in. We were given a description of the car and the two of us got out to see if we could see it, but no car fitted the description we had been given.

We got back into the CID car and ten minutes later further details came over the radio about the suspect vehicle. I looked round again and saw that it was the car parked directly behind us. For the life of me, I don't know why we didn't just leave our car and run. Instead we drove the car up around the corner and parked it again while the area was cleared. We did our best to help with that.

The suspect car did indeed contain a large bomb, which went off and the whole street seemed to disappear completely – it was just mass destruction. It was just fortunate that lives weren't lost that day, but that was just one of hundreds of bombing incidents that took place around that time.

02:38 – CID Office, Tennent Street Police Station, North Belfast

I finally left the crime squad and found myself stationed in Tennent Street, which, along with Oldpark, was one of two stations making up C division in north Belfast. It was an incredibly busy area. I was one of two female detectives attached to the station and had to do night duty every couple of months, which I hated.

One Friday night, after it had been really quiet all evening, a huge incident sparked off in the Oldpark area. The army had searched a house and found an IRA active service unit with a substantial amount of explosives, which, although not yet primed, they were ready to move elsewhere. CID were tasked and, being the only one available, I was taken by army pig [Saracen] into the Ardoyne area. On arrival I could see and hear that a large crowd of unhappy residents had gathered outside the house where the explosives had been found. We came under heavy attack from stones, bottles and any other missile the crowd could find to throw at us as we entered the house to join our colleagues.

I immediately saw four males being held in the front room of the house and, being the night detective, I arrested each one of them under terrorist legislation. They were transferred off to Castlereagh police office for further interrogation. I remained at the house with police uniform personnel from Oldpark and the ATO, who turned out to be a Corporal Howard. All were there to assist with further searches of the house. All I could hear was the crowd outside shouting abuse as they got angrier with every passing minute.

I went upstairs. I had just finished searching one of the bedrooms and moved on to the bathroom to search it. I lifted the lid up from the toilet and saw packets of something down in the bowl, which, rather disgustingly someone had defecated on top of. I stood there, wondering how on earth I was going to get these packets out of the toilet when Corporal Howard appeared behind me and said, 'This is neither the place nor the job for a lady,' and he instantly set about retrieving those packages. I always remembered him for his act of kindness and gentlemanly behaviour, which was not commonplace in an area like that, never mind the circumstances we found ourselves in.

Once all the maps and so on of the find had been completed, I was taken back to Tennent Street where bosses from headquarters, along with our divisional commanders, had arrived, waiting for news of the incident. Four terrorists had been arrested and countless lives had been saved by the recovery of the explosives, which were dealt with by Corporal Howard.

On Monday evening I was back on duty in Tennent Street driving the CID car down Agnes Street with my sergeant, when one of those awful dull thuds reverberated around the area. It was the unmistakable sound of a bomb exploding and it always made me feel sick to my stomach. It was a short time later that we found out it was a bomb at the swimming baths on the Falls Road. Two local civilians had been killed at the scene when the explosion blew out part of the wall of the baths. An ATO man had also been killed instantly as he had stepped on a pressure plate connected to a secondary device: a booby-trap bomb that had been clearly prepared for just such an eventuality. He was part of an army unit carrying out a follow-up examination of the area to make it safe. Corporal John Howard, aged twenty-nine, was married and came from Warwickshire.

02:43 – Special Branch, Coffee-Time Reflections

We used to have a monthly liaison meeting with the Garda. They would come up to see us, we never went down South. The Garda that we dealt with in the Branch were first class. They were fully aware that the real enemy was the IRA, but they were under political control and could exercise very little effort against them – the government at the time was not backing them up. The Garda in those days was a very political organisation. I think it's eased a bit for them now.

They would come up to us with around twenty questions

every time, mainly about the UVF. They were terrified of more Dublin/Monaghan-type bombings happening. Our boys would give them everything and we'd always be asked what we wanted to know from the Garda. Each desk would give them ten questions, but we never got an answer. In the end I just stopped asking, I didn't even bother drawing up questions to give them. One of the bosses at quite a high level would come along and say, 'The Garda are up on Friday. Have questions ready for them or send them to them in advance.' I never bothered because they never told you a damn thing officially. Unofficially they were quite happy to talk to you, but they couldn't be seen to be doing it. The Garda were prevented from helping us, no doubt about that.

I identified 159 murders that were carried out in the UK or the Republic of Ireland. A few of the victims were shot on the border, some were alleged informants, and a couple took place in England. But most of the murders, at least 145 of them, were in South Armagh. Soldiers and policemen. Every one of those attacks were planned, conceived and executed from the Republic of Ireland. The killers could get away after the attack – five minutes was all they really needed to get across the border to safety.

South Armagh Provisional IRA didn't even bother doing forensic washups. If you were in Tyrone or wherever else, you'd go straight from the attack to the washhouse – into the shower, burn your clothes or put them in the washing machine with bags of detergent. It was all part of their routine after an op. In the follow-up to an operation, quite a few of them were arrested in the bath or shower, their clothes burning in the grate. In South Armagh they didn't even bother because they knew the Garda wouldn't bother them. They used to go straight to the pub for a few pints of Guinness after shooting at the army or police in Northern Ireland.

03:10 – Ardoyne Area, North Belfast

I was the military liaison officer in north Belfast for a number of years in the 1970s. Everybody in the area knew who I was as I was always on patrol or at the army base in the area – the walking target in the green suit! On one particular night, I had gone out on foot patrol with the military around the Ardoyne area. We saw this young girl being attacked by a group of male youths – unsavoury types that we knew to be members of the youth wing of the IRA. They were giving her a bit of a hammering and I strongly suspected from their actions that they were about to sexually assault her. I intervened and dealt with the young fellas, then walked the young girl home and handed her safely to her mother. I thought no more about it.

It was months later, and we were coming down the Crumlin Road, just before the shop fronts, when this elderly woman walked up beside me as if she was just walking along. But then she started talking away without looking at me. 'Thanks very much, son, for looking after my daughter, she was going to get a severe hiding or worse. But since you got her home that night, I have managed to get her out of the district. She's living happily elsewhere. I was wanting to speak to you or get hold of you anyway.' She was walking and talking at the same time as if she was not near or with me whatsoever. Then she said, 'I'm going to turn down here, you just follow me down and when I throw my cigarette down at a particular driveway, you'll know that's where you need to be.'

And that's exactly what she did. I made arrangements to have the house searched and it turned out it was owned by Brendan McClenaghan, the IRA's top sniper. In the house we found ammunition, explosives, weapons and a huge bag of intelligence documents – we later learned that these had all been moved into the house to be moved on somewhere else fairly rapidly. We also found the Woodmaster rifle that had been used in the murder of Corporal Marshall from the Gordon Highlanders Regiment. [Corporal Jack Marshall, aged twenty-five, was a married father of two from Dundee in Scotland. He was shot on 28 August 1977 by the IRA when his foot patrol came under fire in the Brompton Park area of Ardoyne and died shortly later in the Royal Victoria Hospital. A nine-year-old girl was also injured by bullet fragments. Brendan McClenaghan received five life sentences for this and other murders. As he was led away by prison officers from the court, he gave a clenched fist salute to relatives in the public gallery. He had played no part in the trial, stating he was a republican prisoner of war and dismissed his lawyers. He stood with his back to the bench as the judge read out his hour-long judgment.]

The woman lived a few doors down and had seen the stuff being brought in, all the bags and boxes going being delivered. The house was well chosen as it was not visible from the OP at Flax Street Mill (this was before the OP at the bus station was built).

McClenaghan had not been at home when we'd raided his house, so his details were circulated among security force personnel with the instruction, 'Lift on Sight'. He subsequently rang us at the ops room in Ewarts's Mill in Flax Street, where the army were based in Ardoyne (they all knew the number for the ops room) and he said he was desperate to get picked up because the IRA were going to kill him. Now, this was a guy who was their top gun when it came to shoots. It turned out he had borrowed money out of funds belonging to the IRA, misappropriating three hundred quid. He had been given the opportunity to put it back but hadn't bothered. He had also fallen out with some of the senior IRA team in the area and had got very,

very cocky and just wasn't behaving himself the way they wanted him to. So much so that when the money had gone missing, he was terrified. He knew that he was going to get nutted [shot in the head].

We picked him up by arrangement at the Butler Street/Crumlin Road junction thinking, of course, that it was a come on to lure us into the killing zone of a well-planned ambush. I put a lot of teams in place all round the area to keep us safe; it was saturated with police and military personnel. But as soon as we had him in the back of the vehicle he started to talk: he admitted to fourteen murders and several attempted murders. Unfortunately, it was of no value; when it comes to evidential admissions we have to wait until formal interview.

I've never listened to anything like it in all my life, it was an absolute cacophony of 'I did this ... I killed him ... I shot so-and-so ... I opened fire at ...' it just went on and on. The amount of stuff he was admitting to seemed endless. He was charged and convicted, I made out my statement of evidence for the court, which I attended, but he pleaded guilty, and I didn't have to present it. He was probably told to plead guilty by the IRA as he was no use to them anymore. I think he knew it was all over; he had done too much.

I can't even hazard a guess as to the number of lives that wee woman probably saved, and it all stemmed from rescuing that young girl from the junior IRA men and bringing her home safety. Just doing my job.

When we had McClenaghan in the back of the car, I couldn't help but notice that he kept looking at me and when I returned his gaze he said, 'You. I had you in my sights more times than you could think of, but I wasn't allowed to shoot you.' He explained that Martin Meehan, the veteran IRA commander in the area, had given instructions that I wasn't to be shot.

Meehan's first wife had died in the mid-seventies and the cortège was to leave the family home in Northwood Drive to make its way to Milltown Cemetery. There had been some concern that, as it passed Alliance Avenue at the Bullring, it might be attacked by loyalists from the Deer Park, Cliftonville and Oldpark Roads, but I got all the necessary security in place at those potential flashpoints. I was actually standing at the junction of the Bullring myself as the cortège came past. I came to attention and saluted as it passed, as we did in those days. The woman lying in that coffin was a mother and a civilian who had suffered badly from cancer for four years. Meehan later rang Oldpark RUC station and thanked the duty inspector for what we had done and for the respect shown at his wife's funeral.

Another encounter came the day that Special Branch rang me to say, 'Martin Meehan needs to know that the UVF are targeting him in just the same way that he is targeting them.' I decided this was something that couldn't be done over a phone call as it was something very specific that had come out of one of the clubs in the lower Shankill Road. I got a message to Meehan to come and see me. When he arrived at the guardroom at Oldpark station, I came out to see him and said, 'Come on, let's go for a walk'. We went out into the yard as I wanted him to feel he wasn't being surveilled; to find out if I could get under his skin a bit. You never knew with these guys, sometimes you can turn them in a heartbeat. We were dandering round, chatting away, then he turned to me, looked me in the eye and said, 'You actually really mean that. You really want to warn me, don't you?' I explained to him that it was my job as a policeman, that I was there to protect life and limb. It's one of the founding principles of policing. He responded, 'If we were in charge and I was in whatever position of authority in this company of ours, how would you react to me?' I told him that I was a policeman and that I would do my job in exactly the same way. I said, 'You confuse what you think of us with what we actually are.'

There were another couple of occasions with him. One day I was walking past his house and he called me, so I stopped. He asked me, 'If the army are planning to carry out any searches in this area do you plan that or organise it for them?' I replied, 'Not at all. The army act upon whatever intelligence they have, or any request from a different agency to do something, then they go and do it. I'm the policeman. My job is to make sure there are no excesses; that everything is properly recorded; and if criminality is discovered, or any complaint made, that it's properly dealt with.' He shook his head and said, 'Great answer.' I was still wondering what he meant by that, when he started talking about school and about who and what we were. Then he said, 'There by the grace of God, go you or I.' 'What do you mean by that, Martin?' 'Well, I could be you and you could be me, that's the flip of a coin.' I said, 'You can call it the flip of a coin, I call it choice. I chose to be what I am. I come from a background not dissimilar to yours.'

I was a Catholic, brought up in north Belfast and played hurling and Gaelic football for Ardoyne in my teens. My father was from the Falls Road. My grandfather was in charge of the IRA in Belfast during World War Two. My grandfather on my mother's side was in the Royal Irish Constabulary and was an ex-soldier. I was lucky. I had the ethos of how to conduct yourself and live your life – my father was a staunch trade unionist who had no time for political terrorism of any description. That was his upbringing. His father had drummed it in him not to become involved in anything because it was a futile exercise.

On reflection I think Meehan got the message. The last thing he said to me was, 'I hear you're getting promoted. Congratulations.' Where he had heard that was beyond me, but he actually stopped me in the street to say it. 'Where are you going?' he asked me. I told him, 'I don't know, probably some bog station somewhere at the border.' His reply amused me, 'You don't want to be going there, that's not safe'. 'You think this place is safe?' He said, 'Oh, you're fine here. It's not been too bad, has it?' With that, it all just suddenly fell into place what McClenaghan had said, that I wasn't allowed to be touched, not that it made me feel any better.

03:12 – CID Office, Armagh Police Station

When I was in CID in Armagh, we used to do callout on night duty. I got called out one night to a car crash: a police car, an armoured Cortina, was involved and several officers had been killed. They were patrolling just outside Armagh city when they received a call to attend a shop in which the intruder alarm had gone off. It was the middle of the night and they had obviously been trying to make their way to the premises as quickly as possible. Those armoured vehicles were always top-heavy and, because of the weight of the armour, difficult to stop, and handling was poor. They collided with a small stone bridge on a country road and three officers were killed, including a part-time reserve girl in the back, the driver and front seat passenger.

It was a very sad scene to have to attend. The most difficult part was trying to get the three bodies into body bags: there wasn't a bone in their bodies that wasn't broken from the impact of the crash. It was the saddest thing. I still have nightmares about it.

The young lad who was driving the car had originally joined the police in England, but he'd suffered badly from homesickness, and had returned to Northern Ireland where he'd joined the RUC. He got stationed in Armagh and was not long there when he and another policeman were attacked while opening one of the town barriers – in those days these were used to seal town centres off to prevent car bombs being brought in at night. As they were out working at the barrier, a hand grenade was thrown at them. It exploded and they also came under fire; both were shot several times. They were both lucky to survive the incident. The young lad had only just come back off the sick after being shot and blown up. So if ever somebody wasn't meant to be a policeman it must have been him.

The other lad that was with him at the barrier also recovered and, while he was doing so, he studied for the sergeant's exam and passed it. He was, however, a terrible gambler and at that time they had gaming machines in the club at Gough barracks. In those days you could have got your pay in cheque form instead of being paid straight into the bank. The club in Gough lifted so much money you could cash your wages at the bar, which was something he did but, unfortunately, he'd stick it straight in the fruit machine. He got seconded to us in CID and, while he was with us, we would have whip rounds among the team to give his wife money for housekeeping because he was gambling his wages. Then, having fully recovered from the gun and bomb attack, he got promoted to sergeant and was sent to Ballymena station. A year later he shot himself.

Jack Herman became chief constable and he made sure that all the gambling machines in stations with big payouts were removed. It was the sensible thing to do. I don't know what happens, but it's surprising the number of cops who drank, gambled or whatever their vice. They needed to have to have something to focus on I suppose to take their mind off work and the dangers that came with it. Really, they needed help, but post-traumatic stress disorder wasn't addressed then so no one knew what to do. Tragic, really tragic.

03:15 – Ballymoney Police Station, County Antrim
I was in Ballymoney RUC station in 1999 and was put into one of the Amber Serials [Temporary Mobile Support Units] that were formed in July to deal with the building tension in the area in connection with the Drumcree/ Dunloy parades. Normally there would just be pockets that we had to keep an eye on but with it being a predominantly Protestant area, tensions were running high across the entire area we had to cover.

During one particular night shift in the Amber Serial, I ended up being the only person in our crew trained in the use of the baton gun. We got a call to the Carnany estate following reports that a petrol bomber had been seen moving around the area. We arrived at the entrance to the estate and saw a lonely figure standing about a hundred yards in front of us at the corner. We got out of our vehicle, which was a borrowed army Land Rover, and watched as this guy lit what we believed to be a petrol bomb. I lifted up my baton gun, loaded it, and got ready to fire in case he came any closer. For whatever reason he did not come towards us but threw the now lit petrol bomb in our general direction, which landed about twenty yards in front of us and started to bounce.

This genius had obviously not done the 'how to throw a petrol bomb at the police' course: he had used a plastic Coke bottle!

03:23 – Belleek Police Station, County Fermanagh
I passed out of the training centre in 1973 and my first station was Belleek – Belleek by name, Belleek by nature –

in Fermanagh. Because our squad was so big, they couldn't take us all at one time on the driving course when we left Enniskillen, so half the squad went on the course and the other half went to their stations. I was in the half that went to the driving course first.

My friend Bertie came out of the Depot on Friday and went straight to the station on Saturday night. On his first night, six rockets were fired at the station – one rocket came crashing through it. I met Bertie on Monday and said to him, 'That was some bloody christening you got.' He said, 'Wait till I tell you, you'll see when you're in it. The bedrooms are small and there are sandbags in the windows but when you go in, you will know mine: my fingerprints are in the lino!'

Belleek station was right on the border, with a river running past the back of it. The Irish army were meant to guard the station from their side; they were meant to have a military post in place there, but every time the station was attacked, they weren't there. The sergeant in charge of the Irish army at that location was from Belleek – he was on our list for arrest when he came home next.

We had a macron Land Rover [before the bulletproof Hotspurs, Land Rovers were made of macron]. We often had to take an eight-mile drive just to get from one end of the town to the other. There was a short way, a distance of 200 yards, but that road went into the Republic and then came back into Northern Ireland on the other side of the town. Unless we were unarmed, we weren't allowed to go over that way. Hence the eight-mile trip. You went out of Belleek, about three or four miles towards Kesh, then you went over a bridge and then back down the Shore Road into the other side of the town. The bridge that we crossed had been blown up by the IRA and the army had put a Bailey bridge in its place. I think it's still there. It was always a nightmare going over it because you were waiting for something to be under it and detonated as you crossed.

We were left with this eight-mile journey to get a distance of 200 yards. We did scoot the short way and chance it the odd time, but the Irish army always tried to stop us. It would have been reported as an international incident and border incursion, so we just said, 'No, we were unarmed.'

I remember we got a call that involved the two sergeants – our sergeant and one from the Garda – who wanted to meet to have a chat. Six of us went out and met the Garda sergeant and another officer at the bridge. The two sergeants stood having chat and I stood on the bridge with my rifle. My left foot was over the border, in the south. The Garda came up to me and looked down at my foot, then looked at me, then back at the offending foot. I noticed the Garda sergeant looking over, so I held my ground. The Garda sergeant came over and tapped the Garda on the shoulder. He turned round and went, 'What?' The sergeant told him, 'Stop making insinuations with your eyes.'

03:32 – CID Office, Londonderry

One night, during the height of the hunger strike disturbances, a colleague and I got called to the shooting of a soldier in the Creggan estate. We had been told the area was clear.

We just drove around in ordinary cars at that time, and I recall that we came in from the back road, just at the top end of the Creggan estate. My first thought was that it was just like the middle of the day because there were so many people on the streets, actively causing bother, though it was actually three or four o'clock in the morning.

There were barricades everywhere, many of them alight, and a lot of burning lorries, buses, anything the rioters could get their hands on. The roads, of course, were littered with debris. As we drove past an entry, I could see down to where the soldiers were standing at the scene of the shooting, but from where I was, I could also see five terrorists organising themselves in preparation for attacking the army. Very seldom did you ever see the terrorists themselves in action, but these were armed to the teeth; every one of them had long arms, a mix of rifles and Armalites.

We were sitting there in a car, roads around us blocked, with nothing but Walther pistols to defend ourselves. All we could do was warn the soldiers below that there were a number of active gunmen and where they were. Then we drove like the clappers to try and get out of the area. With hindsight we should never have even gone into the estate. Two men in suits in the middle of the night in a car, during rioting? We might as well have had 'police' written on the side of it and a blue lamp on the roof!

04:41 – Woodbourne Police Station, West Belfast

My story relates to a time when I was a sergeant in Woodbourne RUC station, west Belfast. I was living with my wife and two children in Newtownards, but my mother and father were living in our family home in Ainsworth Street, Belfast, which is in the Shankill Road area. Significant tension had been building up in the Shankill, a loyalist/Protestant area of Belfast, because of the pending Anglo-Irish Agreement, ultimately signed by Margaret Thatcher and Irish taoiseach Garret FitzGerald. The agreement brought about significant hostility from the loyalist unionist community across the province, which ultimately led to violence. One demonstration against the agreement was held in Belfast and attended by Ian Paisley and Jim Molyneaux. Here Paisley made the famous three 'no's speech and it was estimated to have been attended by as many as 240,000 people. I was on duty myself that day and saw what was happening first-hand.

Regrettably, there were elements in the loyalist community who decided that RUC officers and families of RUC officers should be alienated within the community, despite many of those officers not being content themselves with the agreement. Nevertheless, they enforced it because it was the law of the land and that was their duty.

My parents would have been opposed to the agreement. My father was an ex-Royal Marine and World War Two D-Day veteran. Both worked in the community but, living on the Shankill Road as they did, and having a son in the RUC meant they were well known in the area and of course to paramilitaries. Following the agreement, they experienced a lot of hardship in that little two-up, two-down house in Ainsworth Street. My father would have gone for a drink in the area but after the agreement, he was alienated within his own community and certain elements, particularly those in the UVF, despised the fact their son was in the RUC. This culminated in various threats being made directly to my father, who being an ex-Royal Marine ignored them and said nothing to my mother. He did, however, tell me what had happened.

I was deeply concerned because I was aware that many RUC families were having to move house because of the Anglo-Irish Agreement. I could sense that a similar fate awaited my parents as the verbal threats became more sinister. My mother received anonymous threats by phone that both of them would be killed in their own home or petrol bombed when they were sleeping. If they didn't get out of their own volition, they would be burned or forced out because I was in the RUC.

My mother was distraught about all of this. My father was still determined to face them down, despite the threats coming from members of a local club that he had been a member of for decades. He realised they were becoming more frequent and very real. Over a few weeks, they heightened considerably and graffiti, which read 'SS RUC OUT', was written on the wall of their home. I knew they would stop at nothing to get my parents out. The graffiti was quite unnerving for my mother as she worked in the Shankill Leisure Centre and was very apprehensive when it came time to return home. My father was still adamant that he was not going to move house or be intimidated.

The house was petrol bombed in the middle of the night. Fortunately they survived that, but it became so apparent that these loyalist paramilitaries – the UVF – would have them move. The turning point for all of this was when I was called over to Tennent Street to speak to the authorities there and they told me they had information that my mother and father would be murdered in their own home if they did not leave. I was told the police could keep an eye on the house for the next twenty-four hours to give them time to gather their belongings and get out. The police said it was a very sinister development, but they were convinced the threat was real and my parents would be murdered.

It was over to me to convince them, my father in particular, that they had to move – they had no choice, they would be killed. This was the most difficult thing for my mother and father, who were both born and reared in the Shankill Road. They'd grown up there, gone to school there, all their friends and family lived in the area, they'd been there all their life and it was so deeply upsetting to tell them they had no choice but to leave their home and be taken to a safe house. I cannot put into words how deeply stressed and upset they were. The police in Tennent Street did as they said: they kept watch on the house while my mother and father gathered what belongings they had. Within that twenty-four-hour period, with police surrounding the house, a van arrived, gathered up their furniture, and then in the most undignified manner they left because of loyalist paramilitaries.

The irony of that I don't think could be lost on anyone: my father was a D-Day veteran, my grandfather fought in the First World War and was at the Battle of the Somme, my brother was serving in the Enniskillen Dragoons, yet simply because I was a serving member of the RUC, my mother and father had to sacrifice their home. Having planned to see out their days in peace where they had been born, they now had to start again in the latter stages of their lives.

They moved to Newtownards, where they knew no one apart from me, my wife and the kids. They eventually got another small house there and I suppose they did live quite happily because they were close to my wife and kids and when my brother came back from the army, he settled in Newtownards as well. They made the best of it because, sad as that is, they had no choice. I think to this day the paramilitaries have a lot to answer for. Loyalists? They don't know the meaning of the word loyal.

For the record, this is just one story – mine was not the only family affected around that time. Just over four hundred families had to move out of their homes after the signing of the Anglo-Irish Agreement, most of them serving police officers and the rest their extended families.

05:00 – Hastings Street Police Station, West Belfast

Thursday, 14 August 1969. Sergeant Blair Wallace (later to become an ACC [assistant chief constable]), Eric McAdam, four others and I went to the bottom of the Falls Road at Dover Street to reinforce police under attack. This was the second night of rioting organised to take the pressure off the rioting in Londonderry. We found a serious riot in progress: a mob from the Falls had burned the Scarsdale Hall; a Falls

Road man had stolen a large digger and was attempting to knock down a hydro pole with it – he got chased. I heard transmissions from Hastings Street police station on the police radio – they were under fire from Divis Street flats. I head the person transmitting say they were taking cover under the tables. Police employed Shorland armoured cars and fired Browning .303 machine gun rounds into Divis flats. They killed the suspected shooter, twenty-year-old Hugh McCabe, a Catholic soldier home on leave. He had been firing with a .303 Lee-Enfield rifle. As a result of the use of Shorland .303 machine guns, a nine-year-old child, Patrick Rooney, was killed.

We were at the junction of Dover Street trying to keep the warring parties apart. I saw a young man wearing a white shirt go into the intersection and throw stones up the Falls Road. This was a twenty-six-year-old Protestant named Herbert Roy. I went into the intersection to grab him and to pull him back into Dover Street. He had his right arm raised to throw a stone and his back was arched to his rear. As I reached out to grab him, he fell rearwards landing flat on his back. I saw a red stain on his white shirt. I subsequently learned he had been shot in the heart. I shouted to my nearby comrades, 'He has been shot!' I immediately felt what was like a hammer blow wielded by a giant hit my right foot. I knew I had been shot. I was able to remain upright and I took cover in Dover Street.

A civilian took me in his car to the Royal Victoria Hospital, via the Shankill Road. The scene at the hospital was like a front-line casualty aid station in a war. A police detective put my uniform and personal protection weapon into a large bag, and I was put on a trolley and put in a room with two other wounded. One was a policeman.

He had been driving a Shorland that had been attacked and had crashed. He had a head injury. The other man was a Catholic rioter and when he realised we were the hated RUC, he got down from his trolley and attacked my colleague who, due to his injury, was unable to help himself. I got down from my trolley and went to his aid. The RUC detective who had taken my clothes came in and separated us.

I was then taken away for surgery, which was completely successful even though the bullet had crossed right through from the front of my foot to the heel and over all the small bones therein. The surgeon told us that he could not understand how I had escaped injury that would have given me a limp for the rest of my life. I think the reason was that the bullet, a .38 calibre, was fired from a distance and was an old round from an old gun left over from the previous Troubles of the mid-fifties. It was probably travelling at a relatively slow speed and took the line of least resistance around the bones. Nevertheless, a bullet from the same gun put paid to the unfortunate Herbert Roy. Of the sergeant and six men who went to Dover Street and the Falls Road that night, two were shot and three injured by stones. Only sergeant Blair Wallace and Eric McAdam remained standing.

When I was in the hospital, gunmen opened fire from St Comgall's School upon the police in Dover Street. They used a rifle, a Thompson sub-machine gun [SMG] and handguns. Their fire was returned by a sergeant from York Road, who ran across the road right into the field of fire using an SMG to full effect. The gunmen escaped down the rear of the school and down the rear of the Ritz cinema, where they met my late brother John who had come from Donegall Pass police station. He was a reserve officer at that time. He opened fire on the gunmen with an SMG, and it is believed he killed two or three of them.

While I was in the hospital, my wife, Phyllis, was awoken

from her sleep at 5 a.m. by a knock on the door. When she opened the door, she found her father and her uncle Jim, a detective inspector, standing there. Jim said, without any preamble, 'He's been shot, we don't know if he's alive or dead!' This was quite a shock for any wife but especially one who was eight months pregnant with her second child. Phyllis had to endure the trip to the hospital not knowing if she was a widow. She still remembers this with total clarity to this day.

When we came to Canada, ten years after I was shot, I joined Peel Regional Police, a department between Toronto and Hamilton. I served there for a while and then left. I started a Traffic Ticket Defence Company in the City of Brampton. A friend from Belfast introduced me to her brother, Owen, whom she had sponsored as an immigrant into Canada. Owen had been an alcoholic in Belfast and in Brampton. He had reformed completely and had been responsible for the creation of a halfway house in the city. For this service to the community he had recently been made a justice of the peace operating out of the Brampton Courthouse. This was the court in which I conducted much of my Traffic Ticket defence business. We met at our friends' home for dinner and had a friendly time together.

A number of weeks passed, and Owen asked me to accompany him into Toronto to order his judge's robes. We retired for lunch to an officers' club I belonged to in downtown Toronto. We arrived at the latter end of the lunch period and were the only two in the dining room. While we had lunch, we talked about Belfast in August 1969. Owen told me he had been at the top of the Falls Road while I was at the bottom. He was shooting down the road in my direction. We agreed upon the probability that he was the person who shot me. The subject of Herbert Roy or my brother's action was not raised. Owen and I remained friends and had many more lunches together when at the courthouse. This friendship remained until he died.

05:04 – Life in an RUC Family

We attended friends' funerals, we the wives and widows. We were always silent and in the shadows. Trying to hold a home together and raise children in the midst of a terrible abyss of guns, bullets and death. We never watched or listened to the television news; nor did we read the newspapers. Death was already all around, along with grief, pain and tragedy, and our husbands were fighting right in the middle of it and arranging funerals on a regular basis. We only stayed sane because we truly believed that it wouldn't happen to our husbands ... that it couldn't happen to *my* husband.

The knock came to the door one morning at 5.00 a.m., a loud hard knock to the front door, a policeman's knock. It was pitch black outside. My husband had not come home again, and I was about to give birth to our second child. My father and his brother, Detective Chief Superintendent Jim Cunningham, were at the door. They looked at me and said, 'Brian has been shot and we don't know if he is alive or dead.'

Silence, silence. I pulled on some clothes and went to the hospital. That relatively short journey seemed to take hours. No words were said. I walked into the hospital in silence, then a surgeon came up to me. He asked me to confirm my name, then told me that my husband would live. He said, 'Your husband had an angel sitting on his shoulder when he was shot, the bullet went in at his toe. It travelled the length of his foot and was lodged at his heel. Now, it was physically impossible for his small bones not to be shattered, but his bones are all intact. This means that he will heal and will not have a limp.'

I was in a fog of so many emotions, but mostly my fragile shell of imaginary protection had just shattered: now I knew that it could happen to him. Nowhere to run and hide, no one to talk it through with or help me to gather myself to understand. How could I go on? What could I tell myself now in order to keep him safe in my head and cope, just cope?

Brian was late again another time. He telephoned to tell me and I could hear a weird noise in the background. He said it was bullets bouncing off the armoured plate over the windows. He was taking a class of instruction, studying for the sergeant's exam, right there in the middle of it. You can just imagine the men all sitting in their battle gear with rifles and machine guns beside them, learning stuff for the sergeant's exam as the bullets pinged off the armour.

Or the time when I was in the wee grocers shop at the bottom of the Castlereagh Road. Brian and the two children were in the car waiting. I was just putting my vegetables in my basket when Brian came running to tell me to drop everything and run as local hoods had seen him and had gone running off to get guns to shoot him.

I knew that I had to do something, anything, to help our men in some way. I had heard Brian mention that the gun holsters they were provided with were no good. They had a big flap over the top and it took several seconds to get the gun out and cocked. I went into the city to a local abattoir and purchased a big sheet of black leather. Brian helped me to design a new holster where the men could put their finger directly on the trigger and get the gun out in seconds. I would tirelessly cut, punch holes and hand sew those holsters. Many a member of the RUC had at least one of my holsters. We also designed a much better soft leather shoulder holster for the detectives that were a great success. One evening a sergeant called Jimmy Blakley came over to our home in Bangor to get his new holster. He served in the same station where my husband was his inspector. He brought his wife and we had a great evening – they had just purchased a new bungalow not too far away from us and were about to move in. I remember him telling us about Canada and how he wished that he had the guts to take his family there to live. He said that he dreaded to think of the legacy he was passing on to his family as he didn't feel he had the courage to do it.

About a week later Jimmy and Inspector Willie Murtagh were killed while on patrol. My daughter took the phone call informing us of their murder. Then one year to the day, Jimmy's only son put his service pistol to his head and pulled the trigger. That was the legacy. I remember the day his widow moved into 'their' bungalow; Brian put up the light fixtures and plugs for her. All I could hear was Jimmy saying, 'What sort of a legacy am I handing down to my family?' There were no words: no words to describe the pain, the dreadful picture of Jimmy in our living room and then seeing this everlasting loneliness for his poor widow. I don't know if she survived the emotion or if she too died. For surely it was all just too much to bear, and for no one ever to ask, 'How are you doing?' or 'Can I help?' We had no one and had to shut up and pretend we were managing, never knowing if our family was going to be next, blown up by a booby-trap bomb that had been put there during the night by a killer.

There was absolutely no help for either the officers or the wives and families of wives or widows. In later years they started a Widows' Association, which is still in existence today – they go on trips together and so on – but there was still no emotional help for those with horrible, imprinted memories. Many would just walk about in a daze or zombie-like state. No ordinary person would have a clue.

I think that keeping our feelings so tightly in place and knowing we could never talk or share them with anyone somehow created a shell covering.

Many of the men took to drinking due to stress. When my husband was a sergeant, he sat beside the same driver in the same Land Rover for three years, never less than sixty hours per week. No one knew the driver would go home and consume a twenty-ounce bottle of whiskey every night. No one had a clue until one day he collapsed. He was taken off operational duty but was well looked after by his colleagues.

We lived with a loaded gun. Slept with it under the bed. Police carried their personal protection weapons everywhere they went; we were constantly looking over our shoulders, never ever driving off without checking under the car for bombs. Policemen were being shot in their homes, meaning home was no longer a sanctuary.

We lived in a wee cul-de-sac with about eight houses. It was on a steep hill and we could see the whole city at night when it was dark. One night Brian came home very late and I went to greet him at the side door. Just about one minute after he came inside, we both stopped dead because we heard another vehicle coming up the hill. It was at that moment we both realised that, subconsciously, we knew the sounds of all our neighbours' vehicles. We looked at each other and both said, 'That's not a neighbour's car.' I called 999 to get help and Brian put the lights out and went outside. He crawled on his belly up the driveway towards our closed iron gate. It was very dark, and Brian had his gun out and was ready to shoot. A man had got out of the unfamiliar vehicle and disappeared behind a tree across the road from our house. The police arrived and got him. It turned out to be nothing important. He was leaving our neighbour's girl home from a date and had gone to the toilet behind the tree. He must have been very shocked to be surrounded by armed police.

The truth was, there was no place that felt safe.

My mum and dad had a bakery shop, and I would be there every day along with my two children. Everything was grand while inside the shop, but as soon as I stepped outside, no one would speak to me as I was a policeman's wife and a policeman's daughter. There was no one to talk to or share how this felt. Silence and more silence until I felt about to break into pieces. One day the UDA called for a general strike and although businesses did not want to close, they had no choice – they would have been set on fire or bombed that night. Our bakery shop was just packed with women and the line went right down the street outside to the Co-op grocery shop. Well, mummy and I had been at our shop since about 5 a.m. that day baking away on the gas griddle. Mum baked soda bread and I baked the staple, wheaten bannocks. We were exhausted, but determined to keep going and not succumb to the men who wanted us to close.

The shop was full, and I heard a loud male voice shouting that we had to close. I came out from the back where I had been baking. I saw a man wearing a balaclava over his face – he had a big gun. I am not sure where my rage came from, but it welled up from somewhere deep within and I yelled out to all the women in the shop. I went outside to the queue of women waiting for bread and I shouted to them to say that this ne'er-do-well wants us to close and how did they feel about that. I truly felt that I could have strangled that man. I told my father that we were not closing. My dad, who had spent thirty-four years in the police before he'd retired, said quietly that we had no choice, or we would have no shop in the morning. So the bad man won once more through fear. People gave in and that was the only fuel they, the bad guys, needed. For these were ignorant men. One minute they were unemployed, standing on a street corner, betting their benefit money on the horses and then going home to beat their wives when they lost, to all of a sudden having a gun in their hand and having people fear them. They were ne'er-do-wells, thugs on both sides. Not one better than the other and they were governing how things were going. They decided who got through the roadblocks, or for that matter, who lived and who died.

Jean McConville was a woman who lived up the Falls Road with her ten children. One evening, she went to her front door to find an injured soldier who had been shot by the IRA. She put her arm around him and tried to comfort him and, for that, the IRA came for her. She became one of the Disappeared [people believed to have been abducted, murdered and secretly buried by the IRA]. The IRA denied for years that they had killed her, but the general population knew only too well that they had murdered this wee woman for showing a little kindness to an injured man. Her body was later found in the south of Ireland and it was discovered that it was the IRA who had murdered her.

Brian's best friend Eric, a detective, came to the station to tell Brian that my uncle Cecil, a well-known and respected constable, had been murdered. Brian had to drive up to my parents' house and tell Daddy that his youngest brother had been murdered sitting outside a local bank – he didn't even have a chance to draw his gun. Cecil was a giant of a man in so many ways: he was very tall and had a great big generous heart. The family called him The Cub, even though he was nearly seven feet tall. I remember his lovely wife speaking on the radio the very next evening and saying that there would never be peace until all the children of Northern Ireland were educated together and no child was divided by religion. My dad never really recovered from the death of his brother and died just six years later.

We tried so hard to keep our children away from danger and never spoke about it in front of them. But every night the children would hear the bombs going off and shots being fired. We lived outside the city, but Belfast is in a valley and night-time sounds travelled and sounded like they were on our doorstep. Gillian, our little girl, would pick sores in her face at night, I put gloves on her, but I couldn't stop her. She did not eat properly, the only nourishment she really got was a bottle of Complan I would give her when she was asleep. At age five and a half, she weighed only twenty-seven pounds and wore baby size clothing of eighteen months. Our son, John, had alopecia and his hair fell out in bundles. The children dreaded their daddy leaving. My husband went to England every other week to give lectures to the army before they came to the province for their three-month tour. He had to arrange for the staff car that picked him up to go to the airport to park 500 yards away so the children didn't see him leaving.

As a wife and mother I tried my best, but everyone suffered one way or another. My husband and I made the very difficult decision to come to Canada to give our children a better chance at life. We came as a family of four and now there are twenty, including husbands, wives and grandchildren and great-grandchildren.

Who knows if we were right to come away and leave the land we loved that will always be our hearts? We miss the culture, the soft sweet smells and all our many generations of family who are buried there, and I know Brian sorely missed his career. But we celebrate our family being free to live and not to have to check for car bombs, or sleep with a loaded gun under our bed.

I feel this story represents all the wives who 'kept the home fires burning'.

05:09 – Lisburn Road, South Belfast

I was only nineteen when I got a call to a sudden death on the Lisburn Road in Belfast. It was an old lady, aged ninety-seven, who lived on her own and had just died of old age. We were searching the house – as you must to try and find any valuables for safekeeping – when her grandson appeared. According to neighbours, he was the only visitor this lady ever had. He said to me, 'I think there's something valuable up in the roof space, but I have never been allowed to go up and see what it is.' So I went up to take a look. To my surprise, I found fifty old UVF rifles that were still wrapped in the factory-oiled brown paper. They must have been part of the consignments brought into Northern Ireland back in 1912, during the Home Rule crisis. Just one of these old .303 rifles would have been very valuable, let alone fifty, plus the historical context would add to it considerably.

It was a bit of a nightmare to establish who the new owner would be as the next day, relatives suddenly started to appear out of the woodwork. Every one of them wanted to take possession of these valuable rifles. I already knew that the only one who ever visited granny was this grandson, and he was just pushed aside by these others.

The legal wrangling went on for years as they tried to establish who was to get these rifles. Suddenly everyone was claiming, 'I'm her favourite son … I'm her favourite this that and the other,' and every single one of them promised that what they were saying was the truth and they were the rightful heir. You could tell by looking at them that it was all lies: every single thing that came out of their mouths. It was just a hateful environment, which left a terrible taste in the mouth.

As one of the senior constables in my section commented, 'Where there's no will, there's a relative!'

05:12 – MSU, Cookstown Police Station, County Tyrone

I was stationed in Cookstown in the mobile support unit. I lived in Belfast and was travelling up and down. I was doing huge hours in Cookstown. My breaking point came just after the Twelfth of July in Pomeroy, where that year's parade was held. I had just worked for three weeks solid and been home for only two hours in those three weeks to collect washing.

I went to see the superintendent and said, 'After the Twelfth, I'm taking a couple of weeks off.' 'Ah, no, you can't,' he said, 'I've already let another inspector go off, I need you to cover.' I said, 'He lives in the town, he is working eight hours a day and getting his rest days off, I've been here for the past three and a half weeks, and I'm stuck. Your call, I either go on annual leave or sick leave, but I'm going off for two weeks.' 'Okay, I'll ask if he will swap.' I told him, 'I'm going off sick if I have to. Whether he swaps or not.'

I went home on 13 July. I lived in the Castlereagh area at that time and walked round to Lisnasharragh RUC base. I had phoned ahead and spoke to the chief superintendent in personnel. I told him quite bluntly, 'I've given you two and a half years down there in Cookstown, I want back to Belfast. He told me he did not have a vacancy and I explained to him that I was not going back down there. He then backpedalled and said, 'I have one vacancy in the mobile support unit in Belfast.' I replied, 'That'll do me.'

I had a relaxing two weeks off and was looking forward to returning to work back in Belfast, given all the trouble I had gone to in order to get there. I was due to start on the Saturday with the ebonies. I began a twelve-hour shift at three o'clock in the afternoon. I had just finished giving the briefing to six Land Rover crews – five sergeants and myself – and we were about to head out when we got a call to say there was a bomb in a pub near Corporation Street. There was quite a lot of republican activity in the city at the time as we were in the middle of another INLA feud.

This guy had ambled into the pub, set a bomb on the counter and announced they had fifteen minutes to get out. We arrived and started to clear the entire premises. We had just done so when I saw this old boy sauntering across the road and realised he was headed towards the door of the pub with the intention of going in. I shouted, 'No! No!' and ran forward towards him. He looked at me and said, 'What's wrong, son?' I was just explaining to him that he couldn't go in there because there was a … BOOM! Every window in the building came out and showered us with glass. The doors came out and we were blown off our feet, I didn't even get to say 'bomb'. 'Sure, it's gone off now, son,' he said. 'Come on, we'll go in and get a pint.'

I had just got myself tidied up after the bomb, when we got a call to say there was rioting occurring in the Ardoyne area of north Belfast. Off we went and, as we were coming down Ardoyne Avenue, I saw this thing coming through the air over the top of the grass bank we'd decided to stop beside. It was a coffee jar bomb which had landed on the hill of the grass, rolled towards us and stopped. My driver started reversing and I was banging the side of the truck shouting, 'Stop, stop, stop! That's a bloody coffee jar bomb that has been thrown at us.' 'Oh shit,' said the driver. We got the coffee jar bomb cleared and dealt with by the military. While the army were doing that, we moved in and shifted the republican crowd involved with the riot we had initially been called to. I suspect the riot was only taking place to lure police into the area so that the coffee jar bomb could be thrown, as the rioters dispersed quite easily.

We heard a call on the radio that rioting had broken out on the lower Shankill after local police had attended the report of an alleged rape at a house just off Peters Hill. They had said on the radio that there was a lot of aggravation towards them and there were only two of them in a soft skin car. I informed the dispatching radio controller in 'uniform' that we were in the area and would go down to check it out.

Two of our Land Rovers went down to the area and stopped at the relevant house in Peters Hill to try and assess what was going on. I decided to get out and approach the house. One of my crew, Scotty, was to cover/guard me. He got out of the vehicle as well, armed with a rifle and I started to bang on the door. The next thing I heard was this *doof, doof, doof.* I looked round to my left, and there was a guy standing shooting at me. I said, 'Scotty, that fucker's shooting at me!' 'What? Who?' and he spun round, but the guy was away up the alley. He disappeared. I looked round at Scotty and said, 'You're some star. I'm glad I've got you here guarding me.'

That was it: a bomb exploded, a coffee jar bomb nearly hit us, we were stoned by loyalists and republicans, and I was shot at all in the one day. My first day – welcome back to Belfast. I was near ready to go back to Cookstown!

05:30 – Glengormley, County Antrim

I was living in what would be called a safe area, in Glengormley. But one morning at 05:00, it became apparent that it was not so safe. Unbeknown to me, my garage had been broken into at some stage and the people who did it had been able to identify that a policeman lived there. That information had found its way back to the Provisional IRA who'd put a plan in motion to kill me.

A police patrol in the town had started to follow some people they were suspicious of; they didn't know where they were going, but there was something about them that made the police suspicious. They came into the street I lived in and were caught by police in the bushes outside my house. At 5:30 we were woken by the shouting and screaming of a police assault team arresting them in the front garden. I remember plainly coming down in my dressing gown with my gun. The truth is I would have been useless because I could hardly speak with the shock of it. The good thing was I didn't have to give evidence in court or anything like that.

My wife and I initially thought, we love this house, we will stay here as long as we can. It was the first really good house that we had been able to buy, and it was near where the kids went to school. We planned to hold on to it. We were provided with a guard at the house while waiting to get the security package – bulletproof glass, doors, and so on – but two nights later, immediately behind our house they murdered a guy, a building contractor, as he was walking from his home. He was shot dead on the doorstep. We moved out that afternoon. Our kids never went back to the house at all, never mind the school. We were moved into emergency accommodation and spent Christmas in a real dundering inn of a place.

While we were in the emergency accommodation, there came the Shankill bomb. The PIRA had placed a bomb in Frizzell's fish shop, murdering nine innocent civilians and injuring fifty-seven. One of the bombers also died in the blast. My mother-in-law and father-in-law owned the wallpaper and paints shop next door to Frizzell's fish shop, though they were on holiday at the time. They were lifelong friends with the Frizzells. I received a phone call from my wife's sister to say the shop had been blown up and they couldn't find her brother. We drove down to the Shankill, parked up in a side street and ran down to the premises. The chief constable, Ronnie Flanagan, was there and he let me through to help with the search. The couple killed inside the shop were from Lisburn; my wife's brother had gone out to get something and the two girls who had been at the back of the building were okay.

What my wife has gone through from that first incident is horrific. Having to move home three times under threat; standing outside your family shop which has just been destroyed; thinking your brother was missing in the blast … if you've ever seen anyone in a full breakdown, it is just awful. The chief constable gave her a hug, trying to console her. The people around us that we rely on for support so often suffer the collateral damage. My little girl never went back to that school and when she met friends later on, one of them said to her, 'You had to move because the IRA were trying to kill your daddy.' That stayed with her because to this day she is paranoid about doors being locked all around the house.

While I was stationed in Andersonstown and living in Bangor there was a period of time in which there were a lot of doorstep murders. I ended up keeping a shotgun under my bed. One night, a prison officer's car was blown up in the street beside me and I got out of bed, closed the shotgun and nearly blew my own foot off. I just don't think people get that this was how we lived.

05:34 – Coalisland Police Station, County Tyrone

Jim Seymour was born in Bristol the day before the start of World War Two. When he was old enough, he joined the Royal navy, and when he had served his time, having married a girl from Northern Ireland, he joined the RUC.

That was in 1971, when his children were aged twelve and seven.

On 10 June 1981 his son, Victor, turned twenty-one, but Jim took no part in the celebrations, nor did he attend Victor's wedding the following year. He took no notice of his own twenty-fifth wedding anniversary in 1983, and when his daughter, Dawn, turned twenty-one six months later, he did not show any interest in that event.

Jim was equally unconcerned about events outside his home. Three sets of Olympic Games were held without any enquiry from Jim about heights, times, or distances. He took no interest in Northern Ireland's progress in the World Cup. Watergate came and went; the IRA bombed Birmingham, Guildford, and the Tower of London; sex discrimination and equal opportunities legislation was passed; Idi Amin murdered his way to power in Uganda; Reagan succeeded Carter, who had succeeded Ford, who took over from Nixon; Princess Margaret was divorced; the Yorkshire Ripper was arrested; Bobby Sands starved himself to death; breakfast television came to our screens; and Argentina invaded the Falklands. But Jim Seymour took no notice of any of it. Nor was he aware of the death of Sergeant Bill McDonald on 12 August 1984, the two hundredth officer to die in Ulster.

The only significant day for Jim in all this time was 4 May 1973, when he was shot in the head by an IRA sniper. He was opening the gate of Coalisland police station to admit a police Land Rover when he was hit by one of a number of bullets fired from the darkness opposite. The bullet went into his head between the eye and the ear and reached the opposite side of his skull without coming out. Since that night, Jim had been paralysed and only partly conscious. Now and again he could smile, but what he thought – or if he thought – no one knew, and the world, which had much more important matters to deal with, cared nothing about him. The world that is, apart from his wife.

Every day since 1973, and that is every day with no exceptions for holidays public or private, Jim Seymour's wife visited him in the room in which he had lain since 1973. The world may have forgotten Jim, but Mrs Seymour hadn't.

Jim Seymour died aged fifty-five in South Tyrone Hospital, bringing to an end twenty-two years of quiet, dignified suffering by someone who had been surrounded by the constant love and attention of a devoted family. No words can possibly convey what his family have endured or express what they have experienced.

Jim's wife May was devoted to him. She initially had to walk two miles from her home to a bus stop to make the daily trip to the hospital. She died on 13 May 2003.

05:38 – CID, Carrickrovaddy, South Armagh

In the summer of 1991, a soldier was blown up and killed in Carrickrovaddy – a small townland between Crossmaglen and Newtownhamilton, near the Irish border in south Armagh. The army patrol had been out looking for a photographic montage of IRA suspects in the area – a military patrol had accidentally dropped it some days earlier. The soldiers were making their way towards the rendezvous point where they would be collected by a military helicopter from Bessbrook. They were walking through a wooded area with conifer trees, when a bomb containing 300lb of explosives was detonated. Lance Corporal Simon Ware was literally blown to smithereens and died instantly. The bomb had been buried in the bank of a track that had been cut in the trees to form a firebreak.

We spent our time at the scene gathering bits and pieces of him from the conifer trees; you could have put all we recovered into a plastic bag. We brought what was left of the body back for post-mortem, but there was little enough to investigate. It was terrible, just terrible. One thing I will never forget was the sight of his left hand, which still had his wedding ring on it. We were able to recover the wedding ring, but it was damaged, all bent out of shape, so we took it to a local jeweller who was able to fix it for us so that we could return it to the family.

His funeral service was held at the Guards' Chapel in Wellington Barracks, London. He had been married in the same chapel only five months earlier; just two days before he left for Northern Ireland. His twenty-four-year-old wife looked on as the priest who married them conducted the funeral service, the coffin just a few feet away from the spot where the couple had exchanged their vows.

05:57 – Uniform Patrol, Oldpark Police Station, North Belfast

It was 1982 and I was on the night shift. I had been detailed as part of the crew in CO 90, an armoured Cortina, with two colleagues. We had gone down to Musgrave Street for a break and some food, as there were no canteens or facilities in Oldpark at night. We had just ordered something to eat when a call came from uniform about a suspicious male in Groomsport Street, carrying what appeared to be a wooden board with something attached to it.

Our three gravy chips were hastily boxed and three grumpy peelers set off at speed to the call. With concern growing about the temperature of our food, we quickly found the suspicious person making his way along the footpath in a nearby street. We stopped him and discovered that the suspicious item he had been carrying was the innards of a phone box stolen from Manor Street. He was immediately arrested, placed in the back of the police car and we set off for Musgrave Street to deposit him in the police office.

He was quite talkative on the journey back and informed us that he knew his rights and was entitled to make a phone call, so Andy told him to carry on. He spent the rest of the journey trying to phone his mother from the call box sitting beside him on the rear seat of the police car, but couldn't get through. When he was being processed in the police office he told the custody sergeant that the lads who had arrested him were decent men who had treated him very fairly, however his mother was a bitch for not answering the phone.

06:15 – RUC Headquarters, Belfast

For a while, a particularly popular form of IRA attack was to place a bomb under an officer's car, which made you paranoid because of your family.

We lived in Bangor at the time, in a street that was on a bit of a hill, and every morning I'd go outside and check under the car. Then I'd go driving up and down the hill a few times, slamming the brakes on. When you think about it now, that's ridiculous, but that's how bad it was.

I remember as a recruit being shown a video that gave examples of some of our colleagues' deaths: some had been blown up getting into the car to go to work at various times because of our shift pattern, and even while taking the kids to school. There was one I always remember that had a small blonde-haired boy whose body was blown away from the car by the force of the explosion. When I became an instructor in the training centre, I used to show that video to the recruits at the end of the first week. There were always people who didn't come back on the Monday.

06:28 – Sion Mills Police Station, County Tyrone

In 1994, when I was in Sion Mills, a major case was the murder of a wee boy called Kieran Hegarty, an eleven-year-old from Strabane.

Kieran had witnessed a guy called Brian Doherty putting up paramilitary graffiti in a bus shelter. Doherty abducted the boy, making him walk two miles out of town to a wooded area on the Knock Road, then murdered him in the forest, bludgeoning the little boy to death. A dog walker in the area found Kieran's body and alerted the police.

The duty sergeant and CID guy on call went out to see what they were dealing with. They saw the body, but only had the old VHF radio at the time and it didn't have the range for them to contact the station from such an isolated area. They made the decision to leave the scene in order to organise a full-scale police response to the incident [it would have been too dangerous to leave one member in such an isolated and hostile area]. Unbeknown to them. Doherty was lying in the forest, watching them as they examined the scene, and when they returned to the station, he decided to go down and move the body to a marshy area. When the police officers returned to the area, they had to perform another search in order to find the body again.

Doherty, aged twenty-one, was arrested. When interviewed, he confessed to stripping the child and throwing him in a quarry before bludgeoning him to death. Doherty killed young Kieran just days after signing himself out of Tyrone and Fermanagh Psychiatric Hospital. He was described in court as a menace to society and the judge remarked, 'A more cruel and macabre killing is difficult to imagine.' He was convicted on the grounds of being criminally insane and detained in a high-security psychiatric unit in Scotland. He is still serving his sentence for the murder.

06:35 – Uniform, County Antrim Countryside

I left CID temporarily to take up promotion in uniform and was assigned to 'nurse maid' a senior male civil servant who was visiting from England and staying in a grand country house set in a woodland. Early on a winter's morning, feeling ill from a hangover, he asked to go for a walk in the grounds. The frost lay heavily on the ground and the puddles on the muddy pathways had iced over. We were accompanied by a uniform constable.

Not long into our walk he said he needed a pee and asked if there was a toilet close by. As there was no toilet, I suggested he go behind a tree. As we waited, the uniform constable lifted a stone and unintentionally struck the ice on top of a puddle with it, causing a loud cracking noise like gunfire, which was exacerbated by the stillness of the frosty morning.

My charge came running from behind the tree, his manhood in clear sight as it swayed from side to side like an uncontrollable garden hose, gushing out streams of steaming urine. 'Are we being shot at?' he nervously enquired. 'No, just a farmer in a field shooting vermin,' I answered. 'Thank God for that,' he said. Red-faced and doing his best to hide his embarrassment, he looked down towards his now-concealed manhood and saw his now heavily soaked trousers. To save him added awkwardness I suggested he wear the constable's overcoat while we made our way back to his room.

I would go on to meet him again, but what happened on that frosty morning was never again mentioned.

06:55 – United Nations Detachment, Kosovo

I was involved in an RUC deployment to Kosovo to assist with policing difficulties that had arisen in the country due to unrest; we were part of a United Nations detachment.

There was also a contingent from the Irish army out there at the same time and we got to know quite a few of them.

We were still there on 4 November 2001 when the RUC name was changed and we were incorporated into the Police Service of Northern Ireland (PSNI), bringing a proud chapter of policing to a close. Within eight weeks they had sent over new uniforms and we were told in no uncertain terms never to wear the RUC uniform again – though we did, of course, continue to wear the polo shirts we had with the RUC crest.

We were to receive United Nations medals for our service in Kosovo and, when it came round to the time of our medal presentation ceremony, I asked the Irish captain if he had any pipers in his contingent of troops. He said yes and we invited them as our special guests to the ceremony: we were piped in to receive our RUC United Nations service medals by a piper from the Irish army.

The ceremony took place about eight months after the Royal Ulster Constabulary name was changed, but we had made a formal request to receive our United Nations medals for service in Kosovo in RUC uniform. We felt it was quite significant when this request was granted. It was a big thing for us.

06:59 – Life in an RUC Family

My dad's story starts in 1936. He was born on a farm in County Cavan, the eldest of four children. At the age of nineteen he went to the RUC training centre in Enniskillen and then was sent to his first station, in Keady, County Armagh. He used to see my mum cycle past the station on her way to work in Armagh.

Soon, he had a narrow escape when a booby-trap bomb exploded minutes after his patrol had crossed a bridge in Middletown. The security threat was so high at that time that officers from the south were not allowed to visit their families, although at times necessity caused him to cross the border against orders. His home in Keady police station was run-down and damp in those days – so bad that the water would run down the walls in his bedroom – and, as a result of this he was admitted to Dungannon Chest Hospital with pneumonia and TB. He was there for over six months.

Mum and Dad got married on his birthday, 21 October 1959. He was then transferred to the Derrytagh area in the Lurgan district. He lived and spent almost the rest of his service in Lurgan. My dad was a special man in so many ways – he even delivered me in our home when the midwife failed to arrive on time!

During the 1970s, there was a spate of loyalist attacks on RUC men's homes. Our windows were smashed with bricks, and my sister and I woke up in our beds covered in glass, though fortunately we didn't have a cut on us. We and other families had to move house because of this, but worse was to come as many of Dad's friends and colleagues were murdered and injured in the days ahead.

He was made a detective constable and transferred to Newry CID for a short spell, before going back to Lurgan station. Those were hard days for the family as he was working hours such long hours that we kids very rarely saw him.

On 7 July 1975, Dad was blown up. Sergeant Kennedy, dad's friend, knocked on the door at 3 p.m. that afternoon and went into the kitchen to Mum. She was using the old twin tub washing machine at the time and when it was switched off, we heard a horrible noise coming from the kitchen; it was Mum. I will never forget that wail engulfing me as it took over the house. A police car arrived bringing Mum's friend and my granny. Mum told us that Dad had

had an accident and she and her friend went to the hospital. We didn't see Mum for days.

The police had received a call to say there had been a break in at a local primary school: the headmaster's office had been ransacked. So Dad and his partner, Andrew Johnston, went to investigate. Dad was kneeling down in the office, the caretaker who had been showing them round was in the doorway, and then Andrew opened a drawer. That was when the bomb exploded. Andrew was killed outright; the caretaker had both of his legs severely damaged; and Dad caught the blast in his head. Andrew was only twenty-three years old at the time with an eighteen-month-old baby at home.

Dad was rushed to the local hospital and was in theatre for over four hours undergoing surgery to his brain. He had two titanium plates inserted to replace parts of his skull that were missing. The eardrum in his left ear was blown apart and his eye was badly damaged. He was left deaf in that ear and blind in that eye. Mum was told it was touch-and-go for a while and was warned that, if he survived, they couldn't be sure of the extent of any brain damage he might have. While he was in intensive care, he knew no one and was very distressed, shouting and taking the bandages off his head. As he gradually improved, a radio was brought in for him but in those times when he got distressed, he dismantled the radio and broke it completely.

My sister was thirteen, I was eleven, my brothers were just seven and two when it happened. We were sent off to the family farm in Cavan for three weeks, and when we came home, we were allowed a quick visit. It was an enormous shock for all of us. It was like looking at a monster. There was this man who was supposed to be our dad, but he was like an old man with his head and left side of his face heavily bandaged. He was covered in cuts, bruises and burns. His left hand was heavily bandaged as there was a hole in it. His holster had melted into his chest from the severe heat of the blast. He had shrapnel and stones in his arms and legs (in fact one of his party tricks over the years was to move a stone up and down the inside of his leg, his grandchildren were mesmerised by this, but it was gross).

He made a remarkable recovery, or so we thought, but that was only the beginning: it wasn't our daddy we got home. It was a man who stammered, couldn't walk properly and got cross very easily, mainly because of the headaches he had. We were constantly told to keep the noise down so we didn't annoy him. We were never the same family again.

At the end of August it was decided we would go to Scotland for a couple of days and as soon as we got back, Mum had her first of many heart attacks.

Over the years Dad had to endure many operations, mainly on his eye and ear. He had injections into his eyeball for the pain, but he would never let them remove it, which would have been better for him. He had numerous ear infections and had to have further operations to prevent the infection entering his brain. He had to have several skin grafts on his left hand and he had a hole in his temple which would not heal properly. He often said that the skin graft site was more painful than the damaged area the skin had gone to.

We moved to a bungalow in an attempt to improve his quality of life, hoping it would allow him to get around a bit better. It was then that he had his first epileptic fit. These were very severe and he had to be admitted to hospital each time they occurred. He would lose consciousness for a long time and have a severe headache afterwards. The normality for him was now an epileptic fit each morning.

He couldn't drive anymore so he was dependent on Mum or other people taking him places.

Mum found the change in life unbearable. She suffered from angina and had three more heart attacks before having a fatal one in March 1984. I was with her at the time and performed CPR as we waited for the ambulance, but the fight had gone out of her; she was so tired and just wanted to go. She was only forty-four years old.

Dad coped exceptionally well over the years, remaining as active as he could with the help of his dogs, his friends and former colleagues visiting and taking him out. Although he didn't admit to it, there is no doubt Dad suffered survivor's guilt. He kept in touch with his murdered colleague's family over the years and celebrated the milestones and the achievements in the life of Andrew's little girl. He was so fond of both her and her mum.

In 2006 he was admitted to hospital with pneumonia and sepsis. We were told that he wasn't going to pull through but then the doctors decided to put him into an induced coma to allow his body to try and heal. He fought hard only to awaken from the coma to find he had suffered a stroke while on the ventilator. Many weeks later he was discharged from hospital, but he had to use a walking aid and he hated it! His lungs were so weakened that he ended up on piped oxygen in the house and had to have a cylinder with him when he was out.

He passed away on 7 February 2008.

He suffered greatly during those last few years. He had always been so active, walking the dogs and tending to his beloved garden. His life revolved around his love for Mum, us, other members of the family, his job as an RUC officer, his lifelong friends and colleagues.

He was so proud to have worn the uniform of an RUC (GC) officer.

On 23 November 1999, the Royal Ulster Constabulary was awarded the George Cross by her Majesty Queen Elizabeth II. This was only the second time in the illustrious history of the award that the George Cross had been awarded for an act of collective bravery and the significance of this is not lost on the men and women of the RUC. The only previous recipient was the people of Malta in World War II.

Citation

'For the past 30 years, the Royal Ulster Constabulary has been the bulwark against, and the main target of, a sustained and brutal terrorism campaign.

The Force has suffered heavily in protecting both sides of the community from danger – 302 officers have been killed in the line of duty and thousands more have been injured, many seriously. Many officers have been ostracised by their own community and others have been forced to leave their homes in the face of threats to them and their families.

As Northern Ireland reaches a turning point in its political development this award is made to recognise the collective courage and dedication to duty of all of those who have served in the Royal Ulster Constabulary and have accepted the danger and stress this has brought to them and their families.'

Buckingham Palace, 23rd November 1999

Message sent to all members of the RUC by Chief Constable Ronnie Flanagan just before midnight on 3 November 2001, when the RUC was renamed The Police Service of Northern Ireland.

Message from the Chief Constable

To all members on duty on what is the last tour of duty under our proud title, 'The Royal Ulster Constabulary'.

You are a very proud part of our history, but after midnight you will be the same men and women have always been – dedicated utterly to the service of all the people of Northern Ireland.

I could not admire you more. I know we will carry on in exactly the same dedicated fashion under our new title, The police service of Northern Ireland.

I thank you all from the bottom of my heart.

Your friend and colleague,
Ronnie Flanagan

Acknowledgements

The RUC is a proud force that should never be overlooked or forgotten. This trilogy of books about 'A Force Like No Other' allows our story, told in our own words, to live on.

I would like to thank my former colleagues. You gave your time so willingly and I know it wasn't always easy for you to speak out. Your enthusiasm for the books and your ongoing support have been a source of tremendous encouragement for me. The importance of your testimony on Northern Ireland's troubled past and your place in it can never be underestimated. Historians and people with political agendas can write about Northern Ireland and offer their opinion but you are the people who were actually there. Your accounts are first hand and not a matter of hearsay or agenda.

I would also like to thank everyone I had the honour of serving with. Things were tight at times, but the craic was great, which made the horrors of what we dealt with a bit more bearable.

I am particularly grateful to the family members of officers who came forward and contacted me to tell their stories of what it was like waiting at home while we were at work. These are previously untold stores from a group who have never been given the opportunity to speak. I hope this book goes some way towards representing the many who did the suffering in silence. These are voices that need to be heard. I am particularly grateful to one woman who spoke of how her life was changed after her father was injured at work and his colleague murdered.

Finally, thank you to my friends and family. Gill, you managed, as always, to keep me focused when distractions came along and steered me back to the task in hand. Lynda, yet again your unspoken support and ready smile were greater sources of strength than you will ever know. Thank you to Johanna and Rebecca for providing a gentle nudge when required (and the occasional roll of the eyes). Your future is what all of this has been about. May you both have long, happy and peaceful lives.

ALSO AVAILABLE BY COLIN BREEN

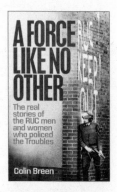

A FORCE LIKE NO OTHER

The real stories of the RUC men and women who policed the Troubles

A FORCE LIKE NO OTHER: THE NEXT SHIFT

More real stories of the RUC men and women who policed the Troubles

For more information visit:
www.blackstaffpress.com

and follow Colin at:

 colin.breen1

 @colinbreen12

COLIN BREEN is a freelance journalist, screenwriter and broadcaster. He has written extensively for many newspapers, including the *Belfast Telegraph*, *Sunday Life* and *Herald* Dublin, and is a regular commentator on local and national radio, television and the BBC World Service. He served as an officer in the RUC for over fourteen years at the height of the Troubles. *A Force Like No Other: The Last Shift* is the follow-up to *A Force Like No Other (2017)* and *A Force Like No Other: The Next Shift (2019),* and completes his bestselling trilogy of books.